D1246918

JOURNEYING
THROUGH
the INVISIBLE

The Craft of Healing With,
and Beyond, Sacred Plants,
as Told by a Peruvian Medicine Man

HACHUMAK

with DAVID L. CARROLL

HARPER WAVE
An Imprint of HarperCollins*Publishers*

If you know or suspect you have a health problem, it is recommended that you seek your physician's advice before embarking on any medical program or treatment. All efforts have been made to assure the accuracy of the information contained in this book as of the date of publication. This publisher and the author disclaim liability for any medical outcomes that may occur as a result of applying the methods suggested in this book. The use of traditional medicinal plants is regulated differently by the laws of each country, the authors and publisher do not encourage the use of such plants and their products outside the corresponding legal frame present in each reader's country.

HarperCollins books may be purchased for educational, business, or sales promotional use. For information, please email the Special Markets Department at SPsales@harpercollins.com.

FIRST EDITION

Designed by Bonni Leon-Berman

Library of Congress Cataloging-in-Publication Data has been applied for.

ISBN 978-0-06-301489-3

22 23 24 25 26 LSC 10 9 8 7 6 5 4 3 2 1

I want to dedicate this book to all the children recently born and yet to come to Earth who have been gifted with Medicine force.

Some of these young people will have the chance to grow in the few remaining traditional communities where they will get the chance to develop their talents and receive the proper tutoring. Most of them will be born in parts of the planet where their culture offers no niche for the thriving of their capacities. Most of them will probably struggle and be dragged down by the negative currents of life, their attention diverted away from the world of subtle realities. But a few will stay close to their callings and make wise choices in their lives. They will seek and retrieve the available fragments of the ancient knowledge within their reach and will be able to offer help to the world while fulfilling the Medicine Force as a vehicle of self-expression.

This book is for the unborn, the newborn, and the very young. The ones, better than us, that are coming next.

"The key to all of your behaviors is hidden in a box that you can't open using normal tools. Your subconscious needs a different recipe than the one you've been using."
—*Gerard Armond Powell, founder of the Life Advancement Center*

CONTENTS

AN INTRODUCTORY NOTE

While a majority of shamans are men, a good number of women in Peru also practice shamanism under the name of witch, woman of knowledge, woman of power, sorceress, and others. Though in these chapters we refer to shamans using masculine pronouns, we do so to make the read flow more smoothly without having to repeat "he/she," "his/her." Please bear with us if our regular use of the masculine is vexing. And while we acknowledge the limitations of addressing the issue in the binary—male or female practitioners—we mean no disrespect to those who identify as nonbinary and who practice as such.

INTRODUCTION

Natural Medicine, the ancient art of healing, has been able to survive through the ages because the practices have floated under the surface of the more formalized culture. Since the oppressing times of the colonial period and the blanketing times of the overrational and industrial-modern culture, the keepers of this knowledge have been forced to protect it in an underground world. Some of the traditional nations that have been able to live relatively undisturbed certainly preserve much of their ancestral wisdom. The rural population around the world that has carried and protected the healing knowledge has never been front actors in our modern history; these are the people that few paid attention to before. This knowledge has always been there, out of view, serving the traditional population needs, the way it always has.

In recent years, predominantly one part of the ancient healing arts has come up to the surface—the use of plant medicines— and it's now in the spotlight of international attention. That is not a negative thing per se, because it can offer so much, and it is probably needed now more than ever before and on a larger scale. But this exposure brings a host of new challenges and dangers— not only for the public but for the knowledge itself.

Now that we are in the twenty-first century, we are once again witnessing a similar clash of cultures that occurred back in the colonial times. When a traditional spiritual knowledge is quickly absorbed without necessary time taken to understand its principles and delicacies, it is transformed into a product of consumption.

The odds that the modern world will need to take in and embrace this traditional knowledge is high, though it's essential that the Western world makes an effort to adapt and explore a respectful mindset for embracing and understanding the benefits of the ancient healing arts.

My personal practice has never been on a large scale. After being a student and an apprentice, I spent many years working in rural areas of my home country, Peru. Most of my friends and clients in Peru live a life strongly connected to the land; their lives are not filled with material possessions, but their inner worlds are of great richness and structure. Later, life brought the opportunity to me to help people from other countries. I have always helped them in the same way I have helped my fellow Peruvians while also trying to assist them in understanding the proper mindset for receiving the Medicine Force. During those years I was told many times, especially by people who were quite experienced in plant medicine ceremonies and other practices, that I should one day write a book. In that book I should share my understandings about the healing force and the plant medicine protocols—how plant medicines work, how to understand and navigate the experiences, the codes of the invisible language, and the nuances of this healing art. I have heard several times, "I wish I had this knowledge before so that I could have avoided my difficult plant medicine experience," or "If I had known this before, I could have understood better my previous plant ceremony experiences." This book has come to fulfill those requests, and it's my hope that it will be a positive contribution to the international community.

It is from a deep part of my heart with gratitude and service to the people in need of assistance as well as to the beautiful spirits of nature and the deceased masters of the past that I am now openly sharing some of my understandings and stories. The work with the sacred plants is a very important part of the Natural Medicine Craft, but this book is not only about that. I want to offer a larger picture of the Medicine Craft and to create appreciation for other important aspects that are endangered or still not well-known.

I have learned from my teachers to be prudent, only stepping out to serve when my skills are needed; then I step back and become just another member of the group. I prefer not to be called by any titles; my skills are not of a higher value than any good hunter, good storyteller, or anyone else. To stay discreet in the visible increases your power in the invisible.

One of the big challenges that we all face is what can be called superstition. Superstition is the great enemy of any form of true knowledge, whether scientific or traditional. Superstition bends the perception of reality, and it creates artificial truths driven by the needs of our personal fears and ambitions. Sadly, superstition has corrupted part of the traditional knowledge, and it constitutes one of the wrong doings that the false practitioners use to take power over gullible people's minds in the name of healing. It's very difficult sometimes for the outside observer to discriminate what comes from a real observation, a real experiential process, in contrast to what is just an artificial construct imposed over the mind. In this book I am writing things that come from direct experience, and I am explaining and denouncing some of the superstitious practices that are out there.

The ancient healing arts are deep and expansive—you never stop learning, and what you learn in a lifetime will always be a small fraction of what is available to learn. There are many things that I have understood through the years, and there are many things that I am still yet to understand. As a man who has learned from both worlds—the modern, rational, scientific one and the traditional one of multiple realties—I have decided a long time ago to base the construction of my knowledge on direct observation. I don't buy everything that I hear per se, so this book is basically a sharing of my experiences and observations.

Reality is perceived through the filters of our internal languages, the languages that we learn from our parents and our culture, and the internal languages created in our mind from our good and bad experiences. Those languages, the filters that we see reality through, differ from the language of Nature and the spirits. The closest thing to the spirits' language that we have in the human culture is poetry. Metaphors, analogies, and symbols talk to our deepest consciousness. They flow in a more malleable and fluid way than the angled constructions of our conceptualities so they can pass through the different grids of our mind and also cross over to the realities of nonhuman beings. True symbols embrace several things at the same time. They are like the knots of a net that connect the strings of different realities. A symbol is a key to access different spaces, a pathway to other worlds, so don't expect a logical succession of concepts while dialoging with the other worlds.

In Natural Medicine, the messages you receive seek to connect with that core layer of one's consciousness that is able to understand that language. That deep part of our consciousness is often dormant or untapped, but it is actually so powerful that when correctly stimulated, it can take over confusion and start the process of dissolving internal conflict, of changing self-destructive behaviors, and navigating the labyrinth of painful memories that haunt us. Beyond that, it can bring the understanding of how to embrace a way of life that will help the world in a constructive and collective manner.

PART I

STARTING *the* SHAMANIC

JOURNEY

CHAPTER 1

THE PATH TO THE PATH

First, a note. In this chapter, please allow me to present a section on my personal history before going into deeper descriptions of the medicine person's Art. In this way I can introduce both myself and the fundamental shamanic concepts that will be explained throughout the book. By gaining familiarity with my path to becoming a *curandero*, it is my hope that you will better understand the ways in which plant medicine and traditional healing contribute to deep and lasting healing.

Trapdoors and False Promises

I had never for a moment thought of myself as a bodyguard.

I was twenty-one years old, it was the late 1980s, and Peru was reeling from the murderous assaults of the Shining Path Maoist insurgency. Several years later the former philosophy professor and leader of the Shining Path, Abimael Guzmán, would be caught and jailed for life. But at the present time, he and his followers were killing both enemies and innocent victims by the thousands with assassinations and bombings. They were even stoning people to death in village squares. Violence and danger were present at every level of Peruvian society.

All this brutality made the capital city of Lima an extremely precarious place to live. So, when my friends Martina and Chaska asked if I would accompany them as an escort—read: guard—to a dangerous district on the outskirts of the city, I was taken aback. During the 1980s parts of this area were risky during the day and downright perilous at night. At the time I had been spending nine hours a day training in martial arts—more on this below— but had rarely thought of using my combat skills as a personal protector.

I was even more surprised when Martina told me they planned to visit a local *bruja,* or sorceress, who lived in this depressed area. This elderly woman was reputed to be a powerful miracle worker who could help people solve whatever problems they brought to her altar, be it making money on the stock market, winning someone's affections, or curing cancer. Martina and Chaska knew I was train- ing in the martial arts, and that I had been in more than one fight on Lima's streets during this unstable time. They needed protection and were afraid to visit this part of the city alone. Would I come?

When the Spirits Are Free to Roam

It was the middle of the night, and the darkness made the house look particularly run-down and sinister. The *bruja,* Martina had been told on the phone by one of her assistants, only saw cus- tomers after midnight when "the spirits are free to roam." Both Martina and Chaska had been asked to send a written statement ahead of time giving their names and a description of their prob- lems. Martina was deeply depressed for unknown reasons and thought she had been cursed. Chaska had lost a good deal of her life's savings in a financial scam and wanted magical help getting it back. Other people would be at the consultation, they were told. The cost was extraordinarily high, forcing poor clients to come up with funds they might otherwise use to put food on their table. I kept this thought to myself as we parked the car in front of the *bruja*'s house and knocked at the front door. It was opened by a well-dressed young man with slicked-back hair and an ingratiating smile. I explained to him that I was here as an escort for my friends and would not be participating in the night's ceremony. He nodded without breaking his smile and ushered us into a long hallway where some ten or twelve people were standing almost at attention looking both frightened and eager.

The young man disappeared for a moment, then returned holding a pot full of empty envelopes. On cue everyone removed a wad of cash, stuffed it into one of the envelopes, wrote their name on it, and handed it to the man. Some members of the crowd did this in such a routine way that I guessed they were frequent visitors.

After the paying ritual was complete, we waited in silence for several minutes until a door at the end of the hall opened and an old mestiza woman appeared. She beckoned us into a room and motioned us over to a large circular table. We all sat down.

She was a large woman, more hulking than heavy, with many colorful beads draped around her neck, heavy silver earrings weighing down her lobes, and large metal rings on every finger. She was most likely in her late sixties, a combination, I thought, of Spanish, African, and Peruvian native. Her face was heavily made up, deeply lined, and unexpressive, with large black eyes that moved constantly but seemed to look at no one in particular. She smelled strongly of several commercial flower perfumes including Agua de Florida. A dagger, a set of rattles, what appeared to be a human thighbone, and several other objects of sorcery were placed in front of her on the table.

After we all took our seats, popular street music began playing on a stereo and the *bruja* started reading names from a list, telling people to raise their hands when called.

As she read, an older man sitting on a bench in the back of the room stood up and began circling the table taking sips from a bottle of liquid and blowing out mouthfuls of spray on each client. The spray had the same cheap, heavily scented smell as the *bruja's* perfume. This fact immediately put me on alert. Though I was unfamiliar with shamanic practices at the time, I knew from common Peruvian knowledge that if you use a flower fragrance in a sacred setting, you always make it yourself. You never buy junk perfumes from the marketplace. I looked around the table to see how other people were reacting. Many appeared nervous or awed, but no one seemed even slightly skeptical. I was touched by their faith and, I was coming to think more and more, their gullibility.

The roll call finished, our host looked around the table several times with a stern glance and asked that none of us cross our arms or legs. This, she told us, would block the flow of healing energy. She then said prayers, summoning a litany of saints and spirits. The audience was quiet and respectful, clearly cowed by the woman's reputed power.

Suddenly the lights went out and the room became black.

Several silent minutes went by, then the *bruja* began shaking her rattles, faster and faster, knocking violently on the table with her rings. As she rattled, she sang, whistled, and made odd choking noises. She also mumbled a strange mixture of prayers and invocations. In the dark I could see the outlines of her body shuddering convulsively and swaying from side to side. Watching this strange dance, I heard a sudden crashing noise on the other side of the room. Something heavy had fallen to the floor. "*Blop, blam, Blom!*" like that.

A moment later the sorceress called out a woman's name.

"Maria! Maria! Let's see about Maria! What can I do to help your father's emphysema?"

She recited several "magic" verses, and I heard another loud

dropping sound. Each time something fell, she called out a different name and announced what kind of healing she was performing. "I'm driving the spirits of the disease out of Maria's father
now," she would say; or to another client, "You've had a spell cast
on you, Arsenio. That's why you had the fire in your office. I'm
taking it out, all the burning energy and curses."

From time to time she would pause, strain in one direction
or another, and bellow out mysterious phrases like "Something
dense, hello! I will go for it! No western wind!" Then another *bom!*
on the floor.

In between each noise the *bruja* continued to rattle ferociously;
good camouflage, I thought, for disguising the noises her helpers
were making, such as the banging of doors and things dropping to
the floor. She was also giving each of her clients vague advice that
could apply to anyone. I see you are having troubles at home, she
would say, or there is some type of blockage interfering with your
ability to make money. Or you have an enemy who is poisoning
your relationships at work, one-size-fits-all generalizations of the
kind that have been mouthed by pretend psychics for centuries.

This performance went on for a half hour or so, until the *bruja*
announced she needed to rest.

The lights went on and the young man who had greeted us at
the door appeared with a dustbin. Moving quickly, he began picking up a number of small flasks and black packages littering the
floor, clearly the objects that had made the banging noises. The
packages were banded with rope and fabric, and the flasks were
covered with slimy wet dirt, as if they had just been dug out of the
earth. Each flask contained a thick, dark liquid, the implication
being that the flasks and packets had been buried somewhere in
secret plots by unknown sorcerers, then magically materialized
by our *bruja*, each package holding the evil energy that had poisoned the life of a particular person sitting at the table.

While the lights were on, I took the opportunity to glance around the room.

The first thing I saw was a trapdoor in the ceiling located just above where the flasks had fallen. In the dark it would have been an easy matter for someone on the roof to open this door and drop the flasks while the sorceress was making her ruckus below. At the time you could buy these flasks for pennies at the local flea markets.

During the break I told my friends that I wasn't sure this ceremony was the real thing, and that maybe they should look at it with a more critical eye. I pointed out the trapdoor on the ceiling and said how easy it would be to feign the so-called materializations. Though my training as a shaman was still far in the future, I knew in my gut that what this woman was doing was clearly not part of the archaic Pre-Columbian approach to the spirit world. It had a made-up feeling about it, like a play that had been rehearsed a hundred times and was being performed once again tonight. When I said all this to my friends, they remained silent. Moments later the lights went out and another round of chanting, rattling, and falling flasks and packets began.

Later, when the ceremony was over and we were driving home in the early morning, I asked my friends if they believed what the *bruja* had told them was true. They considered my question for a minute, then agreed that yes, they basically thought it was real.

"Why?" I wanted to know.

"Well, what about all those flasks coming out of nowhere?"

"What about the trapdoor above them on the ceiling?" I asked.

"Yes, maybe. But you know, it could have been real."

"The sorceress seemed authentic," Chaska said. "I feel a little different after the things she told me." Martina added that she had a strong feeling that something was going to change in her life for the better.

For myself this experience shocked me into understanding just how suggestible and blinded by wishful thinking people can be when they are desperate to relieve their pain.

What I witnessed that night was not only cruel trickery but a blatant show of contempt for people who had come to this woman's home in good faith with anguish in their hearts and so much hope. Her behavior also seemed disrespectful to the ancient art of shamanism itself, of which the woman's performance was clearly a clumsy counterfeit. This understanding guided me later on when I was training to become a *curandero*, or shaman, helping me realize that in order to recognize a true spiritual path, one must first learn to recognize the false ones.

In the following weeks, I told this story to a few friends and then more or less forgot about the incident. I never would have imagined that ten years later life would offer me the chance to learn from true shamanic masters how to do the things that this fake shaman pretended to do—to heal, to work with the spirit world, and to genuinely help other people.

Spiritual Minimalism

For many years I have practiced traditional natural medicine both in Peru and in foreign countries around the world. While my birth name is Jorge Flores Araoz, when speaking of my healing activities I prefer to be called Hachumak, a shamanic name I was given high on a mountain in the north of Peru during one of my training sessions.

Currently I do much of my work in a jungle compound located on the banks of the Amazon River in Peru. From time to time, I also travel to different regions of the country to perform natural healings or to escort clients on road trips along non-beaten pathways through the prairie and mountains. In my compound I cultivate many medicinal species of plants, making every attempt to protect the supernaturally lush rain forest that surrounds my center from commercial exploitation.

Though not a native of the Amazon, over time I have become a member of my local jungle community. The village near me is made up of people with Amazonian ancestry and some with Spanish mixed blood. These people have no electricity, computers, or Wi-Fi, and very few cell phones. Most live in quiet harmony with the rain forest surrounding them and believe deeply in the spirits and intelligence of the elements. Two local families work with me on my property, taking care of the grounds while I'm traveling. I have strict rules against hunting and cutting trees on the land.

Through the years I have practiced traditional shamanic healing in a way that has evolved over time, and which I sometimes refer to as "Spiritual Minimalism."

I call it "spiritual" because the essence of shamanism is based on communication with spirit beings from the subtle world. And "minimal" because working with troubled clients has made me aware that the simplest way to heal is the best way, the way without beads and robes, bones and wands, all of which are a cultural coloring that vary from tradition to tradition, but which in my opinion overcrowd a ceremonial space that should be kept clear and clean. This minimalist approach is even more important today than ever because of the large number of international seekers who are pouring into Peru to take part in sacred ceremonies and who can be easily fooled by costumed practitioners and hyped-up rituals. Spiritual Minimalism also has an instructive side. By keeping a ceremony austere, spirit healing has fewer distractions and can be absorbed more directly by both clients and skeptics, demonstrating the incontestable reality of the shamanic way and the power of this ancient form of medicine.

✢

A shamanic ceremony can be remarkably vast and varied. During a night cradled in the arms of the sacred plants clients almost always undergo higher levels of consciousness. During their odyssey they may experience a sense of freedom from egotistic likes and dislikes, an enhanced creativity, a new appreciation for life. They may acquire a better understanding of their partner or parents. They may gain the ability to forgive themselves and others and in the process acquire increased self-understanding, higher levels of energy, and a sharper pitch of intuition that lasts for years after the session is over. They may derive feelings of oneness with nature, communication with friends and relatives who have passed away, insight into their death and the fear of it, or a new sense of the sacred. And for a few advanced individuals a true breakthrough into the Divine realms can occur.

During my years of practice, I have hosted clients who come for both physical and emotional ailments. As we shall see throughout this book, these people can be healed in a real way only if they are counseled by someone capable of moving psychic energies and who knows how to work with his clients in an intuitive and compassionate way.

Many years ago, I received a message from the plant spirits telling me never to perform sacred plant ceremonies outside of Peru. Due to this caveat, when visiting other countries today, I mainly discuss Amazonian plant traditions with small groups of seekers or lecture to audiences interested in the subject. In some situations, I help serious medical cases by using hands-on healing. This practice has always been an important tool in my lineage, though the method my teachers taught is different from other touch therapy sessions I have seen. At times throughout the years serious seekers in other countries have offered me tempting rewards if I would perform a shamanic ceremony for them using the sacred plants. I always decline, knowing it is essential to stay faithful to the message I received from the sprits, even if I do not entirely understand it.

﹋

During my early years of training, a master practitioner told me that in our profession there are five basic rules a shaman must know in order to work effectively with the spirit world.

First, during a ceremony a shaman should know he will encounter many terrifying and grotesque beings that live on the spirit plane. He may be challenged to fight dark forces or deal with sorcerers who are trying to harm him. A shaman must learn to be fearless.

Second, during a ceremony a shaman can be exposed to the psychic illnesses that lurk in a client's subconscious. The look, taste, smell, or acting out of these illnesses may be offensive or repulsive. A shaman must become immune to the emotion of disgust.

Third, a shaman should be sincere, compassionate, and generous. There are some practitioners of the magic arts who willingly exploit the suffering and despair of the vulnerable. None of them deserve to be called either healers or *curanderos*.

Fourth, an aspiring healer should understand the importance of lineage. Besides knowledge, a *curandero* passes on an initiatic force to his student, an invisible power that becomes the nucleus of the trainee's healing practice. Without having this power, without belonging to an authentic shamanic genealogy, and without learning the dangers and demands of the spirit world from a practiced teacher, even a skilled psychic can damage himself and others. Despite what many recent books on the subject claim, no one can become a true *curandero* on his own. He must be trained in an initiatic tradition.

Fifth, the master practitioner told me how important it is to define what I want to do with the gift of my life and the gift of my Medicine. A shaman must decide which side of *curanderismo* he stands on, white or black. If white, he is a healer; if black, a sorcerer or *brujo*. Evil is not a symbol or allegory to a shaman, the teacher insisted. It is a reality.

The Plan That Was Not to Be

I was born in Lima, the capital of Peru, though a large part of my ancestry is European. Both my mother and my father were educated, and both had a deep love for Peruvian culture and for the richness of our country's art, folklore, and history. My father's ancestors came from the Asturian and Basque regions of Spain. My mother had mainly French and Italian ancestors with some Gypsy blood, plus, like the majority of Peruvians, a bit of native Peruvian and African in the mix. Both parents were intellectuals and well versed in philosophy and history; I rarely saw them without a book in their hands.

My mother's grandmother, who lived in a southern valley of the Peruvian coast, had been a woman of power who smoked cigars and was an excellent tarot card reader. She had peculiar psychic skills such as the ability to tell if a girl was pregnant by observing the back of her neck, an aptitude that brought her fame in the rural area where she lived. Her daughter, my grandmother, was strangely charged with an electromagnetic field; when she walked by the television set the image on the screen would become fuzzy. When we touched her, we sometimes got a quick electric shock.

In grade school I was shy and introverted. My parents enrolled me in a private school in Lima where French and English were spoken along with Spanish. By the time I graduated I was reasonably fluent in both languages. During my high school years, I and most of my fellow students were prepped to travel to France after graduation, where we would continue our education at a European university. Eventually I was to become a scholar like my parents. That was the plan.

But none of it was to be.

During my years in high school, I made two life-changing discoveries. First, Chinatown in downtown Lima. Second, the fact that there were individuals in the world who had special knowledge that was different from the kind espoused by scientists and scholars, the kind of knowledge I was never told about in school but which, once discovered, I wanted to know a good deal more about.

Martial Arts in a Chinese Morgue

One day during the mid-1980s when I was twenty years old, a friend and I visited the Chinatown district of old Lima.

Chinese immigration started in Peru during the mid-nineteenth century, making Lima's Chinatown one of the oldest in the Americas. At the time, its streets were picturesque, lined with food vendors, pushcart peddlers, and many Asian immigrants just off the boat.

That day my friend and I checked out the restaurants and shops in central Chinatown, then explored its more mysterious back streets. On one street we passed an alley that led to a sad, run-down building. For reasons I didn't understand, I felt an irresistible urge to investigate it.

Entering the building alone—my friend decided to go his separate way—I followed a long hallway paved with red ceramic tiles, each carved with Chinese sacred symbols. The hallway had several doors on either side, and at the end was an open metal grill gate. Behind it I could see a dark, rickety staircase.

I climbed the steps to the rooftop, where I looked down on the colorful buildings in the neighborhood. On one side of the rooftop was a large enclosure that appeared to be a temple of some kind with red fluted columns flanking a large door. Venturing inside, I entered a large room filled with antique Chinese paintings, calligraphic hangings, and several bed-like couches. Toward the back of the space were three altars holding weapons mounted on wooden stands.

After studying the interior with great interest and a bit of awe, I walked back down the stairs to the main hall, where on my way out I noticed the words "Kung Fu Classes" written clumsily in chalk over one of the hallway doors. For some reason these words stayed in my mind, and in the following months I thought of them many times. A year later, driven by curiosity and what I later understood to be my fate, I came back and knocked at the same door. A sweaty teenager opened it, allowing me to peer inside, where I could see a number of young men, some Chinese, some Peruvian, all dressed in tattered sport garb—no uniforms—and all performing punching and deflecting motions. There was no equipment in the room, no mirrors or railings or punching bags. The walls were dingy and the room was windowless.

A well-built Chinese man, clearly the teacher, beckoned me in, and we spoke for a few minutes. On one side of the room there were more bed-like couches that I later learned were catafalques used on certain days as a morgue for newly dead members of the Chinese temple.

The teacher gave me a short explanation about his martial art practice without applying the slightest pressure, seeming more anxious to return to his students than to talk to me. But I liked what he told me. A couple of months later I joined his class.

Here I should mention that though my new martial arts school used techniques from a Shaolin lineage that emphasized strength and fighting skills, its core was focused more on breathing and the development of chi (in Mandarin *qi*), a practice known as *nuikung* in Cantonese and *neigong* in Mandarin.

Qi or chi, as you most likely know, is the Chinese word for "vital energy." Its cultivation is designed to build inner power, but of equal importance, it is used to heal a variety of physical and psychological ailments, in both oneself and others. Any authentic Asian martial lineage is both a fighting practice and a medical art.

Around the time I started practicing *neigong*, I entered the national university in Lima to study agricultural engineering. After several terms, I began to feel that it was impossible to do both things well—studying and fighting—and eventually my passion for *neigong* won out. I dropped out of college, moved into a tiny apartment, and gave my full time and attention to the gods of the martial arts.

I trained in this discipline for the next eight years.

During this time, I not only learned routines for creating and projecting *qi* energy; I discovered that *qi* could also be used for self-protection, even against an unexpected attack.

One day in Lima I was crossing a busy street when a car came wheeling around the corner and ran into me, battering my leg. Though I felt strangely heavy, I remained standing and experienced no pain. When the car pulled over to the curb, I saw a sizable dent in its bumper. I realized that after years of practicing *neigong*, an energy field had inflated around me the second I was hit, enveloping me in a protective shield without any conscious intent on my part. The car was more damaged than I was.

The *neigong* I was taught in these years, I should emphasize, had a strong spiritual and also magical component. I absorbed a great deal of refined energy from my teachers, one of whom told me that the spirits of our ancient Chinese lineage were around us all the time channeling insight and discernment into our minds without our knowing it. Revelations like these helped me with my fighting practice certainly. But they also opened up the world of the spiritual and supernatural, a gift that made it easier for me to accept the mind-stretching ideas I was later taught about the spirit realm by shamanic teachers.

As my years of martial arts training passed, and as I assimilated the metaphysical as well as physical sides of *neigong*, an important thing happened: I began to realize that fighting had become an increasingly secondary concern, and that healing was now a far more important goal. With a growing conviction I understood that healing was more than just a useful tool for me; it had now become my lifetime calling. What I really wanted to do, I saw quite clearly, was dedicate the rest of my life to helping people overcome their physical and psychological suffering using the vital energy I had developed from my martial arts training. I wanted to become a healer in every sense of the word.

Tai Chi

After many years of practicing the Shaolin-style arts, I began training in tai chi, a considerably different martial form than *neigong*. Most practitioners of this ancient art are less drawn to its fighting skills (which, by the way, are quite potent) and more toward its slow, languorous movements, which are designed to cultivate vital energy.

During the many years I studied *neigong*, matches among my classmates and colleagues were rare, and most of us avoided tournaments. However, my last tai chi teacher had recently come to Peru from Shanghai and was fond of public contests, having won several important competitions in China. She was eager for our small group to take part in national tournaments, and it was unthinkable to refuse a teacher's request.

For the next three years I competed in tai chi events, eventually becoming metropolitan champion, then two-time national champion of Peru, and eventually champion of South America. These winnings led to exposure in newspapers and TV, which was a bit embarrassing for me, having come from a *neigong* background where public displays of martial skill are looked down upon. Yet though the public's gaze made me uncomfortable, as it turned out this small bit of recognition would take me a giant step toward my real calling.

Learning the Art of Healing

During the mid-1990s the National Social Security Office in Peru, which even in the best of times teetered on the edge of economic collapse, was feeling the money pinch more than usual, especially in the public health sector. Government-run hospitals were draining the state's finances in many areas of rural Peru where physicians and medical equipment were in short supply. Hospital buildings were costly to maintain in these impoverished parts of the country, and thousands of ailing older people were denied medical attention. Was there a way to conserve money and still provide care for the poor and elderly?

In response to this dilemma, several open-minded doctors and officials from the National Social Security Administration started a hospital coalition that took the bold step of using alternative therapies, including tai chi, to heal people unable to afford conventional medical aid. Volunteering to be part of this service, along with several other tai chi practitioners, I participated in pilot programs in several Lima hospitals, using tai chi as a healing tool for a large number of clients. After several months of work, I happened to take a holiday in the northwestern coast city of Trujillo, where a local official from the National Social Security Office asked me to come to her office.

She had heard of our group's work in Lima, she told me. For a sensible salary, would I be interested in providing tai chi classes to elderly clients in hospitals located across the northern coastal regions of Peru? Saying yes would require that I move to Trujillo, which I would use as my base of operations. In the administration's eyes, sponsoring programs that included nonprofessional healers such as myself was a smart way to save money and by the same means help the sick and provide jobs.

The official I spoke with was well-informed about medical matters and knew that in China tai chi had a reputation for restoring health to the aging. Most of the older people in the Trujillo region had worked as manual laborers, many in large sugarcane haciendas, others building stone walls, working with cement, sitting for hours hunched over looms, cutting brush. As the years passed, their health had taken a horrific beating. Many of them were semi-crippled from the agonies of lifting, or from the arthritis that so often develops from bone-grinding labor. Some also suffered from depression and anxiety. The problem, the official explained, was that there was not enough medical care to go around, and these people were going untreated. Would I be willing to help?

Seek

Ever since I had committed my life to healing, I spent a good deal of time looking for a job that would allow me to use my *neigong* healing energies and also to make a living. After all my searching, the job of my dreams was being offered, entirely unsolicited.

Within a month I had packed up my worldly goods and moved to Trujillo, where I taught tai chi classes in small neighborhood hospitals in the metropolitan area but more often in rural towns or isolated coastal regions. In the mid-1990s, I traveled from one healing center to another across the beautiful, unforgiving northwestern terrain of Peru.

In the beginning it was daunting to introduce myself to my would-be clients, most of whom were illiterate laborers between the age of sixty and eighty, and a majority of whom were justifiably suspicious of an educated, Spanish-speaking thirty-year-old kid from Lima who had driven hundreds of miles to treat their rheumatism and back pain for little pay. Why, they wondered, would anyone in the world do such a thing for old, forgotten people who could barely put bread on their table? What was I really up to?

These questions glowered at me from the silent stares of my new wards, especially when I announced that I had no medical degree but had been sent by the Social Security Office in Lima to treat them naturally, with hands-on touch therapy and Chinese exercise classes.

When I told them this, most clients gasped in disbelief or shook their heads resignedly, as if to say that once again the government had screwed them. Many of them had been told that conventional medical help was on the way. Instead, an untrained amateur was sent, and my clients were irate. Some had never heard of China or, if they had, thought of it as a country of heathens. An unfamiliar Chinese exercise routine was outside the frame of reference for these country people, especially when I demonstrated tai chi postures and movements that can look quite eccentric. "*This is going to cure my hip joint?*" one mestiza woman moaned, gazing in despair at the movements that had won me several national championships.

My new clients walked through the classes with boredom and disdain, making few efforts to assume the correct positions, and paying little attention when I tried to explain the meaning of *qi* and how it could help. To make the demanding postures of tai chi easier—certain moves require balancing on one foot or spinning in place—I simplified the form and remade it to suit the needs of those with motor disabilities. Most clients allowed me to place my hands over their painful joints and organs, though it was clear they were being courteous and had few expectations.

During my first year I also started studying the healing qualities of local herbs and plants, spending hours wandering through village marketplaces speaking with herb sellers, some of whom sold items that were clearly used for dark purposes such as dead birds and wax dolls. Most were generous with their information, and I learned a good deal. I brought packages of these herbs to classes with me and handed them out free. A few people reported that the leaves helped relieve their inflammation. Others found them useless and worse, complained how terrible they smelled and tasted.

I persisted. The months passed. Now and then a client would remark that the inner glow generated by tai chi seemed *maybe* to be reducing their pain. Others said the exercises made them feel younger. Still others found that after I had massaged their joints for several months, they started to regain range of motion in a hobbled arm or leg. One woman with crippled hands could now cut meat for the first time in her life. Another man was able to squat again after living for years with unbendable legs. Now and then clients initiated personal conversations, talking to me about everyday things like their gardens or their grandchildren. What gratified me most during these years was seeing the slow, miraculous change in our classes from formal exercise routines into sessions of affection and trust that nourished us all.

Working with indigenous people over many decades, I learned a critical fact: These people care little about your appearance, how much money you make, or what opinions you may have. What they care about are the emotions you generate in them and thus how they feel about you. I have observed this fact with traditional peoples around the world.

This means that a tribal elder will listen less to your words and more to the sound of your voice; less to your assertions and more to your body language; less to your assurances and more to your intentions. If you pass their tests, they will let you into their life and occasionally into their heart.

I, on the other hand, had always been attracted to the quiet presence of the mestizos and the people from coastal and mountain tribes, and I had no difficulty liking almost everyone I treated, even the grouches and misanthropes. Most of them had worked long and hard for many years, and all they received for their efforts was poverty and the contempt of bosses, company owners, and the rich in general who barely considered them to be human beings. Yet they rarely complained and almost never made a show of their pain. By now there was also a growing number of them who seemed to approve of my strange doctoring and a few who wanted to know more about my healing techniques.

On the negative side, I occasionally butted heads with staff members at different hospitals, especially the nurses and social workers, who looked on my healing methods as quackery. Occasionally one of them would tell clients my classes were canceled when they weren't or would disconnect the electricity for night classes. My clients were watching all this. They were very quiet about it and made no comments or suggestions. They were looking at everything I did, how I struggled to heal them despite their resistance and despite the animosity of hospital staff members. Most of them, I could feel, were now beginning to look at me less as an intruder and more as an ally.

A Cosmic Role Reversal

Though the salary for this complicated job was minimal, my needs at the time were simple, and during the first six years that I worked with hospital clients I lived a moderately comfortable life. All this changed in 1999 when a new government came to power and the politics of human services in Peru took a sudden turn. One day a member of the Social Security Administration called me into his office and informed me that he was eliminating the alternative medicine program in hospitals due to "excess costs." He thought it best that I look for another job.

This news came as a sudden and harsh blow. By now I had hundreds of elderly patients depending on me for treatment. I was literally keeping some of them alive, and many were experiencing significant improvements in supposedly incurable ailments. The thought of abruptly walking off the job and abandoning these good people was unimaginable. But how was I going to make a living if I stayed?

I wrestled with this question for some time, finally deciding that rather than return to Lima and look for work, I would take several small jobs in the area and treat my clients for free. Most of them could barely pay anyway, and usually after driving hours over valley and gorge to treat someone in a remote mountain village my remuneration would be a few coins to cover the cost of gas. But no matter. At this point I was working for the sheer joy of it, and for the feelings of affection I had developed for my patients.

Meanwhile, those I worked with saw that I was attending to them without asking for money, and that I was seriously committed to their welfare. Many, perhaps most, were feeling healthier from working with tai chi and the *qi* energy itself. A number of the heavier clients lost weight. After years of wearing dowdy clothes, women once again dressed in colorful skirts and smocks. The men combed their hair and shaved. Even the poorest and saddest of them seemed more optimistic. There was so much love among them, and they started channeling this love more and more in my direction. Soon they were inviting me to their homes for dinner and to their weddings and family gatherings, where I was served all kinds of amazing foods and treated like a friend. They would joke with me in a familiar way or tell me about their personal troubles. Sometimes I had to travel long distances by car to take care of clients in a remote village. After treatment I would be fed a sumptuous meal and stay long into the night, conversing with a particularly interesting villager.

Slowly at first, then more openly, a few of my mestizo and native clients began talking to me about the spiritual relationship they maintained with their ancestors. I started having private conversations with elders who told me about their families' knowledge of medicine, healing techniques that worked with natural forces and invocations. One elderly lady (who I later learned was a good-hearted witch) taught me to read the lines on a person's face as a window into their past. Others took me to remote valleys, where they taught me to recognize rare healing shrubs and cactuses, information I would never have discovered on my own. Some talked about drinking clay as a remedy or making a healing soup with stones. Several laborers told me about medicine that had to do with animals and tree barks, with tiny creatures that lived in streams, and how people who are dead and gone are not necessarily dead and gone.

While I was becoming acquainted with this new knowledge, I was also visiting ancient temples and pyramids all across northern Peru. I took weeklong trips into the desert, studying sacred plants and speaking with spiritual recluses in their wilderness retreats. As I did all this something began to happen between myself and the landscapes I traveled through. They began to speak to me in a tongue I could not yet decipher, but that I wanted to understand with all my heart.

The real turning point came when one day several clients told me that a certain location east of Trujillo was the home of spirits that are sometimes willing to share visionary wisdom with a seeker. Climb halfway up that mountain, an elderly plantation worker told me, pointing to a nearby peak. Go in a fasting state and sleep on the ground for one night; two is better. It's cold and dangerous. There are wild animals. Be careful of wells and pits grown over with grass. It's a rough terrain with thick bush and thorns. If you stay there in a meditative state for several days, they told me, *maybe* the mountain will start thinking of you as a disciple and show you some of its secrets—the hidden places that you cannot see with your normal vision. Or perhaps it will grant you its healing power. Things like that; things I had never heard before.

At the same time, the years I spent with my martial arts mentors made me familiar with the notion of spirits, if of a Chinese variety, and allowed me to feel comfortable with otherworldly thinking. I had also grown up in a country where many people talked about being blessed or cursed, and who depended on the advice of clairvoyants (like Martina and Chaska's pseudo priestess) to make major life decisions. What my clients said about magic fascinated me and educated me but did not surprise me.

Then one day while visiting the home of Pedro, an elderly laborer and one of my closest friends, I was presented with a proposal. Our conversation was short, perhaps five or ten minutes at most. But after hearing what Pedro had to offer, everything in my life went on hold and a new frontier rose up in front of me.

My elderly clients, I now understood, were about to become my teachers.

CHAPTER 2

BECOMING A PERUVIAN

NATURAL HEALER

A New Life

Among the many hundreds, probably thousands, of elderly people I treated during my ten years as a hospital healer, I was befriended by a handful who had special knowledge.

No members of this group ever showed off their insights or acted in mysterious ways. On any village street, a stranger might walk by a raggedly dressed man sitting quietly on a tree stump smoking a cigarette or playing with a grandchild, and never guess that he had the power to subdue demons and speak to animals. Some of these people were powerful witches and *curanderos* who I had helped at the hospitals and who had decided to show their appreciation by inviting me into their world.

Of all those who shared their wisdom with me, Pedro was the most influential. A retired sixty-seven-year-old mestizo adobe mason and agricultural worker, he was a dwarf-like man with a huge head, a scrunched-up face, and a shrewd, somewhat unsettling smile. The proposal that he made to me was straightforward.

"The energy exercises you taught us at the hospital were power-ful medicine," Pedro assured me. "They helped restore my health and the health of others. But you know, there are other ways of healing that you might be interested in learning about. Ways from long ago. I can explain a bit about them if you like."

When I heard these words, my heart skipped a beat. I felt that something dreadful and sublime was being offered to me from ancestral Peru by a man who understood things unseen by most of us. Was this offer gratitude for the care I had shown him? Or perhaps he simply recognized a healing potential inside me that made me a candidate for training.

When explaining his work Pedro never used the word *shaman-ism*. South American persons of knowledge never do. But I under-stood his meaning.

When a shaman speaks of his practice, which he rarely does, he sometimes refers to it as *curanderismo*. More often he calls it his Craft, his Art, or sometimes his Medicine or his Knowledge, terms that imply both healing and wisdom—terms that I capital-ize throughout this book as a reminder that in shamanism these words are sacred. The Quechua term *yachak* is also sometimes used to describe shamanism, especially in mountain areas. It means "carrier of Knowledge," or "one who knows." (Note that when I capitalize the word Medicine in this book, I am describing sacred shamanic practice. When I use the word to refer to the sacred brew, I write it with a small *m*, as in *medicine*.)

I have often noticed that when people from other countries hear Peruvian villagers refer to a witch or sorcerer, they reflexively think that this person is a black magician. Though these names sometimes do refer to infernal business, this is not always true. In much of Peru witches or sorcerers may be white magicians, they may be black magicians, or as is commonly the case, they may be a combination of both.

The terms *witch*, *sorcerer*, and so forth also have a far less sinister connotation in Peru than in North America and Europe, and may even be used by villagers with a certain humor or kindness. In these chapters I use the words *shaman* and *shamanism* simply because they are familiar, and because they avoid the positive or negative judgments we make with words like *witch* and *wizard*. When I speak specifically of a dark magician I prefer to use the word *sorcerer* or *bruja*. The word *shaman* itself, which translates as "one who knows," is Asian, not South American, coming, it is believed, from Siberia or possibly the Caucasus.

Origins

There is a prevailing notion that when the Spanish first arrived in the New World, Inca civilization had ruled Peru for many centuries.

In fact, the sovereign Inca Empire ruled for less than three hundred years. Despite its wonders, a majority of its civic and religious doctrines were heavily influenced by earlier civilizations, among them the Chimu (900 to 1470 AD) from the northwestern coast of Peru and the Chimu's predecessors, the Moche or Mochica (100 to 700 AD) from the same area. The Incas learned from the ancient Waris as well, and from the millenary Amazonian jungle cultures that for centuries exchanged and traded with the rest of Peru. All these civilizations, in turn, were heir to far older social and spiritual traditions that dated back many thousands of years, and whose influence can still be seen on ancient jars, stone carvings, textiles, and architectural ruins.

This patchwork of cultural influences was due in part to the fact that Peru is divided into three entirely different terrains. In no other nation on earth, perhaps, do we find three such contrasting climates and landscapes juxtaposed so close to one another.

For example, the west coast of Peru is mostly coastal plains, prairies, and deserts interspersed with agricultural valleys. The middle part hosts the lush Andes, the longest and, some believe, most beautiful mountain range in the world. The eastern third is Amazon jungle, which takes up 60 percent of Peru and runs thousands of miles through Brazil, all the way to the Atlantic Ocean.

Thriving from around 100 to 700 AD, the Moche nation was situated in northern Peru, its center located where the modern city of Trujillo stands today, the same area where I did a good deal of my hospital work. Known for its monumental architecture and especially its world-famous ceramics, its remarkable pots and jars display complex narrative scenes of Moche life ranging from daily events to deadly rituals. Moche artists also created lifelike ceramic portraits of real people, the best of which rival the finest of Roman portrait busts.

The Chimu culture that followed also had its center in the Trujillo region. It came to prominence around 900 AD, specializing in public works, agriculture, and a complex level of government organization. The Chimu were masters at working in gold and silver. They built reservoirs and irrigation systems using engineering techniques far in advance of anything known in Europe at the time. After many centuries of rule, they were conquered and assimilated by the Incas, who less than a century later, in 1532, were subdued by Pizarro and his ferocious band of conquistadors.

European Sorcery and
Pre-Columbian Wisdom

Just as people often believe that the Incas ruled for numerous centuries, so many Peruvian shamans consider themselves descendants of a magical legacy that comes directly and exclusively from Pre-Columbian times.

But from what I have learned and experienced, this notion is not entirely true.

Though what I am going to say will be controversial and perhaps even heretical in the eyes of some *curanderos*, the methods followed by a large number of Peruvian shamans today are derived as much from medieval European magical practices as they are from Pre-Columbian wisdom.

What does this mean exactly?

If we look back to the year 1532, the Spanish fleet was just arriving on the shores of Peru bearing guns and horses, weapons the spear-carrying Incas could not defend against. But even more irresistible were the soldiers and laborers from different parts of Spain, especially the southern part, who came to the New World well tutored in the practice of occultism.

Their form of wizardry included both black magic and white. It used exorcisms, fortune-telling cards, invocations, charms, numerology, astrology, and medieval books of magic spells known as grimoires (*grimoirios* in Spanish). During three centuries of Spanish colonization, these occult arts thrived in colonial Peru. Like other European magic traditions, they relied on charismatic props or power objects such as daggers, crosses, preserved dead animals, images of saints, human and animal bones, and wands carved with magic symbols, all objects that were unknown to the ancient Peruvians. What's more, since consciousness-altering substances were forbidden by Catholicism, churchmen in the

Americas did their best to eliminate all plant intoxicants, though on the sly Christian acolytes mixed their own psychoactive brews using local roots plus European hallucinogens such as henbane and deadly nightshade.

To make the arrival of European occultism in Peru even more influential, part of Spanish sorcery that influenced *curanderismo* was actually twice removed from Peru since it had strong Middle Eastern affiliations. Since the time of the Middle Ages it had been imported to Spain from across the Mediterranean by the Berbers of North Africa, who had their own powerful magic traditions. For this reason, Peruvian colonial cuisine and fashion, as well as some arts and crafts, have a strong Moorish influence up to the present day. Meanwhile, a certain number of healing shamanic songs that are still sung today from the north coast to the Amazon (though with different lyrics) were borrowed directly from Christian hymns. In short, a large part of contemporary Peruvian shamanism is far from 100 percent ancient Peruvian; some would say it is less than 50 percent.

It is, therefore, clear that many of the methods used by today's shamans trace back to the era of Ferdinand and Isabella, and to archaic sorcery compounded in the magical dens of Tunisia and Morocco. To add to the mix, we know that during the sixteenth through nineteenth centuries magical teachings reached Peru from the Caribbean islands and from the African slave populations sold to Spanish colonists by the Portuguese. After the arrival of literacy and the media in twentieth-century Peru, this magical potpourri became even more widespread, reaching isolated areas deep in the Amazon wilderness. Today in remote parts of the rain forest visitors are often surprised to see shamans giving tarot card readings or using crystals for healing, two decidedly nontraditional Peruvian techniques.

And yet, though today's *curanderismo* is clearly a melting pot rather than a consistent monolithic teaching from the Peruvian past, this fact remains unacknowledged by most medicine people. From my own observations, the reality is that popular Peruvian shamanism (as opposed to the few ancient unchanged lineages that still exist and are found mainly in the northern and remote areas of Peru) is clearly an international amalgam and not an unaltered metaphysic passed directly down from ancient times.

Pedro's Proposition

The techniques of Knowledge that my friend Pedro offered me were, I soon learned, performed largely under the radar in cities and mountains along the northern coast, which is a culturally different world from the rest of Peru. Developed there by civilizations in remote times, their shamanic methods have been passed down from generation to generation up to the present day, while some of these lineages still practice healing traditions developed thousands of years ago with little or no foreign influences. These methods avoid theatrical techniques, relying mainly on the force of the Medicine and the shaman's skills to do the work. Pedro's form of shamanism, in other words, was one of the last remaining forms of the Art that had not been influenced by European magic.

Hearing what Pedro offered that day, I felt inclined to accept his proposition for several compelling reasons.

First, because his way was closely linked to early Peruvian tradition, which I had always sensed held a treasure trove of insight and medical savvy. Second, because what he taught was primarily focused on helping others, especially those with psychological as well as physical infirmities. Third, because his *curanderismo* was based almost entirely on the dialogue between a healer and the spirits. And last, because as a one-time martial artist my experience with the spirit world of *neigong* made me especially inclined to embrace his vision-based approach to healing.

As a result of all these influences, the day Pedro and I had our conversation and he held out his invitation to a new life grounded in the invisible world, I seized it. "Yes," I told him enthusiastically. "Definitely yes."

For a moment Pedro looked pleased. Then he became solemn.

I won't teach you popular healing, he said in his country way. I will teach you *my* way of healing, the north coast way. It is not the common thing you find all around you. It is just the thing I learned for myself.

I told him I would put myself in his hands and follow whatever he taught. He nodded and said nothing, and I fell silent in return. We sat there for many minutes without exchanging a glance or a word. This was our way of affirming that there was nothing more to discuss, and that our arrangement was a done deal.

Blinding in Order to See

Many branches of Peruvian shamanism, as explained, are based as much on European conjury as on Pre-Columbian knowledge. This fact became especially clear to me from an incident that took place during my early training as a natural healer.

One day I was told by my teacher to spend the night on the ridge of a mountain in Viru Valley, south of Trujillo, to make a connection with its spirits. As directed, I camped on the mountain ridge that night and next morning felt inexplicably happy and energized while climbing down, a sign that the mountain had welcomed me. The surface I was hiking on was covered with broken glass-like lava. While walking carefully over these sharp fragments, something odd caught my eye: Three round stones the size of large marbles lay on the ground in front of me forming a triangle. They were the type of stones one normally sees in streambeds worn smooth by running water. But here they were on this glassy, volcanic hillside, three perfect spheres, each stone the exact same color and size. It felt like the rocks were saying "take me, take me, take me!"

I put them in my pocket and continued down the ridge. At the bottom I crossed several fields, eventually coming to a town, where I headed to a local restaurant.

The owner of the restaurant, an elderly, eagle-eyed woman, took my order. Seeing that my clothes were rumpled and I was covered with dirt and sweat, she asked where I had been. I told her I had been hiking in the valley. I could sense that she did not entirely believe me. The mountain I had come down from was considered enchanted and was believed to be frequented by ancestral spirits. Not the kind of place where locals go trekking. Finally, hands on hips, she asked straight out if I was up to *curandero* work.

I shrugged ambivalently, but that was enough for her to know. She then began to launch into a dialogue about magical events in her valley and about nearby Moche temples and pyramids. She chatted on this way for a few minutes, then suddenly stopped, looked at me for a long beat, then bent down close to my ear. She had heard of an ancient Peruvian recipe for helping people see the spirit world, she whispered. To perform it you have to have a black cat. Did I want to hear about it?

I gave no answer, but she went on anyway.

First, she started, you cut out the cat's eyes while it is still alive. That's important, that the cat is alive. Then you take a piece of thread and tie the eyes to a kind of bean that only grows in this part of the country. Without this special bean, she warned, nothing will work.

Now you take the bean and bury it close to a remote mountain where nobody goes. When the plants flower and fruit, you pick the beans and eat them in a certain progression. From then on you can see into the invisible world. I've never tried it, she said with a collusive smile. I don't know about these things; I just hear talk about it in the valley and thought you might like to know.

I thanked the woman for the briefing, ate my breakfast, and left. All during the day I thought about what she had told me. Not the part about blinding the cat. This was typical dark shaman magic that can be quite cruel. What intrigued me was the fact that she had probably never read a book in her life, and clearly had no occult knowledge of her own. Yet she was familiar with the details of this obscure and powerful magic spell. Where had it come from?

The more I thought about it, the clearer it became. To begin, domestic cats did not live in Peru until they were brought here by Spanish colonizers in the sixteenth century. So much for the ancientness of her formula. I also happened to know that there is a prescription in a certain old European book of magic that is *exactly* the same as the one she whispered in my ear. The fact was that the countrywoman's spell, like so much other Peruvian magic lore talked about by villagers throughout the country, was not ancient Peruvian at all. It was strictly colonial, a fact that strengthened my belief that popular shamanism in my country was a mix of the Peruvian old and the European new.

Several days later I told one of my teachers about finding the marble-like stones. She said they were gifts. The mountain had materialized them and put them on the ground especially for me. They were Medicine from the mountain, she told me. They would bring me luck and who knows what other good things.

Mesa Magic

The Spanish-inspired spell that the waitress at the restaurant told me that day is associated with what was said above about the influence of European magic on Peruvian shamanism and especially on what is known as *mesa magic*. Mesa magic is derived from the European practice of spreading a piece of cloth on a table (*mesa* in Spanish) and dividing it into two halves. The magical props placed on the right side of the mesa are used for healing. Those on the left protect and defend, and in certain cases attack and harm. The mesa itself is often fronted with specially energized sticks arranged fencelike for psychic protection. Sometimes the mesa table is referred to as a healing altar.

The types of power objects placed on a mesa vary according to a shaman's goals.

Stones with the power to cure or harm are sometimes used, or bricks that come from a certain tomb or ruin. Flowers may be put on the cloth, or perfumes, shells, candles, bottles with plants in them. Ancient textiles or Inca mirrors are common, along with human bones, mummified hands, masks, and images of saints. Also, animal parts such as the beak of a bird or the head of a snake. Swords and knives, sticks, wands, cudgels, whips, and scepters— each of these props has a particular use for doing good or evil.

Once the power objects are chosen, if the person of knowledge has been correctly trained, he "mounts" (*montar*) the selected objects; that is, he energizes them with his spirit force, giving them a temporary life of their own. Using his inner vision, he sees that certain of these power objects stand out from the rest. Perhaps they shine or glow. They may tremble slightly or transmit silent messages, giving him information on how to remedy a client's specific problem. He then uses these chosen objects to do his work—

break a curse, hurt or push away an enemy, heal an illness, find a lost ring or wallet—whatever his paying client needs.

Mesa-influenced Medicine is by far the most popular form of shamanism in Peru today, especially on the coast and parts of the highlands. In the right hands it is a powerful healing instrument.

Still, it was not the *curanderismo* Pedro offered me. With his form of the Art, there were no power objects or charms; all the Medicine and magic was carried inside you, and all of it was based on direct negotiation with the environment and the invisible world. His way derived its power from spirit animals, ancestors, from locations in the landscape like mountains, forests, and lakes, a practice that made perfect sense to me, dovetailing with what I already understood about Pre-Columbian healing's choreography with nature. I was passionate to learn more.

Shamanic Learning and Practice

During my training under Pedro and other *curanderos* I learned that shamanism, among many things, clears away ghosts and psychic parasites that live off people's negativity. Practiced *curanderos* can interpret omens, conduct visionary ceremonies, translate messages that come in dreams, and speak with dead ancestors and persons of Knowledge. They are experts in constructing invisible protective spaces that cannot be violated or entered by outsiders, either humans or spirits. They know ways of communicating with wild animals as well as animals from the spirit world. They are masters of drumming, singing, and playing the rattle in a way that builds a psychic kinship between the material and spiritual worlds.

When a master shaman enters a trance, he feels awestruck as the veils part and he is escorted into a mysterious universe that in many ways resembles the material world but in other ways is made of dream stuff that, ironically, is more real than the physical reality left behind. Here the spirits reveal the secrets of birth, life, and death. He can move about this magical realm at will, but never knows what he will find or what the spirits will ask of him.

Though I was already well versed in touch healing from my Qigong work in hospitals, my teachers showed me new methods for transmitting curative energy through touch, breath, sound, and distance. When using touch therapy, practitioners work in the spirit world as well as the physical. Just as with sacred plants, they enter clients' bodies on a psychic level, observing their organs and nervous system and finding the physical or mental irregularities causing their distress. The healer then remedies the problems with healing energy transmitted via touch and muscle manipulation.

When performing touch healing, it is not necessary to supplement the process with psychoactive plants. The touch itself is enough. When touch healing is real, clients feel a force entering their bodies from the shaman's hands and sometimes even experience a physical purge.

While hands-on healing remains a vital part of the north coastal medicine, it is found in other Peruvian lineages as well, especially in the Amazon. Yet, though once a prerequisite tool in every shaman's tool kit, hands-on work is dying out in many areas of the country that once practiced it with great proficiency. Today, it is often dismissed by those who do not understand its power or who are seeking psychoactive, plant-induced states of consciousness. For these reasons, the powerful art of shamanic touch healing is becoming more and more a thing of the past.

Some years ago, I visited a museum in Lima to study its collection of Moche ceramics.

The image on one particular pot showed a man in traditional

dress with his hands placed on another man's chest. The caption, which read "An ancient doctor performing a physical examination," was based on the assumption that the man was palpating his client, feeling for a lump or growth. But I knew that what I was seeing was not a diagnosis at all. The image on the pot clearly showed a Moche man of knowledge performing touch healing, and doing so in the exact same way that was taught to me.

Animals and Magic

Throughout the shamanic world, traditional societies have always known that animals have powerful intuitive perceptions, which is why in ancient frescoes and on temple walls they are so often depicted as gods. Shamans are well versed in creature intelligence, sometimes referring to their animal helpers with honorific titles like "Doctor Ocelot" or "Master Alligator." While many humans think of the beasts of the earth as "dumb," when clients take part in a plant ceremony, they are often astonished to discover that certain animal spirits have greater discernment and insight than they do.

The truth is we really know very little about animal thought and reason. Intuitive and aware, animals have their own languages, some of them verbal, some psychic. Animals, unlike humans, show little or no signs of ethical conflict, and are relatively immune to hatred, envy, pride, and greed. The fact that they have no interest in founding civilizations, which, despite the wonders of art and invention, inevitably decline into war and degeneracy, may be a sign of their insight rather than ignorance. In all these contexts animals are a rung above humans in spirit, immune to the currents of mind that end up creating concentration camps and hydrogen bombs.

✴

Spirit animals that are seen during a sacred ceremony are grouped into three broad categories.

First, they are symbols of certain virtues that guide seekers on their spiritual journey.

Second, there are spirit animals that work on invisible levels with shamans and clients, providing them with protection, sagacity, and healing.

Third, animals can be close allies and helpers, both in the physical world and in the invisible, where in some clans or tribes they are totemic. In many if not most shamanic traditions, the *curandero* has one or two companion animals at his side that have befriended him for life, and that he calls on in times of need or peril.

Certain animals can also exert powers over humankind when they so choose.

A hunter who lives in a village near my jungle compound often makes hunting trips to the swamps of a nearby island in the Amazon. One moonlit night while scouting for game he leaped back in surprise when he saw a giant anaconda coiled in his path. The anaconda rose up and from six feet away blew its breath on him. The hunter immediately sensed that something dense and heavy had entered his body. Attempting to compose himself, he fired his shotgun randomly, and the snake slithered into the reeds. He returned home with his legs shaking, feeling deathly ill, and could barely sleep or eat. For days no local doctors could help until a man of knowledge, learning of the serpent's attack, understood that the hunter was not sick but cursed. The hunter had been a victim of *cutipar*, a common jungle term for negative influences that an animal or plant can cast on a human being when feeling threatened or disrespected. It took the hunter several days of abstention and the wise man's help to dissolve the anaconda's powerful spell.

Making Friends with the Landscape

Much of the learning I received from my teachers was designed to encourage self-teaching. A trainee is given direct instruction, certainly. But the core of our practice requires that beginners use this instruction to develop their own methods and personal approach to the world of spirits. This is why we call it a Craft.

Once Pedro casually told me to climb a certain mountain bordering a flooded area known as the Swamp of the Dead. This dreary slough was so named because so many people had been sucked down and drowned in it, with many stories of ghosts resulting.

"This place I'm sending you might be good for you," he told me. "Just go and sleep there for a night. See what comes to you in your dreams. You'll know if it has something to give you."

The next day I trudged past the swamp with its foul-smelling waters and up the mountain trail, pitching my tent at the top. That night I did indeed have a strange dream. A female figure visited me. Her entire body was covered with red hair like a fox, and she had large red muttonchop sideburns. She approached me smiling and asked if I would make love to her. I told her no, I was in a relationship with another woman, which at the time was true. She asked me several more times, and when I continued to refuse, she finally said in a heartbroken voice, "Then at least hold me in your arms with love."

We embraced for several minutes, then she pulled back and said it was time for her to leave. As she was walking away, she suddenly turned and shouted, "Look," at which point in my dream I saw an L-shaped stone bench. "This is what everybody is searching for," she declared. "If you find it, sit on it." She looked at me one more moment with love in her eyes and then vanished.

The next morning the weather on the mountain was clear and cold. My food supplies were gone by now, and I was underdressed, wearing only shorts and a T-shirt. I walked several shivering miles down the mountain ridge until I came to a bend in the trail where under a tree I saw the exact same stone bench the woman had pointed out in my dream. There was no mistake; the exact same one.

Despite the cold, my intuition told me to undress.

I stripped to my undergarments, sat down on the bench, and immediately fatigue, hunger, chills, all the discomforts of a cold night on the mountain, disappeared and I felt elated. I sat on the seat relaxing and meditating in a kind of trance. After an hour or so I got up and found my way down the ridge to a town, where I picked up a lift on a nearby highway and returned to Trujillo.

All that day I felt exceptionally clear-headed and cleansed. By the time I reached home I realized I was beginning to perceive the world in a new way—a clearer, deeper way. In the next few weeks, I discovered my capacity for seeing inside a client's psyche had vastly improved, and that I could address a client's problems in a more sensitive and focused way. Somehow sitting on the bench in my dream had sharpened my clairvoyant perceptions, giving me a heightened intuition and insight that have never left me.

The next time I saw Pedro, I excitedly told him about my encounter on the mountain and about my dream. He was whittling a long wooden pipe as I told him the story. When I finished, he looked up at me for a moment, raised an eyebrow, then went back to his whittling.

Sometimes the Spirits Like You, Sometimes They Don't

Imagine for a moment that you are a trainee asked to make friends with a place in the wilderness known to have hosted spiritual activities in the far past. You approach the site with prayers and songs, asking the invisible beings that guard it for instruction.

These invisible beings may like you and agree to guide you. Or not. Nothing is for sure. And do not even *think* of approaching them without the proper respect or of trying to exploit them and steal their secrets. They will know what you are up to and avoid you. Or they may look unkindly on you for unknown reasons. If you are unwelcome and you keep insisting, they may chase you away or simply remain silent. On the other hand, if they are sympathetic, a transmission will take place that is custom-made to who you are, how much knowledge and energy you are able to process, and what psychic aids will best benefit your needs. This is how your practice grows.

There are also certain signs that appear when the spirits of a sacred site approve of you. You may hear or see a local animal. A bird of prey cries out, a fox watches you from a distance, or a bear or deer—large, memorable animals that rule the area and are, so to speak, spirit ambassadors of this particular pasture or rain forest.

Another indication of welcome is that the earth beneath you starts to tremble. Unlike an earthquake or land tremor, the movement is concentrated directly beneath your feet. Other people may be standing nearby, but you will be the only one who feels it. Sometimes the earth shakes for a few seconds, sometimes for half a minute or more, but it is only for you, telling you that the landscape is pleased to see you.

At other times a magical site acknowledges its alliance with a glow that comes from a tree or behind a rock. You hear spirits inviting you to approach it. Occasionally you may hear a harmonious chord that sounds inside your head and outside at the same time. The chord is unlike anything you have ever heard and can only be described as heavenly.

At still other times, the sky suddenly clouds over and rays of golden light pour down, making you feel wonderfully attuned to the landscape. Or a rainbow appears even if the weather is dry. Seeing it means the spirits are coming down to your level on earth and saying, "I am here. Greetings, nice to meet you. I have fond feelings for you." From this time on, whenever you visit this particular site, it will always welcome you warmly and perhaps send you Knowledge in the form of visions, dreams, or an animal that brings you a message. From now on this is a holy place for you and will remain so as long as you honor it.

Occasionally when visiting a special location, a rock may ask you to come close to it. It does not speak to you exactly, but exerts a kind of magnetism drawing you near. If you tap the rock, it sounds like a bell. If you lie on it, you feel a soft power coursing through your body similar to the feelings one experiences while doing *neigong* exercises.

Bodies of water have their own way of recognizing you. A lake will invite you to dive in and submerge. It wants to look at you and feel your joy while swimming in it. This is how you become friends. Rivers sing to you, inviting you to rest on their banks. Wavelets in brooks splash up and quite clearly dance for your pleasure. A waterfall may ask you to stand under it for a few moments. During this short immersion important life messages are passed on to you.

Finally, when you arrive at a place in the wilderness with the hope of befriending it, you may feel a pressure in your belly, like a soft push or pull. The landscape then asks you to perform a certain task such as pouring water on a baby tree or looking for a lost ring under a rock.

These are just some of the signs indicating that a luminous site is pleased with you and is willing to share its mysteries. There are many others. Being aware and open to them is the first step toward becoming attuned to the secret whisperings of nature that are so vitally important to a shaman's practice.

The Noble Skull

In some traditional areas of Peru, family members keep the bones of parents or grandparents displayed on a shelf in their homes. Of all skeletal parts, skulls are the most common. Piles of human remains are a common sight in many areas of the Peruvian desert and beaches, where for centuries grave robbers have dug up ancient tombs searching for gold or in recent times for ancient pots or *huacos* that fetch large sums of money among collectors. While digging, the robbers randomly toss the bones in all directions; I have seen dug-up beaches in Peru with skeletal limbs and skulls littered as far as the eye can see.

On occasion local people visit these sites, picking up an intact skull, taking it home, and placing it in a favored corner of the house where everyone can see it. They give it a name, offer it cooked food, fruit, alcohol, or sweets, speak to it as if it understands, and generally treat it as a living person and part of the family. In turn they believe the soul of the skull will assume it has found a home and will protect the family from thieves and evil spirits. I know people who swear their skulls talk to them, making predictions or warning them of danger.

Once while I was camping out in a lonely part of the wilderness, an ancient warrior visited me in a dream. Most likely Moche or Chimu, he was handsome and powerfully built with a noble expression on his face. His eyes were transparent and radiated wisdom and trust. Looking at me directly, he announced that I would find him very soon. The only thing he asked was that I take good care of his teeth. If you do that, he promised, I will help you get whatever you want in life.

When I woke up, I pondered what the warrior had asked me but was unable to connect it with anything in my life. Nonetheless, it was one of those dreams you know is real, and that emblazons itself on your memory.

Several months later I was exploring the ruins of a Moche city on a cliff far from any main roads. On the outskirts of the ruin, I came to an ancient cemetery, which, like most Pre-Columbian burial grounds, had been thoroughly despoiled by grave robbers. There were broken bricks, mounds of dirt, fragments of pots, pieces of old fabric thoroughly intact due to the dry air. Here and there I could see piles of bleached bones.

As I was studying this melancholy sight, I had the feeling that a corner of the cemetery was calling to me. Walking toward it I saw a bulbous something-or-other sticking out of the soil. It was a skull, and not just an ordinary skull. Inordinately large and white, it had a huge, perfectly formed forehead, intact facial bones, and most conspicuously an open mouth with almost all its teeth intact, a rarity among ancient skulls and, I would guess, among people from the past in general. I immediately understood that this head belonged to the visitor in my dream.

Realizing what I had come upon, I felt ambivalent about what to do.

Taking this skull home and becoming its protector would trigger the extraordinary powers it promised, of this I had no doubt. It was not entirely far-fetched to say that adopting it would be like having my own genie in a lamp. All I needed was to make a silent pact with the soul of the warrior and keep his skull (and teeth) safe from harm. He, in turn, would give me whatever I asked. It was so easy.

Yet by now I had already given my heart to coastal *curanderismo*, which takes its power from the landscape and from one's healing tools, not from skulls or bones. If I were to enter a relationship with the soul of this skull, I would, in a sense, become its prisoner.

Making pacts with the dead, I knew, always places a shaman on the thin line that separates black magic from white.

And there was something else: By forming a bond with a dead person, this attachment would keep his soul tied to earth rather than allowing it to move on to other, no doubt better worlds. By accepting the warrior's offer of friendship, I would, ironically, be holding him back from his ultimate freedom.

I lifted the skull and gazed at it for a long time. If you say no to a deceased person of stature, you must do so in a respectful way. I dug a hole several feet deep in the burial ground, carefully placed the skull at the bottom, asked that its soul find the peace it was looking for, covered it over gently with fresh soil, and whispered farewell.

A while later I told the story of my encounter in the burial ground to Pedro. After I explained all that had happened, he looked at me with a slight grin. So, you didn't take the skull? he asked, as if to reaffirm what I had just told him.

No, I said, I didn't take it. Was this a test?

He said nothing for a long minute, then let out an odd laugh. Was the laugh a "what an idiot!" kind of laugh? Was it a "This guy is going in the right direction and has passed the test!" kind of laugh? I never asked.

Lessons in the Secret Arts

When stepping into the world of north coast shamanism, I was astonished to discover that the unseen influences our everyday thoughts and activities, usually without our knowing it, determining our behavior in both positive and negative ways.

I began to realize that the ordinary three dimensions where we work and play, fall in love, raise families, make war, do business, live and die—the world we believe to be the only real world—is in fact the bottom layer of reality, the starting point of a hierarchy of planes that extends from our material level upward through increasingly refined psychic realms. This realization gave new meaning to the concept mentioned in so many sacred books and scriptures: that the physical world is an illusion and that most human beings are spiritually asleep.

During the first year of my training, I had two episodes that taught me just how real the invisible world really is. These episodes gave me the humbling realization that all a shaman can do is experience this realm, work with it, communicate with it, but never truly understand its true nature.

During these first months of my apprenticeship, I had a friend who was interested in traditional practices and had used the psychedelic cactus San Pedro several times. He raved about its spiritual benefits so persuasively that I agreed to try it with him. It would be the first time I had ever taken a sacred plant.

With two other friends who were of like mind we took a bus to an arid valley in the north of Peru. From there we hiked across several miles of deserted wilderness, pitching camp next to a stream.

After settling in, we drank a beverage made exclusively from San Pedro. It was bitter and thick, and made me slightly nauseous.

I lay on my side for several minutes sensing very little and feeling like I was falling asleep when I suddenly became aware of odd sounds coming from the nearby stream. When I stood up to look, I saw a group of beings three or four inches tall paddling around in the water. They were talking in boisterous, squeaky voices, playing games, clearly enjoying themselves, and occasionally glancing in my direction. Their faces were humanish, some smiling, some not, while their torsos were like mermen or mermaids, translucent and with scales. I knew instinctively these enchanting mer-people

were the spirit guardians of the stream. After watching them ca-
vort for several minutes, their bodies became jelly-like, and the
entire community melted into the water. I stood there hoping
they would come back. But no.

When it was clear they were gone for good, I wandered around
the area dazed at what I had seen. As I walked, I saw the silhouette of a mountain range ahead. Certain mountains had a subtle
glow to them, while others were dark. This was the first time I
understood that some mountains have a distinct magical character,
while others are simply giant mounds of earth.

Following a path through the brush, I noticed something moving on my right. At first, I thought it was an animal but then
realized the movement was underground. Looking hard with my
expanded vision, I could "see" the body of a dead woman thrashing about beneath the soil, clearly unhappy to be there. As I
passed her grave, she made a strange rattling sound, telling me
in a silent language that she had been murdered and dumped in
the hole. She asked if I could release her from her ghost-like state.

I had no idea what to do in a situation like this—I was, remember, just starting my training as a *curandero* and had no experience
working with the souls of the dead. So, I whispered a long prayer
for her welfare and kept on walking.

Six months later I had another experience with San Pedro, this
time accompanied by two of my closest friends. We spent our
first day in the wilderness exploring the ruins on Cerro Campana,
a huge and important sacred mountain near Huanchaco in the
Trujillo area. Though these ruins are no secret, the north of Peru
is full of lost cities that are totally unknown not only to archaeologists but to native Peruvians as well.

Cerro Campana itself is an extremely imposing sight. A towering rock peak 3,200 feet high, it seems to erupt out of the flat desert, its summit almost always wreathed in clouds. Its mysterious presence is looked on by inhabitants of the Trujillo area with enormous reverence and a touch of fear. The mountain has been depicted in artistic representations from ancient times and is still a popular subject for local artists today.

A *bruja* who taught me many things had recently suggested that when I drink San Pedro, I should first draw a cross on the ground with a stick and pour a bit of the brew on it as an offering. Connect with the place, she told me, as if the place is a person, and ask for its acceptance. Do this, my teacher told me cryptically, and you may see sadness and light.

It was beginning to get dark as the three of us started up the mountain trail. Finding a picturesque ruin along the way, we stopped, set up our tents, and drank the medicine. As I sat there waiting for its effects to kick in, I realized that the mountain was slowly but undeniably self-illuminating, as if someone were turning on its lights with a dimmer switch. When the light reached full strength, the mountain glowed bright gold and green. All of us witnessed it.

Sitting on a stone wall gazing at this radiant sight, I began to feel an overwhelming sadness and nostalgia.

It was difficult to understand what was happening and why, but after several minutes things came clear: I was undergoing an initiation in compassion; that is, for reasons I could not explain I was connecting with the collective pain and heartbreak that my elderly hospital clients had experienced all their lives. These people knew that no matter how much they worked to improve their welfare, they would never achieve the good fortune and security that those higher up on the social ladder took for granted. They saw their parents die badly and could not afford the medicine to help them. Their children and grandchildren had no access to education. They lived in hovels and sometimes could not afford food. While they labored for a few dollars a week at menial work, if they became sick or were injured on the job, their company dropped them without benefits and without pay. It all seemed so unfair—so many people in the world born with so few chances and so many handicaps. How extraordinary it was, I thought, that my clients had carried on with their lives in a quiet, noble way despite such hopelessness.

These feelings of desolation grew increasingly intense until I began to sob convulsively. After several minutes I developed a stitching pain in my chest and started having difficulty breathing. I realized that the San Pedro was undamming a reservoir of sorrow inside me that for my own emotional protection I had suppressed while working with these mistreated people.

Sitting there in anguish, I thought I might be passing out or even dying. I was about to start sobbing again when the sandy earth in front of me quivered and a being less than a foot high pushed his way up from the ground looking partly human, partly alien. His head was like that of a baby, but elderly at the same time. His skin was dark and he was a bit pudgy, looking curiously like an elf but with an ancient Peruvian face. There was a royal presence about him, set off by a jeweled robe that produced a cosmically beautiful light. This sublime little being, I understood, was the monarch of Cerro Campana Mountain. Every major mountain has its spirit king or queen who takes care of the villagers living nearby. Entities of this kind come from a high place in the spirit world and are always extremely generous to humans that seek the Medicine.

For a few minutes he stood there looking at me and I at him. His eyes were glowing, but there was no talk between us or any telepathic communication. Our gaze itself was the message.

Then to my surprise he spoke, telling me that he wanted to give me a gift. What would I most treasure? I told him I would like to become a better human being and bring genuine help to other people.

Without hesitation he blew a chalky substance in my face that tasted like dust. This surprise whoosh woke me up and made my emotions flare.

A moment later a corona of light flooded the sky.

I glanced up at Cerro Campana and fireworks seemed to be going off on its summit, just as they were going off inside me. I felt an invitation from the mountain peak to come closer.

Looking down at my feet, I realized I was barefoot. I had taken off my shoes, when and where I could not remember. The ground around me was covered with sharp volcanic rocks, cactuses, briars, and most likely poisonous vipers. Yet when I started walking, my feet felt no pain and, in fact, felt nothing at all. I was not even looking at the ground as I went; I wondered if I was floating. I kept moving up the trail, the little king now forgotten, my mind intent on the mountain's summons. Gradually the glow shifted again, turning into a rain of indescribably bright light. I was overcome. My legs bent by themselves and I fell to my knees. I was no longer capable—I should say *worthy*—of gazing up. The mountain and the light surrounding me were too majestic. I was too small, too human.

I remained on my knees with my head pressed to the earth for many minutes.

When I finally looked up, the light on the mountain was gone and the royal genie was nowhere to be seen. My breathing had returned to normal and all traces of sadness and despair had vanished. In their place I felt a peace and joy the depth of which I had never known before.

One interesting thing to add about this encounter on Cerro

Campana was that while I was experiencing these marvels—the king burrowing up from the ground, the rain of light—one of my friends was close by the whole time and witnessed everything that happened to me. Back at camp he was the first to bring the subject up, saying how amazed he was at seeing the little being and the burst of light that from his perspective appeared to be burning me to ashes. Though these experiences seemed ultra-real to me while they were happening, as far as the supernormal goes, there is always the possibility that imagination plays a part. When my friend volunteered that he had seen what I had seen, I knew for certain that the secret heart of the world is a magical place.

Inside the Dark Side

When I was still a novice *curandero*, several teachers stressed the need for counteracting the dark forces I would be up against as helper and healer—forces that pervert both clients and shamans, and that encourage seemingly good people to indulge in the most remarkably base behaviors. Learning my craft, they insisted, required that I witness the wicked side of the human psyche first-hand, and that I know how to neutralize it.

As you may remember, I was once told how important it is for a *curandero* to remain unaffected by fear or disgust when healing and when encountering dark forces.

For ordinary people it is rare to meet an avowedly evil man or woman. Most of us are a mixture of the good and not-so-good, and if we do harbor wicked impulses, we have moral and educational standards to oppose them. It is also rare for laymen to witness the remarkably cruel practices performed by certain sorcerers and witches who willingly release forces into the world that can only be described as demonic.

For the benevolent shaman, however, witnessing evil in others is commonplace. This is true first because *curanderos* frequently confront curses, malevolent spirits, and sinister opponents as part of their calling; and second, because many of the problems that clients bring to a sacred ceremony stem from the depraved or hateful emotions festering inside them.

During my training it was my mentors' job to help me develop ways for counteracting evil-intentioned practitioners. Perhaps more daunting, my teachers occasionally choreographed actual situations in which I was intentionally set face-to-face with sorcerers who made no bones about harming people or even killing them. The lessons from these encounters taught me more in a night than I could learn in a year, imprinting demonic impressions on my mind in ways I would never forget.

One evening as I was preparing to take part in a plant ceremony, I began to feel an unusual tension in the air. The shaman I had been studying with at the time was acting uncharacteristically waggish—the way people do when they have a secret and are going to spring it on you as a surprise. This was going to be a memorable evening, for better or worse.

The ceremony got underway, and I began to revel in the effect of the plants. Suddenly I felt my energy body being sucked out of me and transported in a vacuum over a long distance, landing finally on a wild, deserted beach next to a stone cliff that towered ominously above me. The sky was clouded over and seemed unnaturally dark.

I stood there for several minutes getting my bearings, then noticed the silhouette of a man moving around near a fissure in the cliff.

Though the night was impenetrably black, the Medicine gave me occult vision, and I saw the face of the man, a local native of mixed blood. I did not know him personally, but I instantly recognized him as an evil sorcerer.

It seems odd perhaps that I came to this realization so quickly. But to the vision of a *curandero*, even a beginner like myself, an evil *brujo* often has a certain look about him, like that of an animated doll. The man's skin looked inflated and puffy, his lips bulged, and his eyes popped out like the buttons on a rag doll, making him appear artificial, as if someone had sewn him together or drawn him. I watched him move about in the shadows, understanding that he was unclean and, more importantly, that the shaman who was leading the ceremony that night was arranging this encounter for my edification. It was a teaching within a teaching.

As I stood there staring, the area around me lit up slightly, either from the moon coming out from the clouds or from the breath of the spirits—who knows? At that moment I saw the most gruesome sight I had yet witnessed as a student shaman. The shadow sorcerer was holding a male human head, joggling it up and down like a piece of meat. The head was probably stolen from a graveyard belonging to someone who had died recently. Its skin was just beginning to dry and parch.

Though I was standing near him, the sorcerer appeared to be unaware of my presence. Hoping that in my spirit state I could move around without being perceived, I crept closer to see what he was doing. Again, a shock: He was placing passport-sized photographs of men and women into the head's mouth.

Later on, my teacher explained that the *brujo* was sending suffering of one kind or another to the people in the pictures. It might have been a sexual curse or a physical ailment. When you work with the energy of the dead like this, he explained, it is almost always intended to harm enemies or make them sick. Even to kill them. This was the kind of evil, he implied, I could expect to contend with when I became a full-fledged *curandero*.

Perhaps all this was a test, I thought, though I took it more as a training. Still, watching the sorcerer perform his grisly work infuriated me, and I had the impulse to step out of my invisible bubble and challenge him. Immediately I heard my teacher's voice warning me that I was not strong enough to oppose such a potent evil worker, and that if I approached him, he would crush me. In the world of the *curandero*, he cautioned, victory goes not to the good but to the most powerful. He then added that the spirits of the Moches had been watching me the whole time and were pleased, seeing that I reacted with such fury when faced with the outrageousness of evil.

Discovering the Amazon

During my years learning the Craft, I did a good deal of traveling in wilderness areas, attempting to find places of spiritual resonance.

I had always been especially intrigued by the perilous but seductive Amazon jungle, which I visited briefly as a teenager, loving it even then with its lush wilderness and air of secrecy and peril. In the jungle one rarely finds traces of ancient cultures. Unlike the drier areas along the coast and in the Andes, deserted habitations quickly disappear into the hungry mouth of the rain forest, smothered by its web of vines and creepers. Yet the jungle offers endless surprises. Sometimes in the thickest, most remote part of a forest travelers come across huge, deserted cities like something out of *Indiana Jones* with giant stone circles, bas reliefs, and crumbling temples. These sites are mostly unknown to the outside world and sometimes even to the indigenous villagers who live nearby.

During these itinerant years I was especially fascinated by the area south of Cajamarca, west of San Martin, and far east of La Libertad, a transitional region where high peaks in the Andes become hills and then flatten out eastward into green pockets of jungle. This is the ancient land of the Chachapoyas, a powerful jungle nation later conquered by the Incas. Here I traveled from village to village, learning about healing herbs and searching for individuals who still practiced remnants of ancient knowledge. Even today this region has few paved highways, and I did most of my explorations driving over dirt roads in public vans, riding horseback, or on foot. When I found a community inhabited by a *curandero* of merit, I stayed with him for some days, paying rent or working off my stay by helping with food preparation and farm work. If the medicine man liked me, he would share a secret here, a secret there. Sometimes it was verbal knowledge, stories, instructions, sometimes it was a certain body language or whispered sacred plant recipes.

During this period of traveling and searching, I took Ayahuasca for the first time.

New Forms of Ancient Magic

Though I was no stranger to mind-altering substances, having used San Pedro and other psychoactive plants several times by now, Ayahuasca belonged more to the Amazon than to the western and central parts of the country. It was here that I first discovered its remarkable transformative powers.

In my first Ayahuasca ritual I sat in a circle with a handful of journeyers overseen by a shaman who had been especially generous in sharing his practice with me. In Amazonian shamanism Ayahuasca ceremonies are occasionally performed in fields or deserts but far more commonly in an open, hut-like structure known as a *maloca*. The interior of a *maloca* can be forty or fifty feet wide, depending on the number of clients it is built to accommodate. It is almost always round, topped with a high, palm-thatched dome. Considered a sacred space, it is usually set off several hundred yards or more from other buildings in a village.

Within an hour of drinking the Ayahuasca mixture that first night, a parade of spirits began marching through the doors of my consciousness waving a bright banner. Over the flag a small snake floated in the air, its eyes focused on me with disconcerting intensity. The parade stopped and the snake slithered in my direction, gradually growing larger, thicker, and enormously long like a giant anaconda. Drawing close to my chest, it lunged, entering my abdomen and filling my stomach.

The moment the snake entered my gut my state of consciousness became a woof and warp of plant fiber. My chest turned into a netting of jungle ferns and threads. Strange figures, some half-human, half-vegetable, peered at me from different dimensions in this vortex of greenery. My blood veins and arteries became brown vines branching out in all directions and into every cell of my body. Surrounding colors were unimaginably strong and bright. The jungle was introducing itself to me and swallowing me up, making me part of its world and, I thought, part of its universal vegetable consciousness as well. I was, I realized, learning a form of shamanism that was alike in kind but different in form to the one practiced in my northern coastal lineage. From that time on I was a man with one part of me on the coast and the other in the rain forest.

Over the next several years I made numerous trips to the jungle, learning about Amazonian ceremonial procedures and psychoactive jungle plants. I became close with one shaman in particular who taught me a great deal about the Art. In the beginning he let me collect the leaves and vines. Then he showed me ways to plant and harvest the medicine, and finally how to serve it during a ceremony and especially how to understand plant energies and their unique aesthetics. It was during this time that I gradually began to think that when I became a full-fledged *curandero*, I would do much of my healing in the rain forest. And indeed, this is how things eventually turned out.

The Two Golden Rules

There are innumerable aspects to the Craft that an aspiring practitioner needs to understand and learn to apply. I am not referring just to learning how to heal an addiction or ward off spells but also to personal challenges that both shamans and clients are put through during a plant ritual and after, and which I associate with the First and Second Golden Rule.

The First Golden Rule tells us that in a properly run shamanic ceremony nothing ever happens to participants that pushes them beyond their emotional and psychological limits. Ceremony participants can be asked to embrace the ugliest parts of their psyche, but they will never be saddled with a challenge that is beyond their ability to handle. While experiencing a mind trip that forces them to confront their darkest side, clients may feel this moment of truth is too painful to accept, let alone work with. But the moment the encounter ends and a clearing opens into the sunlit field of self-understanding, it becomes apparent why this difficult test was necessary. Whenever clients complain that a session was terribly taxing, I always ask them the same question: Were the harrowing moments you went through during your ceremony worth the lessons you learned? I cannot say that everyone answers yes. But most do.

Then there is the Second Golden Rule, which we will speak of in chapters ahead. It maintains that lessons learned during a ceremony often come back to test us in ordinary life in the weeks and months that follow. The story below offers an example of just how intensely the Second Golden Rule can affect one's life and the life of others.

At one point in my apprenticeship when I was learning Amazonian Medicine, I returned to my home in Trujillo after several weeks of heavy training in the jungle. Two days later I received a job offer from an assistant mayor in a district near the city.

I was currently affiliated with a group of concerned locals who were working to protect the landscape from logging and deforestation. Would I be interested in taking a one-day job with these people to survey a steep mountain just outside Trujillo, the assistant wanted to know. Our mission would be to climb the mountain, map its trails, look for interesting sites and ruins, take photographs, then report back as to whether we believed the area could be promoted as a tourist attraction for hikers and environmentalists.

Ten of us in the group including myself accepted the job.

On the day of our engagement, we piled into an old truck and drove to an impoverished neighborhood at the foot of the mountain. As we chugged through its streets the unfriendly stares and the sight of several townsmen holding sticks and rocks told us we were unwelcome intruders.

Dropped off at the base of the mountain, we started up a rocky, bramble-sided trail that wound its way upward in crazy loops and dips. The members of our group were carrying valuable objects like digital binoculars and cell phones, which at the time were a novelty in Peru. Our photographic equipment was stashed in a backpack that we took turns carrying.

After an hour or so of a murderously steep climb, we reached a plateau. Here four members of the group dropped out, saying they were too exhausted to make it to the top, and that they would wait for us here. A bit farther up the trail three more members did the same.

Three of us continued onward and upward—myself, a university student named Manuel, and a nineteen-year-old woman who called herself Siso.

As we climbed, the trail became increasingly narrow, thinning down to five or six feet. After another hour we made it to the summit where, besides a spectacular view of far-off Trujillo, we found several half-crumbled adobe buildings built centuries earlier. Generally speaking, if one finds ancient constructions on any major mountaintop in Peru, it is safe to assume they were used ceremonially to communicate with the sun or to open conduits to the spirits.

We surveyed the peak for ten minutes or so, taking pictures and writing notes, then agreed it was time to head down. We had not gone more than a few feet when we saw five burly-looking men about fifty feet below us tramping purposefully up the trail in our direction. With bandannas half covering their faces and rifles slung over their shoulders, there was zero chance they were simply hikers or tourists.

Seeing that Manuel and Siso were unaware of the danger, I told them we should prepare for trouble. Both laughed it off. Manuel assured me the men were from another environmentalist group and he started walking down the trail to greet them. Siso stood next to me, shaking her head dubiously at my caution until one of the men shouted, "Hey! How many of you are up there?" When Manuel heard this question, he became nervous.

"There are ten of us up here," he replied, then turned and started walking back in our direction.

The men laughed at this obvious lie. Then in a kind of hysterical voice one of them bellowed out, "Then all ten of you are going to die today!"

This threat excited the other men, and they moved up the trail at an even faster pace. As they climbed one man pulled a long kitchen knife from his shirt. Two of the others carried rifles, and one man drew a pistol from his belt. They were less than thirty yards away by this time.

I stood on the peak watching this alarming scene unfold, my mind racing.

How stupid I had been not to bring a weapon! I knew ahead of time this was a risky area, and that several violent crimes had recently been reported in the neighborhood. When I go to an unknown part of the country, I always take a blade or machete with me. I also have a steel whip from my martial arts years. Today I had nothing.

I looked around the hilltop where Siso and I were standing, seeing only steep rocky cliffs descending on all sides. Siso was terrified and huddling close to me. As I watched the men lumbering toward us, I was reminded of many things but especially of the Second Golden Rule—that the choices a client or shaman makes during a sacred plant rite may come back to test them in the physical world at some future time. In the case of the five bandits swaggering our way, they clearly resembled satanic beings I had met on the spirit plane during a recent Ayahuasca ceremony. The similarity was clear not only by their aura of hateful energy but by their actual physical appearance. Here, I thought, are what demons would look like if I saw one walking down a city street—the same clumsy, powerful creatures with strangely malformed faces, threatening me in the corporeal world as they had previously done in the invisible.

Staring at these men storming in our direction I knew that just as there was no possibility of compromising with demons, there was no chance I could talk them out of harming us. Fighting was not even an option. There *were* no options.

In a few moments three of the men reached us, two of them with guns drawn.

I looked around to see if there was any escape route, but the cliffs were a dead drop on all sides. Below on the trail I could see that the two other bandits had waylaid Manuel. One was fondling his cell phone, the other was beating him mercilessly. I whispered to Siso to stay close to me and do exactly what I did. One of the men pointed his gun in our direction, cursed, and shouted, "I'll kill you if you move!" My only thought at the moment was that I would never allow this dark force to prevail. I instantly pivoted and jumped off the cliff, hoping that Siso would follow, and that the fall was not as steep as it appeared.

After landing fifteen or twenty feet down, I skidded along the ground, banging into rocks, rolling over cactuses, scraping my back and head, but realizing with enormous relief that I was on a precipice, steep but not vertical. My clothes were ripped, cactus spikes stuck me everywhere, and my body was wet with blood. As I continued to roll, I looked around for Siso. She had apparently not followed me on the jump as I told her to do and was nowhere to be seen.

After sliding farther I managed to catch hold of a tree root and stop my downward motion. At that moment a bullet zinged off a nearby rock. Another splattered a cactus, and two more whizzed over my head. One of the men at the summit was firing at me out of anger that I had gotten away, no doubt, but also because I was carrying a backpack that he assumed was filled with expensive high-tech devices. Trying to get out of his sights, I continued rolling, at times having to jump five or six feet off overhanging rocks.

After what seemed like forever, I landed on a plateau out of sight of the shooter.

I lay there for some minutes trying to catch my breath, my arms and legs wobbly and bloody but still working. I wondered what was happening to Siso and Manuel. How could I help them? I felt incredibly weak, and it was impossible, and unthinkable, to climb back up the hill. So, I started to pray.

I asked God and the spirits of the mountain to protect Siso and Manuel, to keep them from harm. I asked that they be spared, and that they somehow come out of this hell alive and protected.

After praying in this way for several minutes I began to feel strangely queasy and nauseated. Then without warning a sharp pain exploded in my chest, as if my ribs were breaking and my sternum was cracking open. It felt like a hole had opened up in my chest and out came—I don't know what to call it—water, wind, Life Force? As it took place, I felt a strange sense of relief plus a colossal burst of energy inside me.

The next moment I heard a bird cawing loudly in the sky. Four hawks flew overhead in tandem, then turned and soared toward the top of the mountain. The arrival of the hawks, I felt certain, was a message from the mountain that all would be well.

I rested a bit longer on the ledge, then continued down. The precipice had become less steep, and I more or less walked the rest of the way. Once on level ground I realized I was dangerously close to the unfriendly village that was also, I felt reasonably sure, the home of our tormentors. I decided to take a path around the other side of the mountain to be safe.

Tramping a mile or so through prairie landscape, I followed the trail, which led to a large dune.

Climbing to the top, I looked down and below saw a settlement of impoverished people living in makeshift hovels made of industrial blue plastic with piles of rubbish surrounding them and pigs wandering from hut to hut. Most of the structures were arranged around a large pit filled with garbage.

At times in my life, I myself have lived in extremely poor areas with no water or basic services, but this was more extreme. I had never seen human beings living in such sad, deprived conditions. When they saw me on top of the dune, someone let out a yell and a gang of them started running in my direction waving sticks.

Their behavior was primal, primitive, territorial. Yet I was surprisingly unconcerned. After the experience of jumping off a cliff, being shot at, and undergoing the purifying burst of energy in my chest, I was feeling fearless. I had faced certain death several hours earlier and escaped. The hawks had flown overhead. Nothing could harm me.

I looked down from the top of the dune at the crowd running toward me. I suppose I was an intimidating sight myself, covered in slime and protruding cactus needles, my many wounds oozing blood. "Okay, bring it on!" I thought to myself. "If you want to die, we'll all die together!"

The next thing I knew, almost despite myself, I was walking *down* the dune in their direction, daring them with my glance to lift a stick. As I approached the crowd it spontaneously parted, forming a kind of alleyway for me to walk through. There was total silence in the air but a heavy tension as well. They were making spasmodic movements and emitting grunts. I quickly walked through the human tunnel, turning my head from side to side, looking in their eyes with a steely glance but also feeling deeply sorry for what their lives must be.

Passing unharmed through the crowd, I continued walking into the surrounding deserted plains. About an hour later I reached town, where I rented a motorized tricycle and drove to Trujillo. Here I cleaned up and took a taxi to the police station, where I met with the commissar.

To make a long story short, all members of my group had been rescued by the Trujillo police. The seven people who lingered behind us on the mountain plateaus were robbed but then let go. Siso was at the hospital injured but unmolested. Manuel was in bad shape from his beating but would recover.

When I went to visit Siso, she told me her story. After I leaped off the cliff the bandits told her they had shot and killed me.

Standing there on the mountain paralyzed and crying, several of the bad guys grabbed her and started pulling her down the trail, shouting in lurid detail what they would do to her at the bottom.

Then suddenly, in this shocked, panicked state, she felt a wave of courage course through her. She immediately turned, freeing herself from the men, who were clearly not expecting trouble from their shaking prisoner. Remembering what I had done, she took several steps and leaped off the cliff, landing thirty feet down and breaking her leg. The bad guys came to the edge and looked over, shouting curses and threats, but not daring to climb down, thinking the drop too steep. Siso lay there in great pain for many hours until a squad from the fire department rescued her.

I asked her how long it was after I jumped that she felt her jolt of bravery. About ten minutes, she said, which was around the time I was beseeching the holy powers for help. To this day I believe that her sudden moment of daring was connected to the gift of mercy from God and the mountain. But whoever knows these things for certain?

For me the events of that day were a turning point in my training. They showed me in harsh but practical terms just how real the Second Golden Rule can be. Weeks earlier I had been fighting evil spirits in an invisible world. Today on the mountain the enemy was here on earth in flesh and blood.

Meanwhile, as time went on, I began to realize that the explosion of pain and exhilaration I had felt in my chest on the mountain precipice charged my internal battery in a powerful way, providing a supply of healing stamina that was far stronger than any I had ever known. That day I also saw the relationship between the spiritual world and the physical world from a new perspective, understanding that the two are not as separate as I once thought. Perhaps, I said to myself, they are simply two sides of the same coin. As above, so below.

This insight too, I believed, was a gift from the mountain.

PART II

PRINCIPLES
of the SHAMANIC
JOURNEY

CHAPTER 3

SHAMANISM AND THE

FORCE OF LIFE

A Word on the Spirit World

Shamanism was previously described as the collaboration between a person of knowledge and psychic forces that live and play in the invisible planes of reality. These forces, as we know, are collectively known as spirits. Though ethereal and disembodied, spirits may take on a visual and sometimes even physical form during this collaboration, creating a reciprocity between human beings and the realm of higher intelligence.

This collaboration can be activated in a number of ways: with psychoactive plants, hands-on healing, sacred music or dance, visions, fasts, meditation, prayer, pilgrimage, and many other reflective practices. When shamans look into a client's body and mind, they identify negative energies that need to be removed, calling on their spirit allies to help. Their job, in a nutshell, is to build a bridge between the invisible world and the world of humanity, inviting benevolent spirits down to the material realm.

Maintaining this bridge can be likened to the original purpose of religion, the word itself derived from the Latin *religio,* which means "to bind" or "unify" (the Sanskrit word *yoga* also means "to bind"). It can even be said that shamanism is the remaining fragment left over from ancient religious thinking. The shaman in this sense is an intermediary between two parallel but interacting worlds.

A misunderstanding I have commonly observed during my years of practice is that people who are interested in otherworldly ideas sometimes tend to confuse the invisible world with the realm of the Divine. In shamanism, and indeed in many world religions, the cosmos consists not just of two realities, heaven and earth, but of three—heaven, earth, and an intermediate dimension sometimes referred to as the astral, psychic, or invisible world. This invisible/psychic plane is a domain of subtle matter that hosts as much diversity of life as our own physical world. Using the European word *spirit* for lack of a better name, it is the place where the redemptive power of plant spirits, animal spirits, and the landscape do their work, where deceased humans roam, and where countless different forms of spirit beings reside.

An important point to reiterate about the spirits is that they have different and sometimes conflicting ethics, just like humanity. They are by no means morally or even spiritually alike. Not everything belonging to the intermediate plane is necessarily divine, enlightened, or even good, and not everyone with the capacity to interface with it is kindly and well-meaning.

At the same time, contact and interaction with the spirit world is a main pillar of shamanism, and in Chapter 5 we explore this domain in detail. In this chapter the structure and practicalities of the spirit realm are referred to mainly as a backdrop to other sacred building blocks, all of which make up the superstructure of ancient Peruvian Knowledge.

Seeing the World Through Paleolithic Eyes

Peruvian *curanderismo* and shamanism in general is very, *very* old. Just how old is impossible to say. Some estimates say ten thousand years. Others go further back. Few experts would dispute the fact that it is the oldest spiritual doctrine known to humankind. From personal visions through the years my impression is that people were highly developed spiritually (as well as a good deal more mobile than is supposed) countless years before historians began to number the centuries. If we wish to gain familiarity with shamanism's original techniques and purpose, we need to see its practice through the eyes of the people who lived at a time when humanity was a good deal closer to the spirit kingdom than it is today, and when every element of life was viewed in relationship to the sacred; a time when contact with illumined energies was an everyday occurrence; a time when people were less accustomed to reaching conclusions about life based on binary logic and dialectic thought, more on intuition, metaphor, and revelation.

This difference in perspective from today and millennia ago is one reason why primeval cosmologies are so misunderstood. According to the understanding of our ancestors, reality was not a three-dimensional box moving through time. It was a series of overlapping realities, literally worlds within worlds, each interpenetrating the next, and all decidedly unlike the linear Newtonian universe we are schooled in today.

The only way to make this incomprehensibly complex mosaic of realities understandable was to present them as symbolic images that speak to the deeper levels of consciousness veiled by our rational mind. The Tree of Life, the mating of the earth and sky, a serpent devouring its tail, a tortoise bearing the earth on its back—none of these images were meant to be taken as literal

beings or events but as figurative expressions of otherwise inde-
scribable truths.

Many of us, moreover, are spellbound by these ancient symbols,
but we are not entirely sure why. The same for ancient structures.
We stand with admiration but also uneasy awe gazing at the Great
Wall of China, the Egyptian pyramids, the perfectly fitted colossal
stone walls of the Incas (who never used the wheel), the mysterious
lines and figures drawn on the Nazca Desert, the miles of stone
towers at Angkor Wat. In present time, I cannot help believing, we
would have a difficult time using jackhammers, cranes, and back-
hoes to re-create the Divine dimensions and sacred aura of these
otherworldly structures. How were such colossal edifices built by
hand thousands of years ago, and by whom? We are riveted by their
mystery but baffled. What did people know long ago that we do not
know today? And what are these extraordinary, dream-like remain-
ders of the past trying to tell us?

In a word, they are speaking directly to our inborn spiritual
intelligence, reminding us of sacred realities we have forgotten yet
which still speak to us—*call* to us—from our unconscious minds.
These realities produce a kind of "itch" bred by the fact that we
sense we are looking at the truth but have no conscious understanding of what that truth is trying to tell us.

When our archaic ancestors looked around them, they saw the
earth; they also saw *into* the earth.

They were, of course, well aware of its physicality. They knew
a stone was hard and water was wet; that the world was a material
formation, yes, but at the same time it was also a reflection of a
higher reality.

When the ancients gazed at a mountain, they did not just see earth and rock; they saw a psychic temple at the center of the world connecting heaven with earth. When they looked at a river, it was more than running water; it was the blood of the planet moving through one of its arteries. If they watched the clouds overhead, they were presumably as charmed by the patterns they saw as we are today. But on a deeper level they understood that clouds are a heavenly message, a reminder from above that the material world is transient, and that permanence lies only in the never-changing sky that the clouds float across. For our earliest ancestors, every element in nature was a message for the soul.

Shamanism Is Art, Not Biology

When I give lectures on shamanism, scientists and anthropologists are sometimes in the audience. After my lecture is finished, they frequently ask my opinion on the biochemistry of Ayahuasca and other plants. What part is played by alkaloids, they want to know, DMT, monoamine oxidase inhibitors, and so forth. Usually, I answer in a vague way and change the subject.

Why?

Because in shamanism the healing that comes from ingesting sacred plants is considered a good deal more important than the chemicals that trigger it. Like any true natural healer, I am less concerned with the causes of an illness than I am with balancing a client's energy system and unlocking its inherent self-healing faculties so that the client's body has the power to cure itself. In essence, all a true healer does is create physical and psychic conditions that allow a client's body to recover on its own.

It is rare, what's more, to see mention made in psychology or biology textbooks of the soul and the spirit, of higher states of awareness, of the prime mover—pillars of spirituality that human civilization has been based on for tens of thousands of years, and that almost everyone who takes the sacred plants experiences. There are, as well, few scientists who acknowledge the fact that otherworldly energies are triggered during a shamanic ceremony. Most would find it implausible or at best anecdotal to speak of sacred plants producing lifetime-lasting visions that heal the human psyche.

So, what then is this prime mover that is ignored by science but embraced by spirituality—this force at the heart of shamanism that powers psychological catharsis and brings us closer to our true selves? Though it has many names, the best English version I know is the term "Force of Life."

The Force of Life

When we sit quietly and gaze at the ribbon of birds flying overhead, at animals, at fluttering leaves, we realize that though the appearance of these living things differs enormously, a single trait unites them all: the *urge to be.*

We all feel this urge. It is stamped into our nature at birth. Among the few drives that all human beings share, the need to exist is by far the most powerful, and we will do *anything* to sustain it.

What is behind this fierce yearning? Animals fight predators twice their size to protect their existence and to shelter their young so that they too can grow up and fight for survival. Plants push up through solid rock seeking food from sunlight. Wounded animals work to heal themselves, never giving up. What is the reason living creatures battle so remorselessly to stay alive?

This battle, shamans maintain, is more than a biological mechanism or a natural instinct. It is an effect of the Force of Life, which, in turn, is a *conscious* energy, a flow of creation that brings animation and awareness to whatever it touches. This flow separates it from other conceptualizations of vital force such as electricity or *qi,* which Chinese philosophers see as a kind of neutral energy that turns the motor of the world. But the Force of life is not a mechanical agent like *qi* or electromagnetism; it is the power of nature itself, of existence itself, driving the cycles of creation and destruction. It both gives us breath and creates the will to preserve it.

In the material world the primary representative of the Force of Life is water, itself an age-old symbol of life.

Water is indispensable for existence. Where there is a river or pond, life flourishes. Pour it on the soil and the earth becomes green. Like the Force of Life, water exists forever, giving existence to every living being. Yet it makes no demands and is infinitely patient. If blocked it goes under, around, through, over; or it simply waits. Eventually it wears down anything in its way, even if the process takes a million years. Water can be transformed to steam or vapor, but its essence as water remains the same. If you heat it or cool it, it returns to its normal temperature; like Life Force, it is always striving to be what it is. One of my Chinese martial arts teachers was fond of quoting the *Tao Te Ching,* saying we should be like water, which is "submissive and weak . . . yet cannot be surpassed when attacking what is hard and strong."

And like the Force of Life, water holds healing powers. It washes away inner poisons. Just to swim in it or bathe in it is to feel healed. In the material world water is life and life is water. If you wish to understand the essence and structure of the Force of Life, think of water.

The Force of Life and the
Three Centers of Consciousness

The Life Force expresses itself in the human condition through our three life centers: the mind, the heart, and the gut/reproductive system. From this three-part division, so important to the shamanic view of life, comes an entirely different way of understanding human behavior.

Starting at the bottom with our abdominal center, the "bag of the belly" (as one of my teachers used to call it) holds many organs, most used for digestion and procreation.

In the middle of our body is a cage—the rib cage—holding the heart and lungs, organs responsible for emotion, circulation, and breath.

Resting on our shoulders is a rounded box with orifices—our head—from which we evaluate the world through mental acuity and our five senses.

Let's look at each of these vital centers in detail.

The first of the centers, the bag of the belly, is where all being begins—in the womb. It is also where Life Force expresses itself in survival mode, causing us to crave food, drink, and reproduction. It is here that fear, acting as a self-protective alarm, warns us when our existence is threatened. It is where sexual intercourse takes place along with the merging of male and female fluids. It is where we store and process nutrients. It is where elimination, menstruation, and most of all the inception and birth of a child occur, all activities associated with the maintenance and conservation of life. When clients in a ceremony harbor self-destructive tendencies and little inclination toward self-improvement, these conditions signal a shaman that the client's energy is weak, and that their abdominal Force of Life needs recharging in the spirit world.

A teacher of mine in the north once explained that a male erection, especially when waking up in the morning, shows that the Force of Life is especially strong when the sun comes up. In the minds of the ancients, erections were caused by solar energy working through the Force of Life. It is no accident that certain ancient Moche pots display figures of men with long, hard members. Or that sometimes a man's body is shown as penis-shaped or penis-headed. Such depictions are not about sex per se, but symbolize Life Force in its most enlivening and robust state.

In some Peruvian ruins one sees stone phalluses shaped like mushrooms, symbols of male fecundity. If you think about it, what better symbol could there be for the Force of Life than the organ that channels it (and, parenthetically, the only external organ with the ability to dramatically change its shape)?

In women one sign of strong day-to-day belly energy is the ability to become wet in the vaginal areas. Certain Moche pots show women displaying open vaginas with liquids flowing out of them. Archaeologists and anthropologists usually describe these images as a symbol of fertility. Actually, they are not only about fertility but also refer to healthy female manifestation of the Force of Life flowing smoothly.

Note too that the belly bag holds the umbilical cord, making it a conduit that connects a child to life itself through the mother and through countless generations of ancestors.

Besides embodying the urge to live and reproduce, the belly bag is also looked on as a sacred enclosure that houses our vital energy.

During and after my martial arts training in Lima's Chinatown, I understood how this potential is expressed in Asian religions. In yoga, for instance, the groin stores kundalini energy, the Life Force that rises up the spine via meditation to the crown chakra at the top of the head, triggering enlightenment. In Zen Buddhism, the belly is referred to as the *hara* and is considered the center of Life Force. In martial arts and Chinese medicine, the lower belly contains the *tan tien* where *qi* is stored and circulated throughout the energy meridians, blood, and bones. Next time you visit the Asian section of a museum, look closely at the Hindu and Buddhist statues. Notice that many of them have protruding stomachs, a sign that their abdomen, their belly bag, is charged with Life Force.

The belly bag, it can therefore be said, is both the center of our survival machinery and a potential route to enlightenment—earth and heaven on either end of the axis of life, responsible for the expression of Life Force on both a material and a spiritual plane.

Next, in the middle of the body we find the second center, where two prime movers are located in the rib cage: the heart, whose constant rhythm is a pure expression of the Force of Life, and breath, connecting us to the outer world of air and to the terrestrial energies that keep us alive.

The chest center, because it is concerned less with reproduction and food, more with feelings, respiration, circulation, and a mystical bond with the universe, expresses the Life Force at a higher level than the belly. It is the part of us that deals with love and courage plus the force of will. It is the part of our body where our arms are connected, which we use to embrace, to pull and push, to defend ourselves, to hold and to let go.

From a modern psychological point of view thought is considered to be exclusive to the mind. But in ancient cosmology insight and intelligence were believed to also be generated by the heart.

In many cultures it is no accident that when people say "I want" or "I think," they put their hand on their chest.

Finally, there is the head, that crowning sphere where more cavities are located than any other part of the body. These cavities—the mouth, nose, ears, and eyes—are the doorways through which we express our thoughts and feelings via speech, and where outside impressions enter our awareness. All this sensory information is then transformed into cognition and mindfulness, helping us negotiate the environment around us. The head is where memory, judgment, analysis, and decision-making take place, and also where our visionary abilities are stimulated through ascetic practice or by the use of sacred plants. The fact that the head crowns the top of our body, the part of our anatomy that is closest to the sky, allows us to gaze up to the sun, moon, and stars for inspiration, making the mind a potential bridge linking us with the cosmos.

Finally, besides existing as independent "organs," our three centers are intimately connected with one another, creating our identity and persona. They are also aligned with the axis of the spine, forming what is recognized in many faiths as the Tree of Life. At the base of this tree the belly bag is rooted to earth. From here it grows upward through the heart, ending with a clear view of the celestial realms seen from the head. From bottom to top, this axis forms a vertical connection between the three centers and, on a contemplative scale, between the three realms of human consciousness: thought, feeling, and physicality.

Symbolic Animals Representing the Body, Heart, and Mind Centers

Though today we speak of the body's basic centers using modern terms, the ancients, whose language was not as concept-rich as our own, preferred describing the three centers using symbols rather than words, especially animal symbols. Through the centuries, *curanderismo* has followed their example.

In shamanism the Force of Life in the abdominal center is symbolized by a serpent curled up in the stomach. Snakes shed their skin, looking young again as if reborn. Their dropped skin is like an empty corpse, yet the snake itself is bright and full of vitality. To people of old this was a visual parable of the Force of Life overcoming death.

Large snakes are also the incarnation of life's continuum, personifying the strength and reproductive powers contained in the belly center. Unlike vipers, which are poisonous and symbolize danger in dreams and visions, the belly snake never bites and carries no venom. In the spirit world it is represented by colossal-sized serpents like the boa, anaconda, and python. If you mention the concept of the belly snake to martial artists, many of them will describe the energy that courses through them during a workout as a snake-like coil winding and unwinding in their stomach. Or sometimes they feel a snake climbing up their spine. Western culture shows the symbol of medicine as two snakes winding around a winged wand known as the caduceus, the scepter of the Greek god of healing, Asclepius.

Moving up to the second center, the cage of the heart and lungs, the symbolic presence of Life Force is represented by visions of animals at the top of the food chain. In some countries this animal is a wolf. More commonly it is a large cat, usually a jungle cat like a tiger or jaguar. When seen in a vision these fierce animal spirits are telling clients that they must increase their compassion and their courage. Do this, they say, by living with more engagement and less fear.

It is interesting to consider that around the world felines are thought to be especially close to the spiritual world. In Egypt, China, Greece, and many other ancient cultures cats were given godlike status. A mighty warrior is said to have the heart of a lion. The lion is the king of beasts. In the Americas the jaguar and its black variant are considered the animals that best personify spirituality. Even house cats have a special mystique. They fight and defeat animals twice their size. They appear and disappear mysteriously. They see in the dark and seem to know things we don't. In short, the heart as represented by a courageous feline is the archetypal symbol of courage, insight, love, and the Life Force.

Moving finally to the head, we come to the center of our mental capability, which, quite appropriately, is symbolized by visions of a large bird that flies higher than all other birds and is usually a bird of prey—an eagle, falcon, hawk, or in Peru and other Andean countries, a condor.

Because these proud creatures soar to unimaginable heights like an elevated mind, and because they see the world below them in all four directions at once, they are a universal symbol of far-sightedness and wisdom. Many birds of power, especially the eagle and condor, are capable of looking directly at the sun without flinching, just as a healthy mind looks at the truth in an unwavering way no matter how difficult it may be to accept. When we see the eye of a hawk or eagle in a vision, we feel the power of our own mental clarity. In human terms, a bird's-eye view is akin to standing on top of a mountain away from the little miseries of everyday existence, gazing down at the display of human life and behavior and comprehending its intricacies in a way we cannot do on the ground. Both bird and spiritual mind belong to the sky. When seen in visions they symbolize a client's illimitable possibilities of development and understanding.

Animal symbols play a large part in almost all shamanic rituals.

If, for example, a shaman looks inside a client during a ceremony and sees that the spirit of a bird, snake, or jungle cat is injured—an eagle missing a wing, say, or a bloodied jaguar—this means that the part of the body the animal represents, the gut (snake), chest (cat), or head (bird), may be injured as well.

In some cases, while moving about in the spirit zone or while having a vision a shaman will morph himself into a snake, cat, or bird, as the healing of a particular client can only be done by using one of these specific animal energies. Looming visions of these three animals sometimes appear all at once, working together to speed a client's convalescence.

When I enter the realm of visions, either in hands-on sessions without medicine or when in deep work with sacred plants, I enter a space that represents the inner world of my client. In this area I see two distinctive parts of the heart. One is spherical and luminous, and is connected to the intelligence of the Force of Life. The other is a formless and slimy fluid covering the heart and containing many different components, like a soup made with multiple ingredients. It is in this beleaguered area where the painful memories and negative impressions from the past are stored, and it is here that most shamanic healing procedures take place.

Through my years of professional practice, I have named these two aspects of the heart the *Soul Consciousness* and the *Suffering Consciousness*. Using these terms helps describe my visions to clients, allowing them to better understand their experiences when taking the sacred plants. Much more will be said about these two terms immediately below and throughout the chapters to come.

When the three internal centers work in unison with each other and with the Life Force, their alliance invariably produces harmonious behavior. When, for example, the Life Force and reproductive functions partner amiably together in the belly, a person feels grounded, healthy, and comfortably at home in the world. In the heart, fortitude, generosity, and love are expressions of a flourishing connection to the Force of Life and thus to life itself. And in the head, when the mind is energized by the Life Force it can reach out beyond the confines of the material world and discover what is real.

Needless to say, this positive collaboration of the three centers provides excellent conditions for a life well lived. At the same time, the question arises: What happens when our three centers and the Force of life are not so tunefully aligned?

Suffering Consciousness

A shaman is entrusted with many moral and spiritual duties. Perhaps the most important of these is alleviating the anguish, selfishness, negative habits, and addictions caused by Suffering Consciousness.

Suffering Consciousness is a form of negative emotional reactivity seated in the ego. It taints our behavior with self-centered and sometimes belligerent desires that are unnecessary and often self-destructive. The role of the shaman, especially the Warrior shaman, who is introduced below, is to regulate a client's Suffering Consciousness and dissolve the knots it has woven in the person's soul. When I work on clients during a ceremony and discover an ugly mass of sick energy in their heart, I know I am looking at some aspect of this person's Suffering Consciousness.

The ego in its essence is not a negative entity per se. It is simply the consciousness of one's self as an individual person. But when one part of the ego sees life only in terms of its own pleasures and needs, self-centeredness and greed are the inevitable result. For this reason, many people commonly speak of the ego in contrary terms ("He's got such a big ego," "That's her ego at it again," etc.), when in fact what they are referring to is the ego's darker part.

And Suffering Consciousness *is* that darker part. It is the aspect of our persona that creates false ideas about who we are and how we should behave, leading us to believe that our conflicted and ever-changing sense of selfhood represents our fundamental identity—that there is nothing more to us than our work-a-day, self-interested personality; that our potential for higher states of consciousness and a sense of soul are unimportant and even nonexistent. Most significantly, by its nature Suffering Consciousness wishes to gain complete control over how we see reality, then to use this false perception to keep us padlocked in a prison of self-absorption and worldly attachment.

If, for example, I have a disagreement at the office with a friendly coworker, Suffering Consciousness may respond in a variety of disruptive ways, from acts of petty sabotage to treating my once-liked colleague as a hated enemy. Or if, say, a child is bitten by a dog, Suffering Consciousness creates a negative image of dogs in general. Later, when the child grows up, he may despise dogs or have a phobia against them, even though the offending dog is long dead and most other dogs are friendly and approachable. Basically then, every hour of the day Suffering Consciousness is busy creating imaginary and unnecessary emotional conflicts that trigger our anxieties and discontents.

Soul Consciousness

But Suffering Consciousness has a counterweight, a powerful moral opposite that is also part of our fundamental nature, more so, in fact, than Suffering Consciousness, being directly connected to the Great Spirit. I refer to it as Soul Consciousness.

Soul Consciousness is the core of our higher being, the most important and benevolent of all our psychic organs but also the most commonly ignored. Contemporary, consumer-focused culture and societal norms encourage many elements of Suffering Consciousness such as competition, obsession with money, anger, and deceptiveness, making us believe these and many other aggressive behaviors are necessary for gaining success in the world. At the same time, it teaches us little or nothing about our Soul Consciousness, which makes compassion, respect, and the spiritual quest the highest priority.

Yet when Soul Consciousness is awakened in a person during a ceremony or spiritual moment, all of that person is awakened and then shown the way to live according to the dictates of conscience and the teachings of the spirits. It is the wise side of our being that tells us that while we are an ordinary individual, we also have the potential for higher understanding. And that as a result, we are obliged to discover this understanding in our mind and heart, and to express it through love, awe, serving others, and feeling part of the greater human family.

Soul Consciousness, Suffering Consciousness, and the Force of Life

Soul Consciousness is the aspect of our being that connects us with the Force of Life and that puts its wisdom into action. It is what some people call our Higher Self or sometimes the voice of conscience. As a child, we connect with Soul Consciousness far more deeply than as adults, who normally live under the rule of Suffering Consciousness. This is why children have a natural sense of goodness and emotional perception. They may not know how the world and human relations work. But they are instinctively aware of Soul

Consciousness, which among its many blessings keeps them forever in the moment. Soul Consciousness, it could be said, is the Force of Life in action.

Our Suffering Consciousness can be compared to an internal body part. During childhood it is malleable, shaped by the environment and the people caring for the child. When adolescence arrives the Suffering Consciousness starts to crystalize. In the adult years it is firmly fixed, while in old age it disintegrates and eventually turns brittle, much like our own skeleton.

If Suffering Consciousness were to be summed up in a phrase, it would be that its dominant goal is to have *what it wants, how it wants it, when it wants it,* using any form of manipulation to get it. And since Suffering Consciousness operates counter to Soul Consciousness and the Force of Life, it mistakes the gratification of its urges for happiness. Constantly invoking "faster," "quicker," "better," "bigger," and "more pleasurable," it is a bottomless well of wants, a condition of mind fed by the delusion that to live to the fullest one must constantly experience dramatic and exaggerated emotions.

This is a key point: To make us feel its importance, Suffering Consciousness generates a variety of excited states, both agreeable and disagreeable: pain, pleasure, frustration, desire, amusement, fear, compulsion, lust, thrills, euphoria, all convincing us that these states are the real stuff of life. This assumption is, of course, the opposite of that championed by Soul Consciousness, which assures us that our thoughts and feelings, nice or not nice, are dreams that come and go like the wind, bringing happiness one moment, misery the next, but never lasting, and never leading us to the true reason why we were born, which is to seek after an existence in harmony with the Force of Life; that is, with spiritual awakening.

❦

Suffering Consciousness feels a thrill when angry and does its best to encourage constant worry and anxiety (after all, you never know what calamities are about to befall you). It is especially partial to addiction. Suffering Consciousness loves to be shocked, upset, manically low or high. It is sure it always knows best. Creating a wall between itself and reality, it has its own version of how our emotions should behave, and it does its best to sabotage any truths that contradict it. As if there is nothing wrong with living a good part of each day in a dissatisfied, agitated, and uneasy frame of mind; as if this is the way nature meant us to be.

According to Suffering Consciousness, generosity is a foolish and unnecessary indulgence, while being concerned with other people's welfare is a sign of sentimentality. Watch out for number one and don't worry about the rest. Suffering Consciousness tells us to take more whenever we can, even if it leaves others with less. When confronted, it tells us to get angry. When crossed, seek payback. Indulge your senses to the limit; self-restraint is for fuddy-duddies and prudes. Avoid apologizing and forgiveness. Do anything to win, and never admit that you are wrong. Lying is good business. And why not lie? Everyone does it. Self-pity is also commendable; I deserve to feel sorry for myself. The world never gives me the things I really want. My dreams rarely come true. If my life seems unsuccessful or if I have a bad self-image, it is my parents' fault, my job's fault, society's fault, the fault of all those people out there who do not understand me. If they only knew how amazing I really am! Finally, never even *dream* of speaking to others of morality and evil. We all know these are nebulous concepts that cannot be defined, and that everything in life is relative.

Obviously, most of us do not constantly think and act in these ways, and there are those among us who are largely free of such self-centeredness. The inventory provided here is meant to give you a sense of the typical vanities and moral vacuums a shaman may encounter when working with clients who are ruled by their Suffering Consciousness.

⚹

Suffering Consciousness starts in our earliest years when we begin to watch, then imitate the people taking care of us. The same way that the food we eat goes into our cells and tissues, the negative feelings we learn in our early years nourish Suffering Consciousness. Our parents, family, and friends are normally well-intentioned, and do their best to bring us up in principled ways. But since Suffering Consciousness is in a sense the ordinary human condition, the people who raise us, usually without knowing it, teach us ways of behaving based on their own bubble of selfishness and desire, passing these attributes down to us from themselves and from generations past.

From the earliest age we are told that people are important or unimportant according to their job, education, appearance, charm, influence, ambition, and social standing. We are taught artificial ways to be liked and to create a false mask of personality that disguises our true thoughts and feelings. We are cautioned that other people's praise is necessary and their disapproval harmful; that money, power, fame, and success are the most important goals to strive after. We are made to believe that our life is always moving toward some golden moment in the future when everything will be perfect and we will be eternally content. Go to school, get a job, outshine your peers, solve all your problems with the money you make and the people you meet, and you will be happy.

But, of course, these imagined rewards never come, and our dashed hopes make us distrustful and cynical. And if they do come, we invariably come to understand that these material benefits do nothing to guarantee our sense of joy, awe, or peace.

Throughout the centuries innumerable systems, both philosophical and religious, have tried to muzzle or at least neutralize the voice of the Suffering Consciousness, replacing it with momentary connections with the Soul Consciousness. Formal religion, and today psychotherapy, certainly have their curative powers. But bringing about emotional change can be grindingly slow, occasionally ending up strengthening the Suffering Consciousness rather than weakening it.

Here, I believe, is where shamanism and shamanic techniques can help. Given a client who is open to change and a *curandero* who is up to the task, psychological troubles that take years to develop can often be rooted out in one or more sacred plant ceremonies. At the least, after a session in the circle clients feel cleansed, clear-headed, and optimistic about the future. At best they feel reborn.

For these reasons, in every shamanic ceremony I perform I attempt to help clients understand why they cling so determinedly to their Suffering Consciousness. I try to help them see how Suffering Consciousness has become their norm; that down deep they do not really *want* to give up their anger, self-pity, and envy. These behaviors have become too deep a part of their habit structure. When people experience a strong emotion or yearning, it creates the illusion that they are alive and passionately involved. For many people, peace and silence feel empty. They need their Suffering Consciousness to fill the hole and maintain the emotional intensity it brings, be it positive or negative. The only way Suffering Consciousness fully gratifies itself is by creating more excitement and suffering . . . and more . . . and more.

꙳

When I work with a person during a hands-on healing or a ceremony, I see that their Soul Consciousness usually has a round or oval shape, while their Suffering Consciousness is amorphous like an amoeba. In some instances, especially in a truly disturbed person, Suffering Consciousness takes on a grotesque shape like a grimacing face, a row of spikes, or a pile of bloody limbs like a drawing in a horror comic.

Sometimes in the middle of a ceremony a cruel or cold-blooded client will psychically appear to me as a gargoyle-like beast. Overflowing with anger and selfishness, this half-human thing sometimes attempts to pierce me with his fangs when he realizes I am cleaning out psychic messes from his Suffering Consciousness. Some people simply do not want to let go of their hatreds. Or, if I see a client in my visions with huge square molars, it tells me this person is carrying a savage sense of resentment, and that when I work to purge him this resentment will be aimed at me, emotionally and sometimes even physically. On rare occasions clients have attacked me while I was working on them, trying to bite, scratch, or strangle me, especially when I am attempting to root out their deepest fears and angers. To delve into the Suffering Consciousness of especially violent or tormented clients is deeply challenging. It makes me understand once again why a teacher warned me that to become a successful *curandero* one must learn to overcome fear and disgust.

Once in a little town in the north of Peru I was told the story by one of my elder patients of an old shaman in the highlands who was approached by a brawny soldier who asked him for his help. The soldier, who was known to be hotheaded and sometimes violent, had been away from his village for many years and had just come home. Since returning he was having terrible nightmares and deep bouts of depression.

The shaman spent a long time talking to the soldier and asking him questions. At the end of their conversation, he told the man that yes, he could help him. But only under one condition: that during the ceremony the man must be tightly tied to a tree.

Needless to say, the soldier was taken aback by this request and wanted to know the reason why.

"Because you are a strong man," the shaman told him, "and there is a great deal of violence inside you. Unless you are bound up during the ceremony you may very well try to hurt me or even kill me when I start shaking the demons out of you."

What the shaman saw during his conversation with the soldier was that though the man's Suffering Consciousness was clearly causing the miseries he complained of, he was so addicted to his brutal side that he would do anything, even kill, to keep it from being exorcized.

But while it is true that during a ceremony a *curandero* can occasionally find himself in dangerous situations when working with a person full of hate, a healing can nonetheless still take place if done with empathy and lack of judgment. Compassionate healing can mellow out the darkest artifacts inside the darkest people, helping them undergo an emotional metamorphosis that eliminates at least a part of the evil and pain that fills their heart.

Finally, it is important to mention that Suffering Consciousness can play a potentially positive role in our psychology as well as a negative one. The relationship between Soul Consciousness and Suffering Consciousness is a convoluted crisscrossing of the high road and the low. In the best of possible worlds, Suffering Consciousness protects us from the pain caused us by others. When it works as a servant of the Soul Consciousness, it identifies an emotional experience as safe or dangerous, comfortable or uncomfortable, gratifying or disturbing. In moments of danger, it advises us whether to escape or confront the situation—fight or flight. It helps us digest whatever misfortunes we may have endured, preventing us from buckling under suffering overload.

In this sense, when working cooperatively with Soul Consciousness rather than trying to quash it, Suffering Consciousness is a purposive and needed tool. When this cooperation clicks in, Suffering Consciousness is not suppressed but is simply put in its rightful place as a kind of a secretary to Soul Consciousness and the Force of Life.

More about Soul Consciousness

Soul Consciousness talks to us in visions and in dreams. Its language is the language of scripture and poetry. In the ancient world, poets had little interest in introspection or random wordplay. Their goal was to provide a fleeting glance into the heart of reality, not only to stress the illusionary and transitory quality of the world but to imply the existence of a higher truth behind it.

During a sacred plant ceremony or sometimes in extraordinary life situations, we connect with Soul Consciousness. Under its auspices, we become more forgiving and optimistic. When we receive unfortunate news, we accept it with equanimity. When we are filled with spiritual goodwill there is nothing in us that Suffering Consciousness can twist or distort. We can relax and let go, feeling free for a few blessed minutes, hours, or days. In truth, the real meaning of that so abused word *freedom* is not the right to do whatever we want when we want, but liberation from the fear, anger, and suffering that keep us a prisoner of the material world and poison our hearts.

✤

Suffering Consciousness and Soul Consciousness both exist in time and space. But each operates under different rules.

Suffering Consciousness time is confined to the length, width, and depth of the material world. Time in Soul Consciousness is ungoverned by the laws of textbook physics. Every second of it is infinite and every moment exists in the present.

When experiencing Soul Consciousness time, clients are in the present moment. Concurrently, under certain circumstances they also experience what I call reversible time, meaning they become free to roam in the past, present, and future, and sometimes in all three worlds at once, unrestricted by clocks or geometry. On this occasion they are, as it were, in eternity. During a ceremony, events that took place a thousand years ago can happen again right now. Just as in quantum physics we know that theoretically it is possible to go backward in time and that the same particle can appear in two distant parts of the universe simultaneously, so in the shamanic world an event that is supposedly over and done remains intact until a person of knowledge chooses to materialize it once again from the past using the power of the sacred plants.

Because of its fluidity, moreover, soul time is also connected to the spirits of our ancestors, family, clan, and even friends or family members born in our future. This is why shamanic ceremonies can heal both previous and future generations, leaping over generational barriers. It is a not an uncommon experience during a ceremony, as many seekers will attest to, for clients to converse with their descendants as if they were seated in front of them, or to swap stories with yet unborn grandchildren and great grandchildren. When these encounters occur, we are allowed to observe our genealogy from a panoramic point of view. At these heights we can look back and assess our ancestral strengths and weaknesses—the very strengths and weaknesses that have come down to us from innumerable generations past and that make us who we are today. All living beings are drops in the river of the generations, the quality of each drop determining the quality of the river.

Throughout our life we are tuned in to the radio station of our Suffering Consciousness. Listening to it is an hour-to-hour habit that allows us to feel stimulated and provides a false sense of security. Unlike Suffering Consciousness, Soul Consciousness does not blare out its messages 24/7 but waits for those moments when we are compelled to turn to it. Such moments can occur when we suffer extreme loss or pain; when we experience the passing of a loved one, a near-death encounter, a moment of intense personal danger, hearing from a doctor that we have a serious disease, enduring a natural or financial disaster, and so forth.

Such distressing incidents shake us so deeply that they crack our psychological defense mechanisms, allowing the voice of Soul Consciousness to be heard above the clamor of Suffering Consciousness, reminding us that despite our belief that we are always in control it is a higher force that determines our fate.

At such moments of shock and self-awareness, Soul Consciousness may effect a complete change in us for the good; what seems like a tragedy can become a blessing.

While under the influence of sacred plants, I have witnessed group members recoil in dismay when their Soul Consciousness shows them undeniably negative parts of themselves. Such moments are made all the more daunting because clients may be perceiving these parts of their personality for the first time and realizing what a large, if unrecognized, role they play in subverting their lives. Or occasionally, as with those who live through near-death experiences, individuals are taken on journeys to the realm of the hereafter, where they witness the god of death judging their worldly conduct, sometimes in a disapproving way. Over the years I have seen deep realizations that Soul Consciousness imparts to clients, transforming the most confirmed unbelievers, and causing an emotional flowering that sometimes lasts an evening, sometimes a lifetime.

Yet another force that evokes Soul Consciousness and, in the process, silences Suffering Consciousness is falling in love or feeling deeply loved and accepted. Because true love is unselfish, Suffering Consciousness knows it has no power over lovers and it quiets down. These moments of freedom brought on by affection may or may not last, but in most cases their memory becomes a milestone in one's personal history.

Soul Consciousness may also present itself during a sacred plant ceremony when clients feel that they are actually dying. They imagine that spirits are about to carry them down to the underworld or that they are being dropped into a fiery hole. Such visions, nightmarish as they may be, are lessons from Soul Consciousness reminding clients that they can die at any minute, and that they need to put their life in order before the final hour comes. Soul Consciousness can also teach people about death itself, taking them on a tour of the land of the dead and putting them in contact with spirits that describe what to expect when passing over to the other side.

Following these and similar encounters with mortality, a curious thing often happens. During a ceremony clients may be forced not only to face their death but also to have memories of life-changing moments they have long forgotten, much in the way dying persons are said to see their entire lifetimes pass before them. When this happens, I ask clients to describe these memories to me and to hold on to them when the ceremony is over.

The next day when clients are in a normal state, I ask them to

write down the most important events of their life. Almost invariably the list includes few if any of the memories they described
to me the night before, including the realization that they are mor-
tal. Somehow revelations that seemed earth-shattering during the
ceremony have faded from their awareness. Why? Because what
clients see during the ceremony comes from their Soul Consciousness, while the list they write in their ordinary state of mind is a
product of their normal Suffering Consciousness.

⁂

Since Soul Consciousness has a quantum-like relationship with
time and space, it can be many places at once, including in our
heart, the part of us where spiritual understanding is born and
develops.

From a shaman's point of view, the heart is divided into two
halves, each half representing a different family of feelings.

In one half of the heart there is love in all its forms—forgiveness,
gratitude, compassion, patience, hospitality, the desire to perform
service and healing for others, and many other caring impulses.

The other half of the heart is ruled by courage and love of
justice in all its manifestations: fairness, tenacity, fidelity, force
of will, discernment, perceptivity, action, and self-preservation.
Allegorically speaking, the love half of the heart is a fountain of
compassion, the justice half a sentinel that helps us navigate the
crooked paths of life, keeping us from wrongdoing. One half is
goodness, the other half is strength.

These two halves of the Divine whole create the power of the
mystical union, which inspires us to help both ourselves and others. The benevolent expressions of this union take place constantly
in our life, though often in seemingly ordinary ways. When we
have the courage to forgive, when we use our will to walk away

from a potentially nasty argument, when we keep a promise, when we let go of a grievance or forgive a debt, when we have an easy opportunity to cheat and remain honest, when we sacrifice our time to help a person in need—these behaviors may seem insignificant to others and even to ourselves. But in truth they open up connections with the Divine. Indeed, such seemingly modest attempts at virtue are like the stones used to build a temple to the power of our own Soul, which, whether we know it or not, is the source and wellspring of all our righteous deeds.

Decades ago, when I was working with my teacher Pedro, he gave me an exercise that sounded easy but turned out to be a demanding training tool that nourished both sides of my heart.

Pedro often sent me on quests to sacred mountains along the north coast. To reach them I had to walk for many hours across rocky prairies. On one such mission he told me that while I was walking, I should think of one foot as the family of love and the other foot as the family of justice. Choose either foot—it was my choice. When I took a step on the love foot, he said, let it evoke tenderness, affection, forgiveness. When stepping with the other, dwell on righteousness, objectivity, and fair play. There was no harm, Pedro assured me, in conjuring up the same sentiments many times. After all, he laughed, how many synonyms for love or justice can you think of in four hours? As it turned out, there were more words for each family than I had anticipated. In many cases, they came automatically as if being piped into my mind from a hidden wireless.

What was compelling and ultimately exalting about talking to myself in this way for so many hours was that when I reached the foot of the mountain, I began to feel I was not only walking with my feet but with my consciousness as well. Memories of significant events poured into my mind that I had long forgotten but that I realized now had deeply enriched my life. When I reached the upper parts of the peak it seemed I was carrying my heart on a tray, and that Pedro had not just given me a reflective litany to recite but sent me on a moving meditation into a sacred space where he knew I would discover wondrous things. The exercise was like gymnastics for the heart.

And indeed, when I reached the top of the mountain, all the good feelings that had passed through my mind during the climb merged together in my Soul Consciousness. My heart was no longer on a tray but was glowing in my hands, embodying the overwhelming joy I felt, and radiating love and justice to every human being on the earth.

Warrior Shamans and Priest Shamans

There are two fundamental approaches to the dissemination of *curandero* Knowledge. These approaches are exemplified by individuals known as Warrior shamans and Priest shamans. These two types of healers are differentiated by their goals and by their style of work.

To begin, most shamans are Priest shamans.

Their purpose is to promote strong, caring connections among the villagers they watch over and with the sacred; and hence to protect and nourish the soul of the community. They work closely with the calendar, overseeing rites of passage and occasions that honor seasonal festivities and important times of the year. They are also village record keepers and cultural historians, deeply learned in local legends, songs, and important historical events that they pass on to townspeople in storytelling sessions that sometimes last an entire day.

When a Priest shaman provides personal council, it is to solve ordinary life problems like marital disputes or hostilities over who owns a bordering strip of land; this, rather than working to eradicate a person's demons and neuroses. Aside from occasional counseling sessions, a Priest shaman dedicates his efforts to the community at large rather than to individuals.

A Priest shaman officiates at sacred plant ceremonies that are open to the entire village, sometimes even including children. He makes sure he is present at official or institutional town gatherings. He cooks, mixes, and serves the medicine brew, and usually drinks it himself. His community devotions, though endangered to some extent by changing times, are still a basic part of Peruvian village life and have been so for thousands of years. They take place on a regular basis in an area of the village set off as sacred, or more commonly in a *maloca*. The medicine brew imbibed at these sessions is different from the medicine used by Warrior shamans. It contains fewer ingredients, and its purpose is to induce a mild communal trance rather than a deep, contemplative state.

During a sacred ceremony a Priest shaman helps followers make contact with the invisible world and encourages a collective unity beyond each member's individual cares and concerns, though some people have beautiful releases and healings as well. Music enlivens the Priest shaman's rituals along with drumming and group or solo dancing. The singing of traditional songs is common, and at times a well-trained Priest shaman performs dream interpretation or forms of divination for the future of the community.

When villagers are in a trance induced by the sacred plants, Priest shamans may also provide social medicine such as mending relationships between families or clans or patching up friendships gone bad. When a village couple builds a house, the Priest shaman visits the site to offer blessings. He uses his psychic skills to help participants find lost objects, recall an important fact, or trace the location of a farm animal that has strayed. During formal occasions like marriages, holidays, funerals, and births he plays the role of spiritual shepherd and master of ceremonies as well.

The task of the Priest shaman, in sum, is to maintain a balanced social order in his village—to encourage town dwellers to maintain a benevolent connection with the land, the spirit world, and with each other. A parallel can easily be made between Priest shamans and priests from other world religions since their goal of promoting group harmony is similar.

A Warrior shaman's task is considerably different from that of a Priest shaman.

While Priest shamans watch over the public good, a Warrior shaman works directly with individuals to address psychological burdens or physical health. He performs ceremonies with small groups or works one-on-one with selected clients, sometimes in sessions that last for many hours and that require extraordinarily psychogenic work from both shaman and client. The sacred plants he uses are a good deal more potent than those mixed in a Priest shaman's brew. These medicines take longer to cook, are often prepared following secret routines, and are given to clients following strict protocols. A Warrior shaman's medicine also includes a larger number of plants than are used in a Priest shaman's brew. In some cases, rare shrubs or vines are needed and the Warrior shaman is obliged to travel deep into the jungle to harvest them. In addition, he may maintain long-standing trading connections with professional providers of psychotropic plants, more about which is described below.

The number of clients participating in a Warrior shaman's ceremony rarely exceeds a dozen, and in general smaller gatherings are preferred. Even if a Warrior shaman is highly proficient, he is never powerful enough to track the unconscious of twenty or thirty people at the same time, or to identify each client's heritage, psychological issues, or acquired curses. The Warrior's way is to delve deeply into his client's mind, erasing emotional afflictions caused by the Suffering Consciousness and sweeping away the psychic debris that obstructs their Force of Life. At times, a Warrior shaman also teaches advanced seekers secret knowledge or even takes them on as apprentices.

In a typical village ceremony, a Priest shaman tends to speak frequently, sometimes with members of the gathering, sometime delivering what amounts to a sermon that invites reflections on spiritual or social life. In a Warrior Priest's circle there is little or no conversation, usually just a few phrases or words of support. While Warrior shamans work for the good, on a personal level many of them tend to be cranky and aloof. On the village streets, which most of them assiduously avoid, they are difficult to approach. While a Priest shaman lives in the center of a village and socializes with its inhabitants, Warrior shamans usually make their homes outside of town. Sometimes they build a hut in a secluded part of the forest or close to a mountain or waterfall. When forced to be in town they keep to themselves, avoiding gossip and chitchat, which makes them uncomfortable and which they believe hinders their involvement with the sacred. Most of the masters who trained me were eccentric and elusive in this way.

As you can see, the Warrior shaman's task is considerably more personal than that of the Priest shaman and more demanding. This is why, when villagers have an urgent personal problem, when they think they are cursed or sick or possessed, it is the Warrior shaman's help they invariably seek.

Finally, a fact to note is that at the present time Warrior shaman lineages are becoming increasingly difficult to find. This shortage is disheartening not only to shamans but to those throughout Peru who still believe in the old ways. Traditionally, Warrior shamans were doctors and healers, and for this reason were targeted as rivals and even enemies when the Spanish arrived in Peru bringing their own form of Western medicine. In today's world, the same prejudices exist, this time with modern conventional medicine leading the charge. The result is that currently Warrior shamanism exists mostly in rural areas of Peru, and even here modern medicine lures away many villagers who in the past would have treasured the opportunity to be treated by a Warrior *curandero*.

Some Common Misconceptions

A prevailing assumption among many people is that a shaman should look, talk, and act in a certain way. Perhaps because they have viewed so many marketing websites, some seekers clearly have trouble thinking of modern shamans such as myself as authentic *curanderos*. I do not look the part—no native costume, earrings, or beads. Also, my mother tongue is Spanish, not any of the indigenous languages of Peru, though I am familiar with traditional wording pertaining to my work. In my experience, some people automatically attach legitimacy to formal appearances without realizing they can be deceived by pretenders playing a part.

Some people I met in Europe several years ago had participated in Ayahuasca ceremonies in the Amazon overseen by native medicine persons fully dressed in traditional garb. Some of these practitioners turned out to be of questionable training and intentions, a fact that deeply upset the group members who thought that because they looked the part, they were authentic. I did my best to explain that shamanic appearances can be deceptive, and that if any of these people returned to Peru for an Ayahuasca night they should base their choice of a medicine person on reputation and positive word of mouth rather than on looks. For reasons I cannot entirely explain, it seems that the more ordinary a shaman looks and the more undistinguished his behavior, the more powerful his Medicine will be.

More on Warrior Shamans

Warrior shamans can be men or women. Sometimes they have families, though more commonly they live an ascetic life. There is no fixed rule. Young people, male or female, who are gifted and recognized as born healers are usually proficient in some particular healing technique and have the potential to become Warrior shamans.

For example, there are young men who have a strong instinctive connection with a certain group of healing plants and who know all about their harvesting, preparation, and uses. These youths are looked on in the community as potential men of knowledge, and through the years some develop deep forms of spiritual refinement. I have also seen women who work as midwives and who are expert at using plants and resins for helping women give birth and for other medicinal purposes. The Warrior women shamans I have met are usually of a certain age. It is common knowledge that after menopause when a woman's natural clock tells her the time of motherhood is over, she becomes increasingly capable of attaining deep levels of soul discernment through her work. Though women shamans are less common than men in Peru, some people believe them to be superior healers. But, in fact, such comparisons are meaningless, and in the long run all shamans, male or female, are judged by their healing talents alone rather than their gender.

There can also be confusion in some seekers' minds about a Warrior shaman's character and frame of mind. For some, a Warrior shaman is not just a traditionally trained medicine person but a combination of Zen master, witch doctor, and Christian saint. But in fact a shaman is simply an ordinary man or woman who has learned to communicate with the spirit world—period.

Here it can be remarked that some visitors and even modern Peruvians anxious to participate in a ceremony sometimes ask a Warrior shaman for "Ayahuasca" or even a popular name like Aya, Mother, or Motheraska. Traditionally, though, native Peruvians tend to avoid asking a Warrior shaman directly for "Ayahuasca," and they absolutely *never* ask for "Aya" or its idiomatic spinoffs. They consider it disrespectful to refer to the vine in slang terms or to single out Ayahuasca at the expense of other important plants that are part of any sacred brew. When villagers approach a Warrior shaman, they may ask for a healing or a purge or for help from the Work. Since they know that each practitioner mixes his ingredients and oversees his ceremony in a unique way, they tell the Warrior shaman they have drunk the brew of Mr. X or Mr. Y, and would now like to try his Medicine.

Warrior shamans can sometimes be confused with black sorcerers. Both work mostly with a small number of clients, and both solve personal needs whatever they happen to be. But, of course, there is a vast difference between the two.

A Warrior shaman works to curtail a client's selfish desires. Remember that the "I-want-what-I-want-when-I-want-it" battering ram of the Suffering Consciousness is the source of most human suffering. It is, accordingly, a given that Warrior shamans steer their clients away from this self-destructive compulsion, working to free them from the ego drives that make their lives lonely and unfulfilled. To do this the Warrior shaman attempts to discriminate between the different motives of the people who seek his services, and to act accordingly.

Dark sorcerers, on the other hand, look on their job as a paid profession and nothing more. In their eyes black magic and white are of equal weight. As part of their work, they make pacts with demons or allow themselves to be sodomized by infernal spirits to acquire shadowy powers. When hired by a client they willingly curse the client's enemy, cast spells, mix poisons, command evil spirits to harm unknowing victims, or create love amulets that force people into undesired unions, all in a day's work. Yet if paid accordingly, a dark sorcerer will also perform benevolent assignments with the same enthusiasm, reuniting lovers, healing the sick, sending blessings to needful persons, and so forth. Nonetheless, the nature of his tools is in truth a loan from a dark source. In a few cases, rare but existent, a sorcerer takes pleasure in gratuitously harming people with his magic, and only accepts assignments that cause ruin, madness, and even death.

Generally speaking, a Warrior shaman is an ordinary person who has developed ways of interacting with spirit energy, and who has learned methods for directing the Force of Life in order to heal. While a shaman may appear to generate supernatural skills during a ceremony, in reality they do not create this magic and power. They may be born with Medicine or develop it to great lengths in their practice. But the skills are always a loan—not a gift but a loan—from the Great Spirit. If misused or applied for selfish ends, these gifts may fade or be taken away entirely.

For most of my brother and sister *curanderos* as well as for myself, this loan from the invisible world plays a central part in our practice, arming us with the protective and dynamic Medicine contained in a kind of sacred tool kit.

I call this kit my Healing Family.

CHAPTER 4

THE HEALING FAMILY

When I speak of my Healing Family, I often refer to it as a psychic tool kit. This kit, in a nutshell, is a group of psychic entities, spirits of plants, animals, and places in nature that over time become friends and allies of a shaman, empowering his ability to heal. These allies may include ancestors from the near and far past, and the spirits of plants and animals that the shaman has met. Also, teachers, the teachers of teachers, and friendly shamans belonging to different lineages. Occasionally a *curandero* aligns himself with long-deceased souls when visiting ruins and settlements. Certain mountains, lakes, deserts, waterfalls, forests, and deserted beaches that have their own power and awareness can all be members of a shaman's Healing Family.

Whenever I am trying to solve a demanding case during a ceremony, the energies I use are a combination of my own personal Medicine and the direction given me by my Healing Family. There are instances when I have struggled for hours to overcome a curse and eventually come to the end of my strength. In such moments, on the edge of defeat, I receive backing from an ally in my Healing Family who gives me the power I need to prevail—power I could not have marshaled on my own.

A Few Members of My Healing Family

Every shaman's psychic tool kit is exclusive to his own work. The spiritual allies in my Healing Family are different from those in another shaman's Healing Family, and this is the way it should be, as each Healing Family evolves from a medicine person's unique needs and abilities.

How do members of my psychic tool kit help? Sometimes a healing ally comes to me as a voice or a whisper while I am treating a client, sparking a sensation that feels simultaneously like an intuition, a prescription, and an inspiration. At other times it appears as a vision, guiding my hands to the right parts of a client's body. Or it sends me its energy.

Interestingly, a Warrior shaman may have a strong Healing Family but for one reason or another decides not to use it. For example, a friend of mine who works in the Amazon and who I consider a genuine and gifted medicine man unburdened himself to me one day, admitting that after years of working with just a few Peruvian clients he now prefers to chaperone large ceremonies populated by out-of-towners. The reason for this approach, he explained in somewhat embarrassed tones, is that large gatherings bring in more money than small. When his *maloca* is crammed full of people, my friend told me, he sings sacred songs and plays the drums, but rarely if ever calls on the spirit world or the powers of his Healing Family. The clients, he assured me, are usually happy with the proceedings, as the sacred plants give them the hallucinogenic trance they crave, if not the healing that only a dedicated shaman can provide.

This reluctance on the part of a *curandero* to use his psychic assets not only depends on increased revenues. Sometimes it is simply easier for a medicine person, especially one with flexible principles, to escort naive clients through a nighttime jamboree of "bells, smells, and spells," avoiding involvement with the allies of his Healing Family and their demanding expectations.

While there are certain secret powers of the Healing Family that I normally do not talk about, I find it useful to describe some of my own Family's most prominent allies when dealing with seekers interested in *curanderismo*. Below is a list, not complete by any means, but inclusive enough to showcase the potent tools and forces that a Healing Family can provide.

THE SPIRIT VOICE

I recall one incident that involved an angry, sexually tormented middle-aged man who was involved in sadistic and nonconsensual forms of sex and who desperately wanted to rid himself of this drive. People predisposed to such behavior often feel guilty, experiencing their urges as an uncontrollable compulsion that they wish with all their heart would go away.

One night on the side of a sacred mountain I performed a ceremony with five or six people including the client mentioned above. This man was very tall with a stocky build and a powerful presence. Socially he was quite convivial, with a wonderful sense of humor and an easygoing manner. In our preliminary discussions he told me that his father died when he was a child, and that this abandonment produced a great deal of confusion and upset inside him.

As he grew up, he became filled with rage, often using his size to bully classmates in school. By the time he reached manhood, his rage had transformed itself into a strong sadistic urge, both sexual and social. He took delight in hurting people with caustic comments and cutting asides. The sexual fantasies he confided to me were cruel, even criminal. Superficially this client was a decent, moral fellow. But a malicious fire burned inside him that he struggled to keep under the surface and under control.

From the start of the ceremony, I worked closely with this conflicted man. Right away his perverse side materialized on the psychic plane in the form of a black demon-like figure. The man was literally possessed. The monster he had allowed to grow inside himself was now visible on the psychic plane.

As I worked on him, I saw the man's body language change before my eyes as the dark spirit grubbed about in his stomach and chest. This was not the same friendly fellow I had chatted with hours earlier but a kind of malicious humanoid that lived to inflict pain on others. The demon was so blended with the man's personality and had taken possession of him so thoroughly that it was impossible to drive it out with normal spells. The creature kept coming into focus for a moment, then fading out, impossible to grab or pin down. Special methods were needed. But which ones?

Then, as so often happens, a member of my Healing Family, in this case the disembodied voice I spoke of, came to the rescue and told me what to do.

Its instructions seemed a bit extreme, I thought, but when a member of your Healing Family gives advice, you take it. Waiting for the right moment, I walked over to the man until I was standing next to him. He looked up at me with an indescribably hateful expression. Before he had time to act on his rage, I punched him hard in the jaw. Stunned by the impact, the demon literally leaped out of the man's body as if it had received an electric shock. A moment later I grabbed and wrestled the demon, tying him like a bull with invisible ropes and then dissolving him entirely, an easy task once he had been disengaged from the man himself.

Naturally the other people in the circle were taken aback by this sudden show of violence, not seeing or understanding the psychic scenario that had just taken place. But the man himself, instead of becoming enraged or fighting back, slumped to the ground and became totally inert. He lay prone for several minutes with a look of shock and wonder on his face, then broke into sobs. For the next ten minutes he cried as I have never before heard a man cry.

The ceremony ended a few minutes later and the man walked quickly back to his tent without saying a word. The next morning at breakfast he pulled me aside and whispered, "It's gone."

THE GOLDEN RAIN

A woman in Lima came to me one day requesting a one-on-one plant session. People in Peru sometimes seek access to the Craft simply to learn what is helpful or hurtful for them at a certain period in their lives, almost like going to a doctor for a wellness checkup.

I agreed with her request, and two nights later we began a session.

Twenty or thirty minutes into the ceremony, visions started to come, and right away I saw ominous-looking dark nodules sprinkled throughout her organs. When a client is healthy, their organs and nervous system radiate light. If they are ill, things look dark inside.

I spent a good deal of time attempting to remove the nodules, but there were so many of them, and they were so tiny, it felt like, as they say, trying to herd cats. After several hours of intense work, I finally isolated a collection of these lumps, only to have them dissolve before I could take them out. This happened several more times.

As the evening wore on, I became increasingly frustrated and finally began to wonder if I had the ability to help this person. The presence of the dark nodules was alarming, though the client knew nothing about them and thought herself well and fit. (In Peruvian healing there is a saying that symptoms are the last and not the first sign of a disease.) I had a strong feeling that what

I was seeing was cancer or a serious autoimmune reaction that desperately needed to be removed. I usually do not need to know the name of the disease I am working on, as I deal only in energies and not physiology. Nonetheless, the word *cancer* hung in the air, and so finally I did what I do in such seemingly hopeless situations: I asked my Healing Family for help.

At first nothing happened. The woman was sitting near me with her eyes closed, breathing quietly and oblivious to any danger. Then my eyes felt drawn to the ceiling, where I saw a watery mist floating above me and looking a bit like melting gold. When a helping force comes during a ceremony, it generates a pleasant warmth inside my chest. This sensation tells me support has come, even if I do not know what it is or how to use it. I was still in my early days as a practicing shaman, and this was the first time my Healing Family had sent this particular tool.

I gazed at the cloud for several minutes, struck by its beauty, when suddenly a light rain began to pour down from it onto the client, sometimes in gentle droplets of golden light, sometimes like a golden torrent. As the drops fell, I could see the light washing the woman inside and outside, infusing every cell of her body. The nodules were quickly loosened due to the force of the Medicine, making it easy for me to remove them. After a few minutes the lumps were gone and the woman, who to this day does not know how sick she was, unconsciously emitted the glow of life and serenity that commonly follows a healing.

From this time on the golden rain became an essential tool in my Healing Family. Often when it falls on clients, I see it washing away ash-like grime that streams out from their fingers and feet. At times a client's body turns completely gold—gold fingernails, fingertips, arms, groin, even the soles of the feet. When this occurs, I relax and go to work on other clients in the circle, knowing that the rain is working a cure on its own. When I come back the person is usually still surrounded by golden light, but by now it is gently fading away.

This coming of the golden rain is an example of how a new psychic resource may appear out of the blue when a medicine person is stymied by a difficult case. Struggling to get the job done with all his heart and with the methods he already knows, and finding them inadequate, he suddenly receives a new gift from his Healing Family that helps him accomplish the healing and then remains with him permanently as a newly acquired tool.

I do not usually call on the golden rain, as it prefers to come on its own when needed. I do, however, wish every reader could someday see the unearthly beauty of this magical cloud and witness the cascade of gold-tinted mist that falls from it.

THE EMERALD GREEN RAY

During my training in the Amazon, I worked with an accomplished *curandero* who sent me on retreats, put me on fasts, and showed me a number of ways to work with the spirit world. He also taught me that a teacher sometimes shows you a healing technique but then leaves it up to you to figure out how to use it. In fact in general, shamanic teachers set the stage, but the pupil must do the work. The bow may be presented to you today, the arrow tomorrow, directions on how to pull the string the day after tomorrow, or next week, or next year, or maybe never. Your trainers expect you to figure out what to do with the tools they offer; there are few systematic, step-by-step explanations. My teachers were guides, not gurus, and we students were expected to learn more from hands-on experience than from formal instruction.

Once during a plant ceremony, I was sitting in the circle with my teacher and several of his clients. After a long period of silence, he abruptly stood up, walked over to where I was seated, and stood looking down at me saying nothing. After several minutes he removed something from his pocket and pressed it onto the spot right between his eyes. Instantly a ray of emerald-green light shot from his brow, hitting my forehead, and lighting up my cranial cavity, as if the inside of my head were the dome of a planetarium and dozens of glaring galaxies and constellations were circling overhead.

In the middle of this vision, as I sat dumbfounded, a small, penis-shaped organ slowly materialized in the center of my skull, erect and pointing upward—this, along with the whirling lights and stars. My teacher said nothing but returned to his seat, and the ceremony continued in silence. The organ remained permanently fixed in my forehead from then on.

In the next few weeks, after a good deal of practice, I managed to teach myself how to project the laser-like green ray from the newly grown switch in my head. But there was a problem: I could not for the life of me understand what the ray was supposed to do. When I asked my teacher, he told me that the ray was now mine, but that I had to figure out its purpose on my own. He had given me the bow. Now I had to find the arrow.

From that time on it took me more than two years of constant experimentation to fully understand the function of the emerald beam and how to use it for different purposes. Though I prefer not to discuss more details about this magical light, I will say that in certain cases it can heal serious and sometimes incurable disorders, mostly mental, and is capable of traveling and connecting with people over long distances. It remains one of the most important instruments in my Healing Family's bag of tools.

GARDENS IN THE CENTER OF A MOUNTAIN

One day my teacher Pedro suggested that I drive to a range of mountains that he considered one of the most important power centers in northern Peru. These mountains were located in the middle of a desert far off the main highway. One mountain in particular was considered the most powerful peak in the range. To reach it I had to drive overland and off-road for many hours before it came into view, sitting isolated in the middle of the desert away from the surrounding hills.

Determined to investigate this legendary power source, I set off with a knapsack filled with food and water and spent several days exploring the mountain from bottom to top. The second night on the hill I drank a psychoactive medicine of my own mixing, a combination of northern plants I called my *yunga* recipe, after the *yunga* region that runs down the coast of Peru.

There was no particular mission I was obliged to perform on the mountain. I came simply to imbibe its power and feel and hear whatever secrets it might whisper to me. Sitting on a ridge in silent contemplation that second night, I heard something calling me. I walked in the direction the voice was coming from until I reached a fissure in the hillside. Inside it was empty except for a kind of nest made of rocks.

I sat down by the rocks thinking I would continue my meditations in this sheltered spot when immediately a dark shadow opened up on a nearby wall, revealing a cavity in the mountain. I entered and took a few steps until the darkness of the cavern opened out to a blinding light illuminating a vast garden inside the mountain, the beauty of which defied description. In a few feet I had literally gone from a hole in the wall to an open field of brightly sunlit flowers and trees.

There was one flower close by that, like many of the other

plants, looked like no vegetable species I had ever seen. It seemed to be summoning me, and I could feel the mountain approving. The plant introduced itself, told me it was a medicine, explained the kind of help it could provide, and that it would become a member of my Healing Family if I accepted it as a gift from the mountain.

Today this plant remains my dear friend and an important part of my tool kit. While performing ceremonies I often evoke its image when I need assistance for a difficult treatment. Before I said goodbye to the flower that night, I asked it if all mountains have secret gardens hidden inside them. Not many, it told me. Only special mountains. Like this one. And these are only revealed to people whom the mountain favors.

SPIRIT LADY OF THE WATERFALL

One day when I was spending time in the northern Amazon, members of a native community asked if I would join them on a trek to a special place. What kind of place? I asked them, but they looked at me blankly. Always game for the unknown, I agreed, and we set off. After several miles, pushing through intense tangles of brush, we came to a bright clearing in the forest where a waterfall several hundred feet high cascaded down over the rocks in a whir of fog and mist. My guides smiled at me in a strange way, nodded toward the gigantic curtain of water, made several hand gestures I did not understand, then walked away abruptly, leaving me alone.

It was a steaming hot jungle day. I disrobed and walked over the rocks to the spray, standing under the falling water for several minutes, enjoying its frigid wetness and the sound of water splashing on rocks. Suddenly I saw a series of visionary flashes in the waves of water pouring down, and then an old woman appeared. She was smiling at me. Though the water was surging down on both of us, her dress remained dry the entire time we talked. She introduced herself, told me she could help me in my healing work, promised that we would see each other again in the future, and faded into the water like mist fades into the air.

One day many years later I was working on a difficult case with a sick woman in a foreign country when the Spirit Lady of the Waterfall appeared next to me out of nowhere and told me she could help. Instantly my client and I found ourselves transported to the same waterfall in the Amazon with the Spirit Lady accompanying us. When we arrived, she directed us to a quiet place approximately a hundred yards from the falls, where I saw a narrow creek with a strong current meandering in several twists and turns until it poured into a small pond.

Here is where the healings take place, the Spirit Lady informed me. She and I then proceeded to work on the ailing woman, washing her diseased limbs with water from the pond bed. After several minutes the client and I were transported back to our ceremonial circle, confused but happy. The woman told me she already felt a good deal better.

Today, whenever I am working on a person with a serious ailment like cancer or heart disease, I often find myself and my client psychically transported to this waterfall and from there, under the Spirit Lady's direction, to the nearby pond, where I wash away toxic energies that are difficult to remove in any other way. Over the years the waterfall has become an extremely redeeming place for me, and even better, the Spirit Lady and I are now dear friends.

Music

According to the ancients, every organic thing has its own visual and auditory vibration, its own pattern and color, and its own song. Humans, animals, trees, mountains, and spirits all convey their individual music, even if we cannot hear it.

Knowing the impact melodious sound can have on both Soul Consciousness and Suffering Consciousness, people of old learned how to transmit musical harmonies by means of instruments: percussion, plucking, wind, and the human voice. Since ancient times, a number of music-making devices have been used by shamans in their ceremonies, usually with salutary results. As a traditionalist, I prefer the drum, rattle, and voice only, as they get the job done without need for further help. Importantly, anyone who is interested in shamanic music must realize it is not meant to please or entertain. Its purpose is purely for healing, and it does not matter what instruments are used or whether the sounds produced are soothing or harsh.

THE DRUM

The most effective sound for imparting mystical Knowledge is often said to be the beating of a drum. There are a number of reasons why this may be true, though many would agree that the most important is due to the fact that the first sound we ever hear is the twenty-four-hour, low-frequency, rhythmic heartbeats of our mother while we are in the womb and under the care of our Soul Consciousness. As a result, the sound of drums has a stirring impact on our soul for the rest of our lives.

Whatever style of shamanic drumming we listen to, and whatever its meter or cadence, it creates a series of positive connections, first with the memory of the womb, second, with the beating of our own heart, third, with the beating of another person's heart, and fourth, with our heart's relationship to the resonating pulses of nature surrounding us. As said, every natural being has its own song.

Think of how a large spiderweb vibrates from the footsteps

of a tiny insect. In the same way even a small drum can convey a mighty emotional tremor that connects the hearts of all participants in a ceremony. When a shaman pounds the skin of a drum during a ritual, he is sending loving and protective energy to everyone in the circle. Everything on earth has a heart, and drumming is its language.

Though some people think drumbeats are mostly monotone, the *curandero*'s instrument, depending on how it is stretched and played, produces so many subtle tones and harmonies that I have heard clients compare it to a mini orchestra. Besides the sounds themselves, when clients ingest the sacred plants, they sometimes see the beats pouring out of the drum like a tapestry of energy. There are moments when the facilitator needs to drum messages for everyone in the circle, telling them a story. There are also times when he focuses the rhythms on a single client who alone receives the drum's gift of Medicine.

After drumming for several hours during a ceremony I often see that the instrument has changed shape. Classically round, it has morphed during the evening into an oval or ellipse, on occasion producing sounds that no one in the circle including myself—and perhaps no one on earth—has ever heard before. The drum may also become larger or smaller, wider or deeper, or even twist itself into a weird sculpture-like object that has no resemblance to its original shape.

For Warrior shamans a drum's primary use is to produce a deep meditative state in members of a ceremony. The style and techniques of their drumming differ from ceremony to ceremony, and no two drumming sessions are ever alike.

In a Warrior shaman's ceremony, drumming can be unhurried and measured like a slow boat crossing a calm river. Most of the time, though, Warrior drumming is rapid with intricate patterns that continually merge one into another, and that help clients navigate through the labyrinth of their Suffering Consciousness to reach the world of spirits.

When he drums, moreover, the Warrior shaman is also modulating the energy of his beat according to the rhythms his clients need that particular night, to what the spirits ask him to do, or to what a member of his Healing Family tells him to do. Occasionally the beats are so loud and asynchronous that listeners clap their hands over their ears. At other times the beat is sonorous and restrained. Sometimes there is little or no drumming at all.

Occasionally a Warrior shaman needs to extend a drumming episode for long periods of time, sometimes several hours or more without stop. Though such an effort is exhausting, a dedicated *curandero* forces himself to continue until his inner voice tells him to stop, knowing that the magic of the drum's voice has brought a needed healing to one or more of his clients.

THE RATTLE

In deep states of concentration clients may hear a strong, high-pitched rattling or buzzing sound inside their head. Or they may sense a vital force pushing inside their belly and chest, producing a vibration that goes from low to high. Hence the ancients found a valuable use for a dried fruit with seeds inside—a rattle to reproduce this buzzing or vibration. Shaking it rhythmically, they could induce a state of trance.

A drum is a low-pitched vibration vehicle, while rattles are its high-pitched equivalent. The two produce opposite yet wonderfully complementary sounds and are often played together. Generally speaking, the high-pitched tones of the rattle echo in the lungs and in the nerve pathways that lead to the head, while the low-frequency drum resonates in the abdominal areas and in the chest. Both drum and rattle are equally ancient.

Commonly decorated with traditional symbols or mystical designs, most Amazonian rattles are made from a gourd of dry fruit filled with seeds. Sometimes these seeds are taken from different plants and placed inside the rattle, each set producing a different pitch. Rattles are also made using large seeds strung on a stick with a cluster of feathers attached to the end. Variations on the rattle's construction differ throughout Peru, and for that matter in countries around the world where shamanism is practiced, a testament to how universal this instrument truly is.

The type of sound produced by this hypnotic instrument, besides its seeds, depends on its shape and size, how fast or slow it is shaken, the way it is held, how high or low the tone, the kind of energy the *curandero* sends through the instrument, the rhythms created by shaking two rattles at once, and a number of other variations, most of which go unnoticed by clients but are of vital importance for helping specific types of maladies.

In my own work I usually use two rattles, one in each hand and each with a slightly different pitch. The process is similar to weaving. When the rhythm is consistent, each rattle emits short threads of energy that vary in color and intertwine, as if woven. This method of conducting energy always makes me think that I am covering the body of a client with a blanket of healing, sliding a flying carpet underneath them, or even wrapping them with ribbons.

Rattles are commonly used to summon spirit animals or send curative energy. Also, to push away and disperse bad energies. During a ceremony, rattles can cause a fog or mist to form over members of the group, raining down colors, sparks, flower petals, and sometimes spiritual gifts. Toward the latter parts of a ceremony when clients are taking stock of what they have experienced, I see these gifts floating over their heads and I use the rattle as a catalyst to make their contents scatter evenly below.

An example of a typical rattle's gift is the "calabash of prosperity," a large gourd that appears to float over one or several clients during a ceremony, usually close to the end of the night. When it opens it releases colorful drops, covering clients with petals or a colored confetti that brings spiritual and material prosperity. I find this practice especially relevant, as it confirms my notion that certain modern entertainments such as hitting a piñata to pour out toys or the release of confetti during celebratory moments are replications of ancient shamanic techniques that over the centuries have become purely secular, appearing in everyday life in the form of a children's party game.

In certain instances, the sound of a rattle can be used as a weapon in the spirit world.

The *curandero* shakes it and activates its Medicine. In response the rattle shoots out an invisible line of sound, cutting, cleaning, and chopping up unwanted parasitic forms. Here we see the psychic versatility of rattles, capable of causing a gentle rain of mercy or, when needed, producing a blade that cuts through demonic beings as effectively as any magical sword.

Finally, during a ceremony a rattle can be used as a kind of psychic compass, showing in a brief visionary flash the route clients need to follow in particular day-to-day situations or even on their spiritual journey through life. This vision appears to the client, the shaman, and sometimes both at the same time, becoming a goal for clients to pursue, literally pointing like the hands of a compass. The shaman may also use the rattle's vibrational powers to keep clients following their visionary road after the ceremony— a long-term effect that protects them from temptations sent by the dark powers to divert them from their spiritual destiny.

During the time I was practicing shamanism along the north coast, a middle-aged worker named Luis once came to me complaining of several painful disorders. Luis was known to be a bad-tempered and insulting man, abusing everyone he knew including his friends, family, and coworkers at his office. On first seeing him I instinctively knew that if he was to recover his health, he needed to take responsibility for his nasty ways and change them.

The ceremony that night was small, just three or four people including Luis, who was constantly telling others about his heart problems and other infirmities. Less than an hour into the evening's ritual, the vision of a powerful Peruvian native standing in a far-off desert with a whip in his hands flashed before my eyes. Images of this kind are usually of a real person rather than a spirit, perhaps a ghost or shadow soul, or sometimes a Person of Knowledge. The man started walking toward our circle with great urgency, though he was miles away. His eyes had a hard, determined look as he trudged over the dunes cracking his whip.

At this point I looked over at Luis and saw that he was trembling.

He was also seeing the man, and he knew the man was seeing him. A member of my Healing Family explained that the whip holder was Luis's ancestor, and that he had been sent by past generations of Luis's family to make their delinquent relative see the error of his ways.

As the stranger approached, Luis went into a state of complete avoidance, closing his eyes, looking away, then standing up and trying to leave the circle. But the man with the whip was not having it as he walked at an ever-increasing pace toward Luis, who might have been his grandson or great, great grandson—who knows?

At this point I began working with the rattles, using a combination of their high-pitched and low-pitched waves that allowed me to psychically travel the long distance I needed to get close to the man. Standing face-to-face, I told him I was here and ready to help. The man told me what to tell Luis to do: He must come out of his bubble of denial and sit on one side of a large psychic funnel. He, the whip-cracking ancestor, would be sitting on the other side. I didn't fully understand the purpose of these instructions until an actual funnel appeared out of nowhere, serving, I guessed, as a time tunnel from the desert to our circle. In a flash Luis's ancestor was standing next to him, raising his lash as if to strike him. All the while I was shaking my rattles and watching this drama unfold.

At this point Luis let out a scream and fell to his hands and knees, weeping uncontrollably, crying out that he was sorry, begging for another chance. As quickly as he had come, the ancestor disappeared and Luis curled up on the floor like a wounded dog.

In the morning he was recovered, and his face glowed like a serene child. He had vomited out much of his anger and guilt during the night's encounter, comparing himself now to an empty vessel. When I spoke with him several weeks later, he told me that his heart problems had improved but, even better, so had his heart.

SONG

Even more ancient than the drum or rattle in sacred ceremonies is the human voice. Besides transmitting sacred stories and messages, singing articulates emotional states and wishful feelings in a way that cannot be expressed as profoundly by any other means of communication. From sounds in the animate world like birdsong, crickets chirping, and wolves baying, to the melodies of the environment like thunder, rain, and the rippling of a stream, early humans had an immense pallet of sounds to incorporate into their songs at a time when knowledge was still passed from generation to generation by singing and oral recitation.

As a result, many songs sung by shamans today come from old masters and old lineages. Others are sent by revelation from the spirits or are learned during a fasting retreat, while still others are received in a state of trance. There are instances of medicine persons who remember melodies heard in a dream and who include them in musical compositions that eventually become popular classics.

In some areas of the Amazonian jungle a healing song is known as an *icaro*, a name that in recent years has been incorporated into the general vocabulary of the shamanic community. There are three qualities that characterize an *icaro*.

First, the melody must come from deep within the shaman's heart, lungs, and gut. When sung from these depths the song elevates people's moods and can open up a direct channel to the spirits.

Second, the melody of an *icaro* provides stronger Medicine than its verses, though words are still a valuable part of a song, imparting spiritual information to the cognitive mind. In some traditions, the words of a song are tonal prayers, meant to focus a client's attention on the Great Spirit. In still other *icaros* words are not words at all but syllables strung together to help carry the melody. An *icaro* can be spoken, mumbled, or whistled as well as sung.

Third, and most important, an *icaro* transmits healing force. When a shaman is singing, the life-giving energies in his breath are sent into the ceremonial circle and into the hearts of each client. This deployment of the Medicine through song can take a moment or two to reach full expression. During this time, if the shaman loses his spiritual focus, the energy of a song drops and becomes simply a stimulating tune rather than a therapeutic tool.

It is similar to manipulating a ribbon in rhythmic gymnastics—the gymnast must skillfully pull the ribbon to keep it flowing evenly while she performs her movements. If it slackens, her form slackens with it.

When *curanderos* chant, they charge the melody with their own personal Medicine, sometimes creating songs that are different from the originals and unique to their particular Art. New songs may also be taught to the shaman by his Healing Family, eventually becoming part of his lineage. Over time I learned that a shaman can also use the vibrations of an *icaro* to make plants grow faster, tame wild animals, and communicate directly with the Great Spirit.

On certain occasions a shaman will surprise everyone in his group by singing secular and even goofy tunes. I once attended a ceremony in the jungle overseen by a first-rank facilitator. After many hours of serious work and traditional *icaros*, he suddenly began singing popular songs from the 1960s and 1970s, the kind of radio hits one would likely hear on an oldies-but-goodies station. Everyone in the circle including myself was taken aback by this abrupt intrusion of worldliness. But as it turned out, these tunes carried just the right rhythms, tempo, and harmonics needed by certain clients to heal. Never mind that the tunes were not art; they were Medicine.

When speaking of the magical effects of sound and vibrations, it is interesting to note that there are two groups of insects whose songs are believed to produce a healing uplift similar to that of an *icaro*, and which were both considered sacred by people of old.

The first of these are bees, whose buzzing lightens a heavy heart, and whose murmur soothes anxiety and reduces emotional pain. The second is the cicada, whose song-like chirping drives away useless thoughts and reduces hostility generated by the

Suffering Consciousness. The bees heal the heart and cicadas heal the mind.

Another example of Medicine transmitted by song is a lullaby. When a mother, brimming with adoration, sings to her toddler, love passes into the child through the emotional vibrations of her voice. Besides filling the child with grace, the mother's song transfers a sense of safety to a certain part of a child's mind, helping the child grow up feeling strong and secure. What a wonderful thing it is, really: By singing to her child, a mother imparts Life Force through the medium of melody. Life Force is everywhere, but it moves most naturally in the flow of love and music. Singing lullabies to young children is one of the most important things a parent can do.

Finally, as we saw with piñatas, there are many cultural amusements created by the ancients that demonstrate truths from the invisible world in the form of stories, songs, and fairy tales, or by toys whose origins go far back in time, promoting a child's intuition. Certain songs and nursery rhymes come down to us from as far back as the Middle Ages, and have a spiritual wisdom hidden in their childish lyrics. Children with their open and fundamentally mystical minds absorb this learning far more easily than adults, receiving seeds of Knowledge that can someday bloom into spiritual awareness. Such is the power of song, poetry, and the music of spiritual healing.

CHAPTER 5

THE LANGUAGE

OF VISIONS:

SPIRITS AND

THE SPIRIT WORLD

Throughout this book I use stories, examples, case histories, and personal experience to make the case that traditional societies from time immemorial have believed in spirits and recognized the part they play in human existence. Of course, spirits appear in different forms in different parts of the world. There are leprechauns, spirit hawks, elementals, dragons, fairies, genies, devas, dryads, trolls, and many more. Since these beings are nonphysical, their appearance is conditioned by time and place, cultural consciousness, and the genetic background of the people perceiving them. We see the spirit world not as it is—it is formless and can take on any appearance—but as *we* are.

Europeans in the deeply religious twelfth century, for example, saw beings from the subtle world in the form of demons, angels, and gargoyles like those carved on the archways of Gothic cathedrals, all in tune with the zeitgeist of their time. Elves, fairies, gnomes, the entire family of fairy-tale beings, have belonged to the green Druid hills and deep virgin forests of Europe since the Neolithic era. For some North American natives, the spirit world is a prairie world, governed by eagle spirits, magic cactuses, totemic animals. In the Middle East, there are ghouls, ifrits, genies. And, of course, Western society perceives the spirit realm based on its obsession with technology: kindly or malevolent extraterrestrials and alien scientists experimenting on human beings in hovering spacecrafts. This is not to say that UFOs do not exist, only that at least some of what appear to be alien beings are spirit creatures from the hidden world.

Spirit forms, in short, are as old as humanity itself. Yet if I told an American friend that elves exist, he would probably think I was deranged. At the same time, if I told the same thing to a Peruvian native or an Irish countrywoman or a Dayak tribesman in Borneo, they would tell me about a jinn or spirit or wee person they recently saw gamboling on the grass on a moonlit night. Countless civilizations use oracles, clairvoyants, divination, and psychoactive plants to communicate with beings in the higher worlds. Almost every work of art created before the time of the Renaissance was based on some form of otherworldly belief.

Many people today, assured by our materialistic worldview that spirit-oriented civilizations of the past had no scientific understanding of how the world really works, steadfastly deny the validity of the supernormal and the existence of an immaterial world beyond sensory perception. According to shamanic thinking, this type of profane thinking is one of the major reasons why the human race currently balances on the razor's edge of extinction. Since the dawn of time, thousands of civilizations have interacted with the spirits in their myths, religions, rites, theater, and music, and profited accordingly. Without this connection today we live in a secular vault, denied the very spiritual forces that can give our lives purpose and meaning.

These secular ways of thinking also show how far contemporary society has strayed from nature. Such thinking prompts us to conceive of the earth as a place whose only purpose is to provide natural resources for industrial development and physical pleasure. We imagine our techno-driven, environment-unfriendly society to be the status quo, something normal and progressive or even the pinnacle of human achievement, rather than an aberration that has never before existed in all human history—an artificial world that would have both puzzled and horrified our ancestors. We are living a dream of material reality that we know in our hearts is false, but which has been sold to us by those who make the money and who sometimes are, to varying degrees, consciously working for the dark side. A friend of mine once quoted me a phrase from the American authority on shamanism Martin Prechtel that so aptly puts it: "We live in a kind of dark age, craftily lit with synthetic light, so that no one can tell how dark it has really gotten. But our exiled spirits can tell."

We are living in the most perilous period in human history, and we are running out of time. Most importantly, as a result of our precarious position, once unnamed sacred plants are intentionally making themselves known again in our culture, sounding an alarm via the spirits and offering us answers to many of the problems imperiling human civilization. These magic plants are right at hand, growing in the gardens of the world's backyard, there for the using and the taking—but I hope an honorable kind of using and a respectful kind of taking.

The Language of Visions

While there are considerable differences among the many types of spirits inhabiting the invisible realm, all have one feature in common: They speak the language of visions.

Many of these visions are triggered by using the sacred plants. But not all of them. They can also be induced by fasting, meditation, breathing exercises, praying, and other traditional spiritual techniques. Spirits may appear to seekers in the form of birds, insects, human-like beings, mythological figures like genies and gnomes, or pictorial narratives that tell a story, flowing across the screen of the mind like a motion picture. There are the spirits of ancestors, ancient shamans and witches, animals, spirits of the drum and rattle, spirits of gems and precious stones, spirits that rule over a special place in the wilderness like a volcano or waterfall (viz. our friend the Spirit Lady of the Waterfall), spirits that guard a flowing body of water (like the tiny mermen and mermaids I saw when I took San Pedro). There are also what I call sister and brother spirits, which have a strange and sometimes bizarre appearance, belonging to a reality entirely different from our own, like beings from another planet, yet who are extremely generous in helping heal clients and shamans alike.

All these and many other invisible entities speak in the language of visions, each with their own accent and dialect. Their message can be conveyed telepathically, visually, musically, or via a combination of all three, with many variations on the theme.

How does one tune in to this language? After undergoing visions during a sacred plant ceremony, even many skeptics are convinced of the existence of the spirit world. It is, after all, difficult to be a doubter when you see the spirit of an anaconda or a monkey or your long-dead uncle standing in front of you clear as day, explaining the solution to a problem that has tormented you for years or opening you up to a state of consciousness in which your entire life unfurls before you in a millisecond.

At the same time, from the skeptic's point of view, it is also accurate to say that certain visions *are* in fact projections of the mind and imagination, and not a metaphysical visitation.

Ironically, both cases can be true: Some visions are indeed from the invisible world, others are thoughts from the depths of one's mind. There is no contradiction here, just two different sources of information, one from the outside, the other from the inside. The fact is that in a ceremony a client can clearly have dialogues with otherworldly spirits who tell him things he would otherwise never know, reveal facts about the future that come true, or provide spiritual insights. At the same time, with the help of the plants, his deeper mind can also come awake, inspiring him with mental and emotional insights from his Soul Consciousness that have been buried up till now but which rise to the surface with the help of the healing force.

The language of spirit visions combined with the wisdom of one's unconscious, though they may not heal or transform everyone who undergoes them, invariably show people parts of themselves and the world they never knew existed. In all my years as a shaman, though clients may occasionally be apathetic about their experience, I have never been told that a sacred plant ceremony was meaningless and without lessons.

The spirits, a shamanic teacher once told me, are very close to us and yet very far away. Most people in today's modern world, he said with a wry smile, assume their existence is a myth or even a joke. But even as they laugh the spirits laugh with them. Forms of invisible life, he said, swirl around us constantly, and indeed, the earth is populated with countless beings too subtle for our five senses to perceive. Some are friends, some are indifferent. A few wish—or are directed by dark agents—to injure or destroy us.

In ancient days, communication with spirits was common, he went on to say. But today the world is a different place. Due to both the destruction of nature by technology and a belief that the material world is the only world, it is far more difficult to network with ethereal beings than in ancient times. Because of these changes in the zeitgeist, the spirit kingdom has receded from human consciousness. Or perhaps better said, the quality of human consciousness has become increasingly lessened over the past hundred years due to the diminution of spiritual belief, making us less capable of seeing into the deeper realities that exist beyond material form. As a result, we have now come to see nature and the world less as a reflection of a higher reality, more as a stockpile of material goods and resources.

In ancient times, intermediaries like sacred plants and shamans were an integrated part of society. Today, though still used by healers in some parts of the world, people in the West who were once brought up with these medicines scarcely know about them today. And yet, my teacher told me, these intermediaries are needed now more than ever before.

✼

Throughout this book, I have continually spoken about the spirits but only on occasion described their appearance, behavior, and personality. In this chapter I will introduce you to some prominent inhabitants of the higher realms along with their most salient characteristics: how they look and act; the different ways they can harm, heal, or teach you; what they want and expect; and the ways in which their influence can linger for years after a plant ceremony is finished.

An important point to remember is that benevolent spirits who visit a shaman's circle are there because they *want to* be there. Because they care about humankind, and because they are the principal force that make all ceremonial healing and transformation possible. If and when you participate in a plant ritual, the sight of these beings will leave you breathless and more often than not fill you with the resolve to become a better person. Here are some of the more relevant players you may meet.

Types of Spirits

Basically, there are four "species" of spirits: animal, vegetable, landscape, and human (including ancestors and ghosts).

Let us begin with animal spirits.

During a sacred ceremony one or more spirit creatures from the animal realm may approach clients, sitting close or touching them. Sometimes they reveal only their face or a small part of their body. A fox spirit may only show its muzzle, an eagle its beak. Clients feel the animal's fur or they smell its not always savory odor. At other times the creature's entire body appears in its full magnitude, a decidedly startling experience if the creature happens to be a tiger, anaconda, or bear.

Happily, for those in the circle, the type of healing force a spirit transmits is tailor-made for each client's particular needs. If a hawk is sent from the spirit world, it brings the exact Medicine a client needs to recover from his problem or ailment. If another animal brings their particular kind of Medicine to the same client, it will not work as well, if at all; their Medicine is meant for other clients with other problems but not for the client at hand. In this case, only the hawk's particular healing energy can do the job.

Speaking broadly, there are two forms an animal spirit can take. It may be an actual spirit bringing help. Or it may be Medicine embodied in an animal's form but not an animal itself. A spirit that appears as a bat or an owl may not literally be a spirit bat or owl but a formless vital force that "wears" the bat's or owl's body to make itself visible and familiar in order to convey a message.

The first three animal spirits I would like to introduce are familiar from the previous chapter: the giant snake, the large cat, and the predatory bird. These, you will recall, are the representatives of our three centers of consciousness: the gut, the heart, and the mind.

SNAKE SPIRITS

Found in shamanic traditions throughout the world, the snake is probably the most common spirit to appear in a plant ceremony.

According to both ancient and modern Peruvian Knowledge, two types of spirit snakes play a part in the *curandero*'s work. The first are ordinary-sized field and grass snakes, some of which are poisonous. The second is a nonpoisonous jumbo-sized serpent, a boa constrictor or an anaconda. According to Peruvian Medicine, these massive creatures, some of which reach lengths of thirty feet or more, are the incarnation of the Force of Life, protectors of the waters and the forest. If one appears in a client's visions lit with bright colors and precious stones covering its body, or if it emerges from the center of the ceremonial circle where both shaman and clients see it clearly, be grateful: The cosmic forces are pleased and will do everything they can to help.

Sometime snake visions appear in our dreams delivering messages to us weeks or even months after a ceremony. If you dream that a viper bites your hand, someone you trust may be betraying you. Sometimes dreams remind you of important lessons taught during a ceremony, or they goad you to follow advice you were given during a ritual but are neglecting. Not infrequently a large snake appears in a dream to help a client overcome an unreasonable fear of death.

At still other times a snake spirit may invite you for a ride. Clinging to its neck, you soar over the continents, passing landscapes not of this earth, looking down on ruins of bygone civilizations peopled in the way they were ten thousand years ago. Or the snake may take you to a brush circle deep in the jungle where you are told to harvest a plant that will heal your particular ailment.

Occasionally clients in a ceremony see a giant boa or anaconda spirit zigzagging in their direction, and immediately assume they are being attacked. They may shriek for help or try to run away. Then the snake rears up and smiles at them. It blinks its eyes in a friendly way. It may give clients a kiss on the mouth. Sometimes it goes inside their bodies through their mouth or belly. This is the Force of Life telling the client "Do not be fooled by my snake-like appearance. I am the *great cosmic force of healing* here to bless every cell of your body. Be glad!"

Often as the weeks and months go by after a ceremony, clients forget many of the remarkable visions they have seen. But for the rest of their lives no one—*no one*—ever forgets their encounter with the spirit of a giant snake.

I remember once during a ceremony I had a vision in which I was imprisoned at the bottom of a pit with dozens of seven-foot-long serpents slithering over my neck and head. They were not the mind-their-own-business backyard variety but angry vipers with fangs that leaked venom. I knew that if I made any awkward movement or sudden sound, they would bite me.

So here I was surrounded by agitated snake spirits, feeling certain I was about to die. At this moment my teacher who was presiding over the ceremony saw what was happening and told me to not be afraid, all was well, and to simply let go of my fears and connect with my personal Medicine. Doing what he advised, my Medicine responded by telling me to release all tension in my body and enter a state of selflessness, a mindset in which I literally no longer existed but was empty as a cloudless sky.

Not an easy task, to say the least, but I did the best I could. After several minutes of trying to let go, I felt the snakes slowly relaxing around me. I realized at that moment that it was my fear, not my physical presence, that had excited them. After a few minutes they were weaving and bobbing around me with affection, wanting to be near me, to bathe in my Medicine. After five or ten minutes of what had turned into a weird sort of love fest, they said their goodbyes and faded back to their place in the invisible world. The lesson I learned from that encounter was that it is possible to maintain an undistracted flow of Medicine energy, even if a life-threatening situation occurs. That event actually turned out to be a specific training for me to improve my handling of the Medicine force.

Several months later while traveling in another section in the jungle, I visited a professional compound where snake-handling experts were removing venom from deadly vipers as antidotes for certain kinds of poisons. In the middle of the compound was a small, grassy corral where around forty shushupe snakes (*bushmasters* in English) were slithering around. Shushupes are considered by some to be the deadliest snakes in the world.

I had just recently experienced the vision of being trapped in the pit of poisonous serpents as described above. Now in front of me was the real-life thing. Being young and daring and wanting to test my training skills, I made an arrangement with the man in charge, who allowed me to enter the corral.

Stepping into the wiggling, hissing mass, I picked up several vipers with fangs bared, handling them gently and managing to calm them with my Medicine force. There were some tricky moments during the session, and the man in charge, watching the snakes squirming ominously in my hands, became nervous, no doubt regretting that he had let me in in the first place. He begged me to put the snakes down and climb out of the corral.

Handling poisonous snakes is certainly not something I would recommend to anyone, including an aspiring *curandero*. Yet in retrospect, I realize that I handled these snakes not simply to prove my competence but also to honor the Second Golden Rule, acting out on the physical level my vision of being trapped in the snake pit and remaining confident in the Medicine force.

CAT SPIRITS

In most parts of the world including the Amazon large cats are the number one beast of prey; predatory felines that represent our second center of consciousness. These magnificent creatures are remarkably cunning and aggressive and generally get the best of any animal that attacks them. When they appear in our visions, they give us will, heroism, and love. Though not as common as snakes, large cats are frequent spirit guests, and in Peru they mainly appear as jaguars, though occasionally as ocelots and cougars.

During a ceremony a giant spirit cat like a jaguar may suddenly appear and gently nestle up to you purring like a kitten. It may nudge you to pet it or curl around you like a house cat. Sometimes it roars to show off its strength. It may speak to you, give you advice, or take you on its back through secret glades in the jungle, the sight of which causes your worries and anxieties to fall away.

During a ceremony, large cats also visit people who have spent much of their lives conning and cheating others, forcing them to open the windows of their conscience so that they can, perhaps for the first time, look inside themselves and see how fraudulent their lives have been. A profound inner turning and spiritual conversion may then result. While not every underhanded person undergoes such a metamorphosis from interacting with a spirit cat, a surprising number do.

During a ceremony clients may also be assailed by savage spirit creatures with fangs and burning eyes. These animals have a catlike shape but hairy, colored, or misshapen bodies. While they move in a slinking, catlike way, they are not really cats at all but mythical beings that are formed from a client's negative thoughts and actions. Their appearance forces clients to see the shadow qualities that they have so long kept hidden from themselves.

In my work I meet many sincere people, both Peruvian and other, who are working tirelessly on their spiritual development. When these people are visited by a loving cat, snake, or other animal spirit during a ceremony, they often believe that the creature must be their totemic animal.

It is, of course, natural for people who crave spiritual companionship to think in this way. But the assumption is usually incorrect. When an animal spirit visits clients during a ceremony and becomes their chaperone for the night, the relationship is usually a one-night stand. As mentioned several times, many animal spirits are not animals at all. In reality, they are the Medicine assuming an animal's shape, such as the snakes that menaced me in the snake pit. I make this point mainly because I have seen clients do dangerous things in the name of embracing their so-called power animal, such as going unarmed into the forest to speak to their "companion" jaguar, or to embrace a giant anaconda. The outcome, as you might imagine, can be catastrophic.

BIRD SPIRITS

Large birds, especially birds of prey, are the animal symbol for the third center of consciousness, located in the head. Birds fly high (like the mind), and are able to look directly into the sun, drawing close to its healing rays, which they disperse to humankind through the beauty of their flight and song. Since large birds have remarkable vision (an eagle can see the whiskers on a mouse from a half-mile up), they take in knowledge of everything that is happening below. This 360-degree optic is native to an eagle or condor spirit—a feathered spirit ally that can take you for a flight, show you how the world looks from above, or impart a guidance that can come only from a being that soars near the eye of heaven.

Finally, bird feathers, used in shamanic practice all over the world, represent spiritual understanding, and in this capacity may be placed on an altar, used to stroke ailing clients, or waved in the air to fan smoke or breath into a ceremonial environment to purify it. Wearing a feathered crown during a ceremony is common for native *curanderos*. The feathers channel the healing energy of the bird they belong to, and are worn as a headdress among many native people, indicating that the wearer has high mental and spiritual understanding.

DEER SPIRITS

When seen in visions deer ordinarily represent a relationship with one's ancestors and hence a person's generational heritage. Or deer spirits may represent a tribe or culture a client belonged to in the past.

Why are deer associated with human ancestry? Primarily because the forked shape of their antlers resembles the branches of a tree, each branch representing a separate ancestral lineage as well as the network of psychic connections that join people with their past relatives. Before it was frowned on by current convention, families would mount a deer's head on a plaque and hang it in their living room over the fireplace. While most householders had little idea of its deeper meaning, this tradition stems from long ago when it was known that a stag's antlers can act as a kind of tuning fork—a receiving station for ancestral spirits of the family that lives in the house, much in the way a radio receives waves through its antenna. I mention this connection because once again I am so often intrigued by the fact that many of the activities people perform every day, unbeknownst to them, have magical origins tracing back for centuries.

Like most herd animals, deer spirits have a leader, a magnificent stag or a human being with the head of a deer. One night while working with plants on a rocky plateau in the Andes, I saw a herd of spirit deer grazing on a ledge, the same ledge they would have grazed on every day while alive. This species of deer was now extinct, which made the sight even more striking. As they munched away, several of them looked up at me with surprise, somehow knowing that I was seeing them in their spirit form. Just looking at these elegant phantoms filled me with admiration and gratitude.

Suddenly the ranks of the herd opened and a stag much larger and more imperial than the rest stepped forward.

I say that I saw a large deer, but this is not entirely correct. Though the creature had four legs, a tail, and a set of magnificent antlers, it was nonetheless part human, though how its parts combined in this impossible way is beyond my ability to describe. The giant deer-man stood in the center of the herd contemplating me silently for several minutes. Then he stepped forward a few more feet, made a bowing movement that clearly said "Hello," and romped away with the other deer over the ridge and into the night.

BEAR SPIRITS

Of all animals in the forest the bear makes the most thunderous sounds, especially when hunting. People usually assume the howl of jungle cats on the prowl is louder. But this is not the case. Relying on silence and stealth when stalking their prey, the ocelot, mountain lion, jaguar, and other feline predators, when forced to make a noise while hunting, breathe out a soft, high-pitched snarl or sometimes just a hiss. Bears, on the other hand, roar. They do this not out of anger or hunger but as a show of power, telling the forest *I am here and now: every animal within earshot should take note.* While large spirit cats need to blend in, spirit bears want their shout to be heard round the world.

During a plant ceremony the vision of a bear spirit signifies the potential force of a client's voice and hence the strength of their will; that is, when the bear spirit visits clients during a ceremony, it helps them release pent-up energies by speaking or even shouting in a bold tone of voice they normally suppress. Emoting in this way helps introverts express what they have long kept bottled up inside themselves, making bear energy the perfect Medicine for those who are sheepish and self-effacing. In the process of talking loudly or even hollering, clients also shed many insecurities, having the strength after the ceremony to speak out and assert their needs at home, with friends, at work, all without feeling guilty or that they have overstepped their bounds. This is one reason why all over the world bear organs in traditional medicine are used to cure tongue, throat, and respiratory maladies, all parts of the body related to the voice.

Once when I was traveling in Arizona several years ago, I visited a roadside tourist shop to see if they sold Zuni or Hopi artifacts. Searching the shelves, I saw an interesting stone amulet with a painted image of what appeared to be a bear with an arrow passing through its mouth into the center of its body. The owners told me the arrow was a sign of luck, and that it had been shot into the bear's mouth to bring the amulet wearer good fortune. But when I studied the image closely, it was clear to me that the "arrow" was not an arrow at all. The triangular "tip" in the center of the bear was actually the bear's heart, while the shaft was a thunder and lightning bolt shot from the bear's mighty heart out onto the world. The talisman was not a good luck charm at all but was meant to help those wearing it use the force of their voice like a burst of thunder to express themselves, keeping in mind that both the roar of a bear and the clash of thunder and lightning are among the strongest sounds in nature.

SCAVENGER SPIRITS

A scavenger is an animal that eats dead meat. In Peru carrion-eaters include crows, vultures, dogs, condors, and many other creatures.

In the shamanic realm, scavenger spirits may help people who have suffered a great loss or who are in the process of dying. When the spirit of a hairless scavenger dog visits a terminally ill person, it helps prepare that person for their upcoming passage to the next world. The same with a vulture or jackal. Scavenger spirits also help people who are near death to disengage from their hates, loves, and attachments, helping their soul become free in its last days, and allowing them to make final amends unencumbered by their past.

Not to worry, though. If you see a scavenger animal spirit in your visions, this does not necessarily mean you or anyone else is about to die. Usually, it doesn't. Just as carrion-eating animals strip bones of rotting flesh, so scavenger spirits cleanse a client's soul from the remains of harsh memories and attachments. They also help clients disengage from a friend or associate they were once close to but who now acts toward them in a malicious way. They likewise help clients through their little deaths, meaning the small, sometimes painful interactions and conflicts we pass through every day. They act in a Delphic role as well, forecasting coming changes in clients' lives or alerting them to an upcoming crisis or breakthrough.

Finally, during a ceremony scavenger spirits will on occasion show clients the actual realm of the dead, guiding them through its maze-like corridors and revealing the otherworldly landscape they will encounter when they die. In the process clients may meet their ancestors, see old friends, reunite with beloved pets, or receive messages from the angelic realm. For those who are obsessed with their mortality, scavenger spirits will help discourage their morbid fantasies and pacify their fears.

OWL SPIRITS

In Peruvian shamanism the owl is believed to see everything around it in the physical and spirit world during both day and night. It is a classic symbol of philosophical and mystical wisdom. When a spirit owl appears in a vision, it brings understanding, sometimes bestowing knowledge that helps clients see into normally hidden parts of the spirit realm. I have also seen owl spirits tell clients they are looking in the wrong place for answers to their problems, and that their issues can only be understood in a spiritual rather than psychological way.

Such knowledge is what makes owls a frequent companion of witches, sorcerers, healers, gods, and goddesses of true knowledge. It is not by accident that they also frequently appear in children's books and cartoons as a teacher or professor wearing spectacles. Because they know and see the world in depth, owl spirits sometimes serve as counselors for a Medicine person, allowing shamans to take on aspects of their owlish appearance and wisdom in the invisible world. This psychic change into half owl, half human is often depicted in ancient northern Peruvian art, especially in the designs on Moche ceramic pots.

MOCHE DRINKING POTS

Though obviously not an animal spirit, Moche bowls and pots are mentioned here because a majority of their painted images represent aspects of the spirit world. Next time you visit a museum displaying Moche pottery, I suggest that you read curatorial descriptions with some skepticism. The scholars who write these tags have limited knowledge of the language spoken by ancient ceramics. Nine times out of ten they describe the paintings as depictions of ordinary life events, completely missing their inner meanings. You will remember mention was made earlier of how the image on a Moche pot depicting a man laying hands on a client was described by museum curators as a medical diagnosis when in fact it was a full-on shamanic healing. As the saying goes, "Scholarly knowledge is hearsay knowledge."

Many Moche water pots are designed in such a way that the water they hold takes on the shape of a certain spirit. When sipping from such a vessel the spirit enters the drinker's body. In this way Moche pots, as well as ceramics from many other ancient Peruvian cultures, are neither decorative crockery nor museum relics; they are spiritual instruments, designed to raise the level of consciousness of the people using them and sometimes to cure them of certain disorders. It can be said that in ancient Peruvian art, many if not most jars, bowls, figures, and drawings have a religious message and often a curative use as well.

LARGE FISH SPIRITS

Fish spirits are almost always large—spirit whales, porpoises, stingrays, electric eels, and assorted monster-sized creatures with fangs and sharp teeth similar to those that swim in the Amazon. In the visionary world, these creatures embody the concentrated power of the Force of Life.

Spirit fish often appear to clients who suffer from fear of drowning or who have a water phobia. They may take these clients for a ride deep in the spirit ocean, showing them that the water surrounding them is benevolent, that it is healing, and that it is, in fact, a manifestation of the Force of Life itself. Besides helping clients overcome unreasonable water panic, fish spirits also comfort those who are emotionally scarred or full of anger and confusion.

When large fish appear in visions, I have seen their great size frighten clients who may already be on the emotional edge. Then to the client's surprise these giant swimmers behave in a playful and friendly way, frolicking with clients, dancing for them, poking fun at their useless fears, modeling good feelings, and encouraging them—like a fish—to swim smoothly and effortlessly through the waters of life.

TOUCAN SPIRITS

The toucan bird, multicolored and tropical, lives in forests from Mexico to central South America and is, in the spirit world, a medical expert. Sometimes it provides shamans with little-known information about mind-expanding leaves and vines. Or it points out where to find rare plants and explains how to harvest them.

The toucan spirit is expert at reducing the symptoms of mental and nervous disorders. Once I was working with a young man suffering from an advanced case of epilepsy. During our session the spirit of the toucan flew down and gently pecked him on both shoulders in a way that reminded me of a king knighting a warrior. Though the man was never cured, the intensity of his seizures was reduced and has remained that way up to the present. Sadly, the toucan bird is hunted today for its beak and tongue, which are made into a powder that supposedly helps mental illnesses. The tragedy and irony here is the fact that making a connection with the toucan spirit during a ceremony has a similar mental healing effect, but without the need to kill the doctor.

TAPIR SPIRITS

A large pig-like quadruped with a flexible proboscis (it is part of the elephant family), the tapir is the largest animal in the Amazon jungle, weighing from three hundred to four hundred pounds. It is known in Peru as *sachavaca*, or "the cow of the rain forest."

During a plant ritual, a tapir spirit helps calm hysterical clients, especially those who are mentally unstable. Sometimes they nudge them on the nose with their proboscis, bringing them down to earth and quieting their mania. At times this contact is all that is needed to help agitated clients gain a placid state of mind.

Besides "the cow of the rain forest," the tapir is also nicknamed "the nail of the great beast" in Spanish because its hoof makes the deepest footprint of all animals in the Amazon. When it lopes in a pack, people can feel the ground tremble so violently it seems as if a bomb has gone off. The spirit tapir is thus strongly anchored to the earth, helping the shaman "ground" clients when they lose their way during a ceremony. The dried hoof of a tapir is also known by many Peruvians to provide a number of medical benefits, and as a result poachers sell it as a medicine in the mercado.

This is a highly unethical as well as illegal practice, as the tapir is an endangered species.

SQUIRREL, PORCUPINE, AND SKUNK SPIRITS

The spirit squirrel speaks the language of many animals. On the rare occasion that it visits, it comes in the company of other animal spirits and deciphers what they say. For this reason, it is known to *curanderos* as the "universal translator."

Both the porcupine and the skunk spirits are masters of defense and protection. Using its quills as weapons, the porcupine's sword-like barbs shield a client from the attack of demons, as well as from spells and curses. Porcupine spirits can also raise quills directly on a shaman's body—the shaman himself may not know it is happening—affording him safety against psychic attack. It is not uncommon in the Amazon community to see bracelets or chest ornaments made from porcupine quills and worn by children, warriors, and villagers as a safeguard against enemies both worldly and invisible.

Just as the porcupine provides personal protection, the skunk is master of protecting a client's surrounding space, especially within a ceremonial circle. It does this by laying down power lines of scent that cannot be crossed by psychic invaders or enemies, even though the scent is not necessarily smelled by the client.

ANIMAL PART SPIRITS

Parts taken from dead animals—never live—such as claws, bones, scales, and fangs, if activated properly by the facilitator, can be used to summon the healing force of the psychic animals they belong to. When necessary during a ceremony, a shaman may take a tooth or a feather out of his bag and place it in the hand of a sick client to provide protection and facilitate recovery. Or sometimes he may pass the animal part over the afflicted area, reciting certain healing formulas as he works.

As a last thought on animal spirits, and at risk of repeating a point made in earlier chapters, it is sad to see that both traditional and modern people are so often attached to props and specifically to props made from endangered species. This is another reason why I default to spiritual minimalism and the aid of my Healing Family, avoiding dependence on at-risk animals. Instead, I attempt to heal in cooperation with nature and the helping spirits. This approach demands commitment and discipline, but it has always been recognized as a higher level of natural medicine, especially since it allows animals of the field and forest to go their way unharmed.

HUMAN SPIRITS

Over the course of my career, I have often been asked how clients in a ceremonial circle are shielded from harmful occult forces, especially from ghosts and dark human spirits.

In response, I remind the questioner of the First Golden Rule, which maintains that during a sacred ritual, clients are never confronted with a psychic or psychological challenge they cannot overcome. I also tell them that when the ceremonial circle is constructed, the shaman builds a protective psychic dome over the spot, not only to keep the bad guys away but to filter out any force that harms members of the shaman's Healing Family. When a *curandero* oversees a ceremony in a secluded natural area, especially in a ruin or an abandoned city where a great deal of activity took place long ago—human activity, which means shamanic activity as well—spirits of people long deceased may still lurk about on the grounds, and it is here that one must be especially watchful.

When a *curandero* creates a sacred circle and generates radiant energy inside it, the effect is like lighting a psychic fire in the middle of the night; a tall, bright fire that can be seen by the spirits of the human dead miles away, arousing their interest. These phantoms, both good and not so good, are especially intrigued when a ceremony takes place late at night in an unvisited, out-of-the-way part of the world.

What kind of human spirits are we talking about?

There are basically three kinds. For lack of formal names, I call them human spirit Type one, Type two, and Type three.

Human Spirits: Type One

Type one human spirits are unhappy and unfulfilled; they have been psychically injured during their lives by accidents, wrongdoing, misfortune, or self-harm. Their misery stems from attachment to some aspect of their previous life. Sometimes they are emotionally connected to objects, locations, beloved belongings, family homes where they grew up; sometimes to the people they loved, needed, or hated; sometimes to the way in which they died—by murder, say, or sudden accidental death, in which case they may appear as ghosts haunting the location where the violence took place.

When Type one spirits appear in a ceremony, they are often clothed in a mantilla or cloak, the kind Spanish and Italian women wear to church. These cloaks are ragged and threadbare, looking more like spiderwebs than clothing. The spirits' hands and feet are smudged, as if they had been playing in the dirt. Sometimes they are covered in oil or grime. Their faces are indistinct and sometimes totally blurred.

The emotional temperament of these stained and unsettled beings runs the range from preoccupied to tormented, usually, as said, because they are afflicted by memories of sad experiences or sometimes cruel or destructive violations that went unresolved while they were still alive. When I witness these spirits lurking around the ceremony perimeters, I see them as souls caught in a net of Suffering Consciousness that has "stuck" to them after their death, much in the way that Buddhists speak of a people's karma following them into the afterlife. In all their longing and painful memories, it is as if a weight is anchored to their hearts, and they cannot escape from the worldly plane until this weight is lifted—that is, until they are released by an external healing or they let go of it on their own.

In their solitude, Type one humans crave contact with people. When they see a sacred ceremony take place, they search for any astral bridge or tunnel that can connect them to the circle and allow them to participate in its rites.

Interestingly, when a poorly trained shaman conducts a ceremony, these Type one spirits are the first to slip past the inept practitioner's unguarded senses, inveigling their way into the ritual circle, where they may simply watch the proceedings or under certain circumstances cause mischief. These spirits may also sneak into a ritual by telling the shaman they have a message for a close relative in the circle. Or the spirit may fake their identity entirely, convincing the bumbling practitioner it is the father of one of his clients or an important personage like an Inca king. To tell if these appeals are true or false a shaman must use his experience, intuition, and sometimes the advice of spirits from his Healing Family. If he has none of these, he will never know how easily the Type one human spirits can use him.

Now and then in my own practice, Type one spirits really do have a relative or loved one in the circle, and they beg me to allow them inside. These requests are usually a brusque interruption. After helping them for a brief time, as I sometimes do, I ask the spirits to leave the circle. Remember, at the moment *curanderos* begin a ceremony, it is their moral duty to use this time strictly for the sake of the people in the ring, most of whom have paid for the right to be there, and all of whom need every moment of guidance they can get. Giving attention to an uninvited spirit is a waste of clients' precious time.

I remember once a woman who I often worked with in plant and healing sessions asked if I would conduct a ceremony with her in a secluded setting. We had shared ceremonies in my jungle compound many times. Now she wanted to know how the experience would unfold one-on-one in a remote wilderness under a starry sky.

Several weeks later we visited the remains of an ancient citadel on a craggy hill. We set up camp, relaxed, and waited until the evening dusk turned dark. It was a quiet night, and we sat on a ridge overlooking a breathtaking sweep of valley below. All was peaceful with no reason for tension or worry. At around eleven o'clock we drank the medicine and entered the higher spheres. We were beginning our work in earnest when suddenly a horde of wandering spirits appeared from nowhere and surrounded our circle. They did not look angry, and their demeanor was more pleading than aggressive. It was sad and obvious that they were asking entry into our ring simply to interact with live human beings.

Who were they? Where had they come from? Had a massacre taken place on this spot long ago? The ruin of the citadel had been thoroughly plundered over the years by looters searching for gold and ancient decorated pottery vessels. There were no shaman spirits nearby who could fill me in on the place's history. Finally, I decided they were what they seemed to be—a group of bedraggled and adrift Type one spirits begging for human friendship. Meetings like this can break your heart.

There was only one thing to do: I stopped the ceremony, telling my friend that the presence of the crowd (which she could half see, half feel) was too distracting to do any meaningful work. We would have to try again another time in another place.

But closing things down would not be that easy.

I crawled into my shelter and tried to sleep, but I felt unbearably pressured by the throng of spirits crowding outside my tent. They were all around me and clearly had no intention of giving up. What could I do? I crawled out of the tent on my hands and knees, stood up shakily to get my bearings, and spent the next five or six hours trying my best to give these wraiths some form of consolation from their guilts and regrets. Eventually it turned out to be a time of service and compassion, and by the end of the night at least some of the Type one humans who had importuned me seemed hopeful and reassured.

Then at first light the spirits faded away. The sun rose and my friend came out of her tent. She realized I had been up all night and had been interacting with our visitors, but that was all she knew, and I avoided talking about it.

After breakfast we broke camp and headed down the slope. At the bottom was a village I had visited several times during my expeditions. Here I saw several peasants I knew standing nearby. I told them what a difficult night it had been on the hill, and how the mob of spirit beings had surrounded us. The two men glanced at one another with knowing smiles, then told us that there are certain nights of the year—the previous night was one of them—when centuries ago elaborate celebrations took place on the hill where we had camped. Without knowing it, my friend and I had performed our ceremony directly on the spot that once hosted a major ritual in which the crowd of spirits I had worked with that night had no doubt taken part. Now forgotten and abandoned, these same spirits waited eternally for visits from human company and perhaps for their ceremony to take place once again.

Human Spirits: Type Two

Type two human spirits look like ordinary people. They dress in normal clothes, are clean and well-mannered, quiet and decorous, though they often look melancholy or preoccupied. These spirits show no anguish but neither do they seem at peace.

Their brooding attitude is almost always because they have died recently and are still strongly attached to certain people or things left behind. Nothing violent or grasping here, just strong connections, usually affectionate, that were left unsettled or unfinished during their lifetime, and that they now wish to complete.

Type two human spirits are usually strongly linked to loved ones, often protecting them from certain dangers or giving them counsel in dreams and inspirations. Though the connections they maintain with people from their past are almost always based on service, they also tend to be obsessive and enslaving. In order to become free from such exaggerated attachments they need to let go and to move on to other realms of being.

Unlike Type ones, Type two spirits are ordinarily welcome in my shamanic gatherings.

During a ceremony clients may be working through a difficult conflict, feeling overburdened from harsh memories and too weak to get through the process of self-purification on their own. In such cases, it is beautiful to see a Type two spirit materialize and help expedite the cleansing.

During these sessions it also sometimes happens that a client is fixated on a Type two person rather than the other way around. The spirit may be a dead relative, a spouse, or a friend that the client was particularly close with. In such cases, it is extraordinary to watch how during the very process of helping the client let go of them, these spirits in turn are able to drop their own attachment to the client and thus to the world. Once liberated in this way, Type two spirits are then free to continue on to the next stage of their fate.

In still other ceremonial situations, the meeting of client and Type two spirits proves a clumsy affair. I have, for example, seen a Type two mother or father visit their child during a ceremony and watched how past discords crop up between them. Quarrels and accusations follow, and in the end neither parent nor child expresses forgiveness.

Human Spirits: Type Three

Witnessing the serene expressions of Type three spirits, it is clear they have gone beyond the chafing miseries of the human condition—the ambition, resentment, and selfishness that so typify the Suffering Consciousness. Almost all members of this group project a shining aura, some radiating a spectrum of colors—cream, teal, yellow, soft purple, kindly colors that speak with humility. When you see them, you understand that these human spirits have cleaned their hearts of all defilements and gained a lofty rank in the world of souls. Why then are they here at all when they could be resting forever in higher mansions?

No doubt you have guessed the reason: They enter the ceremonial circle to provide assistance for a client with a particular need. And when they come, they are among the most potent and gentle of all spirit healers.

A man who later became a good friend traveled to Peru once a year to participate in sacred plant ceremonies. Several years later he brought his son, a boy of eleven or twelve years old who was both cordial and intelligent beyond his years. The father thought it would be a good idea if his son participated in a plant ceremony, which he did. Though things were difficult for him—at times he felt overwhelmed—after the ceremony the boy said the plants helped him understand his life more clearly.

In the following years the boy took the plants several more times. He was growing up to be a reflective and self-aware young man when, to everyone's shock, he died suddenly at seventeen from a heart problem. He had, in fact, been born with a cardio deficiency, but through the years he seemed perfectly healthy, and his family rarely worried about it.

Crushed, the boy's father called and asked if I could help his son beyond the grave. I agreed to try, though at that time I had made few attempts to heal a person in the afterworld, having worked only with the living. I had, however, liked the boy a great deal, and we had such a close friendship that I felt obliged to do as much as I could.

From that time on I took a few minutes each day to check on the deceased teenager's state of being. In the beginning it was clear he felt agonized over being snatched out of his life at such a young age and losing contact with his beloved family. But as time went by, a surprising thing happened. The young man already had a certain amount of inborn understanding plus the Knowledge he had gleaned from his plant ceremonies. Gradually, he worked at accepting his fate, then on turning his death into a blessing by becoming a helping spirit.

The young man put this determination to work in several ways. He appeared in several plant ceremonies that I conducted in the following months. He communicated with the father, showing him that death is not the end and that for him, the son, it was the beginning. He then branched out, helping many other clients in my ceremonies and others, focusing his healing wisdom on young people who had lost their way. In the end he became a universal ally, a prime example of a Type three human soul whose only aim is to lend a helping hand to other people trapped in the pain of their Suffering Consciousness.

As a corollary to this story, it turned out that recently the boy's family moved their son's body to a cemetery located in another city. During the days when the transfer was taking place the boy's vision appeared to me in the early morning hours, explaining that his Soul Consciousness always knew that because of his genetic condition he would die young. This was the reason, he said, why during his teens he overstimulated his body with exercise in an attempt to accelerate his heart failure, thus preventing him and his family from experiencing a long, chronic period of suffering. A very interesting fact is that when he appeared to me, it seemed as if his biological clock had continued to tick, making him now look like a young adult. I keep the memory of this boy and his story in a very special part of my heart and memory, a beautiful example of the Soul Consciousness at work.

One interesting aspect of ancestral visits that I find both glamorous and endearing is when a group of Type three spirits from a particular culture visit a client of their own ethnicity dressed and groomed in the garments of their heritage—robes, scarves, hats, turbans, cloaks, capes, jewelry, all in the fashion of the client's lineage, be it Celtic, Nigerian, or ancient Peruvian. Seeing these impeccable spirits meeting their living relatives and displaying thousands of years of native elegance somehow captures the magnificent clan identity of human civilizations past and present.

Dark Spirits

By now it is no doubt clear that the invisible world, like the human world, is home to wicked spirits as well as good. While these powers or potencies are known by many names, I usually refer to them simply as dark forces.

Dark forces are malignant spirits that both exploit people's negativity and use their perverse energies to do harm for both profit and pleasure. The worst of these parasite-like beings are committed to destroying not only the human race but the entire natural order. They are sometimes referred to as "Satan's children."

Dark forces allow themselves to be used as tools by sorcerers to serve the selfish desires of a client's Suffering Consciousness. The sorcerer first makes a pact with a malignant spirit, which, in turn, agrees to carry out whatever nefarious deeds the sorcerer wishes, be it a curse, a spell, making a man impotent and a woman infertile, harming or even killing a client's enemies. In return the magician must promise to give the dark spirit that is helping him some of his power. Or he may provide the spirit with opportunities for disrupting goodwill and unity in peaceful communities. Sometimes he offers his own soul as collateral.

As people around the world have understood for eons, the soul is a real if ethereal force that can be bought, stolen, or imprisoned. Skeptics who ridicule this idea would be astonished to learn the number of high-profile celebrities who secretly work with sorcerers (known euphemistically as psychics), and how many of these people, especially rock musicians, actors, politicians, business executives, and athletes, have bargained away their moral essence for fame and power. Some celebrities have even been known to admit their connection with dark forces in interviews and in the lyrics of their songs, though the public takes these admissions as jokes or metaphors rather than confessions and thinks nothing of them.

Yet the path of black magicians is ultimately a degrading one, a downward spiral that eventually sucks the offender into a yawning void. Once sorcerers are of no use to a dark spirit because they have nothing more to offer, the spirit loses interest and no longer provides help or protection. When this occurs, the magician becomes weak and listless—he has lost all potency—and eventually begins to turn rotten. Literally rotten. The flesh on his body decays and molders, until finally even family members cannot tolerate his smell and avoid him. I have heard more than one story of *brujos* who had imposing reputations but who in the end came apart in this way, showing how base and corrupt they actually were.

Where these dark powers originally come from, and why they seek to harm humans and the world, is a mystery, which, like all other mysteries of creation, is known only to the Great Spirit. Whatever their origins, a good deal of shamanic training is centered on techniques for identifying the appearance and lineage of dark entities, and on learning ways to counteract them. Nothing illustrates these practices better than stories. Here are two, one short and one long, to show how black the sorcerer's way can ultimately be.

The first story comes from an elder I knew in the north who told me about one of his relatives who had knowledge of shamanism but never practiced it. He lived in a small town in the highlands with his ten-year-old son, and his job required that he travel a great deal, forcing him to leave his son with relatives for months at a time.

As the boy grew into his teenage years, the father spent longer periods of time at home. During these stays his friends and family members whispered to him that his son was showing an inclination for the dark arts. The boy was spending a good deal of time with an old man, they told him, who everybody in town knew was a *brujo* of the lowest kind.

Alerted to these facts, the man saw to his chagrin that indeed his son's normally lighthearted and engaging personality was changing. He was becoming morose in the manner of his *brujo* mentor, and at times threatened to cast a spell on his friends if they disagreed with him or even to do occult harm to their family members. From time to time, he announced to others that someday he would like to be initiated by his dark-hearted teacher and practice his teachings.

One day the man took his son aside, saying he wished to ask him one question. The boy agreed. "Who is the person you love the most in life and is closest to your heart?" the father asked. "You!" the son replied without hesitation.

When the man heard this, he immediately sold his house and moved with his very unwilling son to a village hundreds of miles away. The reason he made such an impetuous change was not simply to shelter his son from the shaman's corruption. The father also knew that in this black magician's lineage, if a man wished to be initiated as a sorcerer, he must first murder the person he loved best in the world. The father was caring for his son's soul, yes, but he was protecting his own life as well.

I had recently completed my shamanic training and was working with clients across northern Peru. Though still young and learning, I was becoming confident in my skills, regularly taking groups into the desert or jungle for ceremonies, healings, and exorcisms.

One day I led a group of nine clients, all with nighttime gear slung over their shoulders, deep into the desert to a power spot where many *curanderos* had set up camp in past centuries. It was here, at the foot of a large mountain, that I prepared the space for the night's ceremony. I had already worked in this lovely, isolated part of Peru several times before, always receiving gracious help from the mountain itself with its many local spirits.

On this occasion we arrived at our camp just as the sun was setting. The moon was out, the sky was a deep evening blue, and the air had that special desert quiet and fragrance, a perfect summer's night. I made a circle in the sand, constructed a psychic dome, and conducted a silent observance summoning the spirits and giving thanks for their help.

Among my clients that night was a couple I knew from Lima. Happily married, they were much in love but had a seemingly unsolvable problem: The woman could not conceive.

Over the past several years, this difficulty had created a growing tension between them. After visiting endless doctors and specialists, and being told that they were both fertile, the couple, as is common in Peru, began to consider the possibility that someone had placed a curse on them. How or why this had been done they did not know. They hoped a ceremony with the sacred plants would help them find out.

The darkness came quickly as our group made ready for a long night. Sitting round the circle in silence for several minutes, I poured out a tumbler of my coastal plant brew and drank a dose. Then I poured a cup for each person. I played my drum and sang sacred songs, and presently the spirits of the plants began to appear. Sometimes when they come, they dance in a circle, but that night they arrived quietly and in pairs. After working with several clients, I turned my attention to the husband and wife.

As I stood on the edge of the circle observing the woman, several clues to her infertility jumped out at me. The area around her womb emitted a damp, unpleasant smell. According to shamanic understanding, we all have spiritual senses that parallel each of our five senses—psychic receiving stations that take in sights, sounds, and odors on the invisible plane, the same plane where sacred visions appear. From past experience, I knew the type of putrid smell emanating from the woman is often associated with black magic.

This impression grew stronger as I started feeling or seeing or hearing—it was difficult to say which—a humming noise emanating from the woman's lower body, a shrill and steady *zzzzzz!* sound as if coming from buzzing flies. Taking a step closer but still maintaining my distance, I saw extremely grotesque and even demonic beings swirling around her vaginal area.

The couple had not been wrong. Someone had cursed the wife.

Studying these and other signs, I was able to identify certain facts about the sorcerer who had cast the spell. I did not know who he was personally, but I was fairly certain I could name the lineage he belonged to. Among shamanic lineages, each type of curse has its own structure and particular way of affecting a victim. Part of a shaman's training is to recognize these different types of enchantments, puzzle out how they work, and undo them. I could also see that the sorcerer had placed protective forces around the spell to prevent other shamans from looking at it too closely or figuring out its secrets. Each curse has its own unique set of locks and keys.

From about ten feet away, I started to psychically work on the woman, tracking the dark, aggressive aura surrounding her. After several minutes, I could see a kind of etheric curtain shrouding her lower parts. On the other side of this curtain the whole story revealed itself at once, along with an ominous truth: A spell was there for sure, and more amazingly, I could see in my visions that it had been bought and paid for by the mother of the woman's husband.

A fiercely jealous woman, I later learned, the husband's mother had always despised her son's wife, and over the years had done everything possible to destroy their marriage, always without success.

They were too much in love. The mother knew that if the couple ever had a child, a bond would be formed between them that could never be broken. As a last resort, she consulted a black magician and hired his services.

A highly accomplished spell caster, the magician implemented his curse by literally plugging up the woman's womb with a mass of dark, squid-shaped energy designed to block any chance of impregnation. The only way to get rid of it was to psychically pull it out and destroy it.

As I was considering how to do this, I became aware of a sudden change in the weather. When our session had started hours earlier, the air was dry and clear. The moment I began to attack the curse a cold, damp wind blew up from nowhere and massive thunderclouds swept low overhead, moving across the sky at an enormous speed and cutting off all light from the moon and stars. Within moments the wind became so fierce that twisting towers of sand spiraled around the campsite, showering down small rocks and pieces of thorny brush. The ground literally began to quake underneath us and even the mountain seemed to shudder.

I was sweating and shaking all this time as I tried to calm the members of the group, who were panicking at the violent winds. Simultaneously, I was trying to pull the squid-like lump out of the woman, who had started making strange jerking movements with her legs, painful noises, and having sensations of pain in her abdomen, as if giving birth.

As I psychically tugged at the lump, I became aware of a shadowy figure standing close to me on the spirit plane watching everything I did. Within moments this figure—clearly it was the subtle presence of the sorcerer who had cast the spell—began to block my efforts. Soon we were engaged in psychic tug-of-war. I would pull at the lump, which was waving its squid-like tentacles and fighting back, trying to bite me. Several times the blob seemed about to slide out, but then the *brujo* morphed it into another shape, and I would be forced to start over again.

After several minutes of this angry duel, I began to feel that my own personal power was not strong enough to do the job. Calling on my Healing Family for help, I continued to yank at the lump with the tools they provided while the sorcerer continued to thwart me with clever and interesting transformations.

This arch battle of push and pull went on for several minutes as the winds reached gale force and members of the group began clutching at rocks, afraid of being blown into the darkness. Finally, with one strong tug the wiggling mass came dislodged and I wrestled it out of the woman's body.

But this was not the end of it. Once removed, certain curses are designed to reboot and return to the cursed person's body. I spent the next several minutes dismantling the dark mass, taking it apart piece by piece on the spirit plane and, in a manner of speaking, grinding it down to essential atoms so it could not resurrect itself and do more harm.

The moment this infestation was fully stamped out, everything changed. The sorcerer disappeared from my awareness, the harsh winds subsided, and after several minutes the moon came out bright and clear. I glanced at the woman. She was relaxed and reached out to hold hands with her husband, who had been beside her the entire time. During the ceremony the husband did not know the particulars of what had taken place on the spirit plane, though he assumed that a titanic battle of some sort had just been waged.

In the weeks following their session, I met with this couple several times. During our conversations I described what I had done to exorcise the spell and how I had seen that the man's mother was responsible for unleashing the curse.

This was a tricky matter, to say the least, and I knew this disclosure would infuriate the couple and perhaps alienate mother and son. Nonetheless, while in training a *curandero* takes a vow to tell his clients the facts as accurately as possible both before and after a ceremony. This work is about truth, I was taught— mandatory Medicine for a client no matter how difficult it may be to accept.

Shortly after my conversations with the couple, I traveled abroad and was gone for some time. On returning home I received a happy surprise. The woman called to say she was pregnant, and that she and her husband were happier now than ever.

After this exchange we fell out of touch, and last I heard they had moved to southern Peru. I must admit, I've often wondered what happened on the inevitable day when the couple confronted the guilty parent, telling her that they knew about the satanic forces she had loosed on them, all in the name of motherly love.

Celestial Spirits

Besides the Type three human spirits that inspire, heal, and give us love, we are sometimes visited in visions by spirits that are pure intelligence and compassion. During a ceremony, these higher beings appear to clients with a serene or smiling face or a look of deep determination and a sense of duty. They are quite large compared to human beings, and appear to come down to our level from some heavenly place above. When they arrive they bring a selection of gifts that include visual symbols, healing tools, and occasionally revelations or oracles about the future. Their visits are usually short, though during this small window of time they teach us wondrous things about ourselves and the world.

Several times in the middle of a ceremony I have been poked

on my leg or shoulder by a spirit of the forest saying, "They are here!" and telling me to look up. When I do I see these celestial spirits seated in an architectural structure floating high in the air. Sometimes they come down to the ceremonial circle simply to say hello. At other times they cheer me up or help me with a difficult healing procedure. After several minutes, they say a warm goodbye and disappear. I do not believe I am qualified to say what these higher spirits really are, whether they are creatures from other galaxies, angelic beings, or advanced teachers that were human eons ago. I do not think any of us will ever know or even that it matters. What is important is that their visits always bring goodness.

Common Visions of and from the Spirit World

So far, we have talked a great deal about the spirits but not much about the spirit world itself. When taking their first steps into this invisible domain, some clients find themselves in a hell-like ghetto. For others the environment is celestial. Still others see a crisscrossing of paths, a city of pagodas, rooms within rooms, a moldy cave, an ancient ruin, a prolonged visitation to one's childhood—the list is endless. The reason for this diversity is that what clients see while wandering in the spirit realm is not a permanent place but a reflection of their own history, psyche, and level of being.

Because the spirit world is so subjective and dependent on an individual's personal nature, each client will have a different story to tell when asked what things look like down the rabbit hole. For many, most perhaps, the invisible world is not only a place but a sequence of experiences that deliver a particular lesson, insight, enlightenment, shock, or healing. The first of these experiences is common to many plant takers. I call it the Corridors of the Suffering Consciousness.

The Corridors of the
Suffering Consciousness

The encounters one undergoes when taking a sacred brew vary from the Divine to the terrifying, with every shade in between. But because an experience is frightening does not mean it causes harm. On the contrary, the fear one undergoes in the shadowy parts of the spirit world is a form of tough love and usually takes place in the first quarter of a ceremony. When clients are confronted by terrifying images, their initial reflex is to believe they are having a bad trip—that instead of a gentle teaching they are trapped in an inferno with no exit. Yet when the ceremony is over, clients often look back on these harrowing moments as the most healing part of their session.

One such encounter is a walk through what I call the Corridors of the Suffering Consciousness, a tunnel or maze-like series of dark, moldy passageways filled with gruesome sights and sounds. The walls in this tunnel are lined with mangled faces, creatures with sharp teeth and claws, skeletons, skulls, spikes, chains, sharp objects, and drooling brutes. As you walk through the passageways, monsters may lean out to bite you, grab you, or make you lose your footing. A number of clients tell me that the skulls, chains, and spiky objects they see when walking this maze remind them of images on heavy metal album covers and T-shirts.

While much can be learned from walking this labyrinth, the prime takeaway for clients is the understanding that this harrowing maze was built brick by brick from their own contentious thoughts and feelings. The appalling sights seen on the floors and walls of the corridor have no objective reality but are personifications of the ugly emotional forces bred by a client's Suffering Consciousness. This is the darkness they have long been hosting. As a shamanic song goes, "They think their house is clean. Hey! Come to the closet here, look what is inside! Look at all these monsters you are keeping inside!"

When clients are shown these undeniable realities, it is crucial that they respond to them like a warrior, laying down the law and saying, "No! I will not let these cruel impulses rule my life any longer!"

The power of this resolution made in the Corridors of Suffering Consciousness is different from decisions made in a state of ordinary consciousness, the reason being that when under the influence of sacred plants, a client's Suffering Consciousness is silenced and Soul Consciousness rules. Influencing the deepest parts of their subconscious where real psychological change can take place, Soul Consciousness empowers clients with an urgent desire to live a righteous life. As a result, the decisions clients come to while under the influence of sacred plants is usually far more potent and enduring than those made in everyday life.

Once clients take their stand, moreover, something inside them shifts. Seeing their noxious behavior portrayed in graphic images helps them understand, perhaps for the first time, how profoundly their hurtful actions have harmed themselves and others. From a spiritual perspective, this moment of witnessing one's malevolent side and rejecting it for the light is akin to the awakening of conscience. Once it takes place, very few people ever entirely go back to their angry habits—yet another way in which the sacred plants free us from pain.

⚜

When I tell people interested in shamanism about the disturbing experiences clients may undergo in the Corridors of the Suffering Consciousness or other scary places in the invisible dimensions, they are often alarmed. Don't such confrontations harm people? they ask. Walking down a dark tunnel filled with screams and monsters trying to grab you? Can't such an attack overexcite a weak heart or make a person with emotional problems even more disturbed?

I answer such questions by saying that when clients take the plants, they are automatically under the protection of their Soul Consciousness and, as explained in the First Golden Rule, nothing can harm a client when their Soul Consciousness is in charge. I also tell them that though it is mandatory for certain clients to go through extreme trials, the role of the shaman is to guard them while these trials take place. In short, if a shaman is well trained, no physical or mental harm can ever be done to those who take the sacred plants.

Eyes Everywhere

During a ceremony seeing visions of eyes that float in the air or appear on trees, plants, or flowers is a common experience, especially for clients who are new to the sacred plant journey. Floating eyes help clients use their psychic senses to read the language of the ethereal world. If you see these eyes in your visions, this is a good thing. It will help you discern a subtle reality that is hidden from ordinary vision, and which reveals the world of helping spirits.

Healing Spirit Fountains

During a plant ritual, it is not uncommon for a Healing Spirit Fountain to suddenly spout up from the center of the circle, spraying everyone with fine jets of water, wetting clients' heads and chests, penetrating their organs, and washing away bad thoughts and feelings. This otherworldly geyser can be seen clearly by the *curandero* as well by many participants. Even clients who cannot see the fountain often sense its presence and feel its healing spray.

The water from a Healing Fountain is sometimes coral colored, sometimes orange, teal green, or rose purple. Occasionally it is crystal clear. When the fountain sprays or when its water pools on the ground, a spontaneous feeling of appreciation is often felt by group members, inspiring them to give thanks to the spirits for their charitableness. This burst of gratitude, in turn, acts as a healing force for those who feel it.

A Healing Fountain may also at times manifest as a cloud of floating liquid energy or a pond in the center of the circle that ripples from the rhythms of the *curandero*'s rattles and drums. At other times water spontaneously gushes out from the midpoint of the circle, covering the floor and making members of the group feel they are sitting on the edge of a mirror.

Throughout the entire world, water fountains are placed in the busiest parts of cities and towns. They are commonly seen in village squares and plazas, in front of churches, in parks, schools, gardens, libraries, museums, and skyscrapers. It is no accident that water fountains are often decorated with sacred images of angels, gods, heroes, or giant birds. Traditionally a fountain is a holy place where people come to drink, to take water, and thus to live. Those who come in contact with its spray during a ceremony feel that their very existence is being empowered and refreshed.

A water fountain, be it in a ceremonial ring or city center, is a universal reminder of the Force of Life.

The Magical Parade

While the name "Magical Parade" sounds symbolic, it literally *is* a parade, a festive caravan moving through clients' heightened senses in a visionary procession that includes any type of vehicle imaginable: horse and wagon, gondola, jet plane, Roman chariot, painted bus, railroad train, holiday-in-Rio-type floats, each transport carrying aspects of clients' lives that were once close to their hearts, but which they now minimize or take for granted.

For example, clients may see a flatbed truck go by on which people are performing an art or skill that they were once devoted to, but which for whatever reason they dropped. The skill may be painting, carpentry, a sport, gardening, learning a language, playing a musical instrument. Now they are being asked to give this art another chance. It misses them.

Perhaps clients see people in a Magical Parade who were once dear to them, who were hospitable and generous. Rediscovering them, clients realize how fortunate they were to have known these people, and how much these people enhanced their lives. They wonder why they are no longer close. Or an ex-lover appears on one of the vehicles, a person the client cared for deeply but then abandoned. The ex-lover gazes at the client with affection and sadness, making the client aware of how exquisite their relationship really was. Why did I leave this person, clients ask themselves, after all the intimacy we shared?

Common also is seeing ex-friends go by in the Magical Parade: a relative or partner they fell out with, a business associate who they assumed spoke badly of them, a once-close teammate or schoolmate they parted with on unfriendly terms. With their heightened awareness, they now realize this person was not their adversary at all, that if they received criticism from the ex-friend, it was quite legitimate, and that they now see the ex-friend liked them and felt bad when their relationship ended. Clients realize they have been carrying grudges against these imagined enemies for decades. Now is the time to drop them.

Hidden Enemies, Hidden Allies

An encounter with Hidden Enemies can be deeply unsettling, causing you to realize that certain friends and associates are not who you think they are.

When Hidden Enemies appear during a ceremony, you see people you deal with all the time—coworkers, fellow students, lovers, teachers, your dry cleaner, your manicurist—anyone in your circle of life. Their faces appear in front of you in a hazy light or sometimes on a dark screen. These images are not simply photographic representations but X-rays into their real thoughts and intentions toward you, at times revealing contemptuous or even hateful emotions that you never suspected. The friends or business associates you see may be privately angry at you, hold a grudge, nurture a secret desire for revenge over an incident you have long forgotten. They may be plotting a way of muscling you out of your position at work. They may lust after your mate and wish you out of the picture. They may not like your tone of voice when you make a request or the way you dress or how you put on your hat.

The variations are endless, but the bottom line is always the same—disguised negative feelings felt toward you by friends and colleagues are revealed in a clear and shocking way. Indeed, clients who frequently use the plants sometimes participate in a session strictly as a precautionary measure to help them make a yes or no choice about a certain associate. Seeing the associate's face during the ceremony, clients can read their true inner feelings and act accordingly. Used in this way, the Hidden Enemy revelations serve clients as a powerful analytic tool for making decisions and protecting themselves as well.

Intriguing to discover is that during a ceremony, clients are often surprised to see mischief aimed at them from individuals who they barely know, and who they have few thoughts or feelings about one way or the other.

For example, a young woman who sold technical books to medical establishments was approached by a man who made a play for her. The woman rejected him and soon forgot about the incident. As it turned out, the thwarted seducer ended up being made principal of a school where a friend of mine worked as a librarian. My friend and the principal worked on projects together from time to time and were reasonably friendly. By chance, after working in the school for a few years my friend happened to meet and fall in love with the same woman who had rejected the principal years before. The two of them were soon married.

One day several months after the wedding the mother of the principal visited the school and struck up a conversation with my friend, who by then was a regular participant in my shamanic gatherings. The mother then started visiting the school several times a week, always complimenting my friend, telling others how creative and industrious he was, bringing him chocolates and cookies, and incessantly smiling at him with beaming eyes. It seemed strange to my friend that she lavished such attention on him, but he shrugged it off and thought little about it.

Several months later my friend was taking part in one of my plant rituals. In the middle of the session the face of the principal's mother suddenly appeared to him glowering with hatred. He sought my help with this disturbing image, and I was shown that the mother wanted to separate my friend from his wife so that her son, the principal, could hitch up with the woman he had attempted to seduce years earlier. During the ceremony I was taken by the spirits to see the mother's house, where a mesa table full of black magic props stood next to her bed. There were candles, little beans, grains, shells, figurines, and bones, very low sorcery, which she was using to hurt my friend and perhaps even kill him.

Invoking members of my Healing Family, I destroyed the spells attached to each prop, making them useless. I did not accost the mother herself, who knew nothing of my visits and who, when her spells failed, I am sure blamed her props for not being powerful enough. In such ways the Hidden Enemy tool discourages black magic and saves lives.

Finally, besides the power of Hidden Enemies to ferret out unknown adversaries, there is an opposite force at work as well: Hidden Allies. Under its influence clients in a ceremony may see into the hearts of acquaintances from their past and present, not realizing how much sympathy and admiration these people feel toward them. Facial expressions, eyes, and body language reveal the true facts. During ceremonies throughout the years, it has been deeply satisfying to see clients who feel lonely or disliked realize how much goodwill is actually coming their way each day from others, and how this goodwill is theirs to accept and enjoy if they so choose.

Human Cartoons

During a ceremony a client who carries a great deal of anger and pain may see visions from the spirit world in the form of animated cartoons. This bit of theater starts with fun pictures of peaceful spirits or playful animals but then suddenly morphs into a bedlam of disagreeable and sometimes monstrous cartoon-like beings and events, all of which represent the client's irresponsible and/or disreputable behavior.

Why monstrous cartoons? Because these grotesque visions make clients aware that their wayward behavior is, in fact, cartoonish—that is, it caricatures and distorts proper human conduct. Seeing scary animations may, for instance, indicate that clients take no responsibility for their unethical behavior or that they reject their moral obligations. Cartoon images may be related to a client's relationships, finances, profession, or strategies of social interaction.

Basically, when clients are hounded by these nasty comic strips during a ceremony, their Soul Consciousness is sending visual messages to the Suffering Consciousness telling it to behave. These images are quite clear in their moral message and are almost always understood by the client who sees them.

Comic strip moving images will, of course, only appear to those from Western culture who most likely grew up spending hours watching Saturday morning cartoons, and whose Suffering Consciousness was strongly imprinted by these dream-like depictions. Traditional people without computers or television receive visual lessons during a ceremony as well, but the images they see are based on their art and folklore rather than on animated scenarios.

The morphing of pleasant visions into ugly cartoons can also serve as a mirror to help clients understand the negative sides of their childhood. Clients who were exposed to emotional chaos when young or who lived in a childhood environment where events could turn from nice to nasty in a moment often fall into this category. As grown-ups, these people are conditioned to expect discord and betrayal in their everyday life and to twist positive social interactions into negative ones. When they see a grotesque cartoon vision of early traumas during a plant session, it may help them understand the nay-saying thoughts and behaviors they express as adults. This vision can, in turn, provide the self-knowledge needed for self-change.

I have, incidentally, often seen ugly cartoon visions appear to clients who by nature are derisive and sarcastic. Over time, bitterness has made these people see life through a filter of ridicule and cynicism; for them human nature is driven by lies and callous behavior. Once again, cartoon visions sent by the spirits may help these people drop their cynicism and begin to understand that there is just as much wisdom and altruism in the world as there is falsehood and vanity.

Gifts

During a ceremony spirits or ancestors commonly bring gifts from the spirit world to favored clients.

The gift may be a positive feeling like courage, love, or determination. It can also be a spirit object like a leaf, a type of hat, a feather, a weapon, a crown, or a piece of clothing. Since clients are under the influence of Soul Consciousness during a ceremony, they know intuitively that this mysterious gift will bring benefits and put them on a healing path. Spirit gifts are usually given with no explanation concerning the way to use them. Clients must figure it out on their own.

As a consequence, seekers spend hours, sometimes days or months, trying to understand how an offering from the spirits can help them. I worked with one longtime client who received a gift of strength from a spirit puma, but who had no idea what to use it for until a year later when she was in a high-speed bicycle crash and had to use medical techniques she knew little about to dress her wounds and those of other people involved in the accident. "At the time," she told me, "it was as if my entire body was pumped up with a knowledge and toughness, which I recognized as the gift of strength doing its healing work on me and the others."

There is also a strange anomaly that occasionally takes place when clients *refuse* a gift from the spirits, thinking themselves undeserving or unready for it. They thank the spirits for their offer but tell them they must first dissolve certain poisonous thoughts and feelings before they can profit from the gift. The spirits respond in their gentle, ambiguous way, saying only, "We will come again another time."

There are two gifts that can help clients overcome such self-doubts. The first is a special place to sit: a throne, a jeweled chair, or any seat of importance. Directed to sit on it, clients are told it will help them see the positive sides of themselves more clearly, though again the client may refuse the offer due to lack of self-confidence or emotional blockages.

A similar aid comes when animal or human spirits place a jeweled crown on a client's head to acknowledge their goodness. As before, a client may refuse the honor. Given such unnecessary diffidence, it is a joy to see that some clients, after being shown the generous and philanthropic sides of themselves by means of gifts and spirit intervention, finally realize their self-worth. They then gladly accept gifts like a throne or a crown, which they now understand are their due, and which will someday increase their capacity to help and heal.

Keep in mind that all benefits that reach clients from the spirit world are meant to teach lessons. Sometimes, for example, clients prone to vanity or pride are offered gifts like a crown or a throne, but in an ironic way, to show them the absurdity of their self-importance.

How to discern which is which? A gift of the spirit or a gift of reprimand? That, in a word, depends on the degree of a client's spiritual insight and intelligence. But remember, there are no absolutes. A good person may be blind and dense but still deserving of a gift, while a vain person may be perceptive and knowing but still warrant a scolding.

Talking to One's Ancestors

It is difficult for many of us to believe that the soul of a relative who lived two thousand years ago has any pertinent advice to offer us today. This reluctance to believe in the unseen prevents us from recognizing that the thousands and probably millions of our relatives from eons past are alive as spirits in the afterworld, where they share a collective clan consciousness and thus a pooled ocean of knowledge based on the achievements of family members. This amazing reservoir of insight is alive and living in the memory of our own blood, where our DNA is a library as well as a code, and where every ancestor we meet in a ceremony is a reference book devoted entirely to our generational identity.

Given this reality, when clients come face-to-face with an ancestor during a spirit session, their blood kinship allows them to tap into this relative's past and receive critical information about family history and genetics, information that cannot come from any source other than their own genealogical clan.

While taking sacred plants it is also possible that clients will be greeted either by a deceased relative they once knew—a beloved aunt or cousin, say—or by a stranger, a long-ago spirit relative from Siberia or China. No matter. Wherever one's ancestors come from, they are always ready to advise and guide, urging clients to take the right turns and avoid the wrong.

During a meeting with their forebears, clients can also become acquainted with their racial history in ways that would otherwise be impossible. Several years ago, a staid, gentlemanly black man named Emil took part in one of my ceremonies. Though his roots were African, he was born in a South American colony, where he lived a conventional family life. Unbeknownst to his family and friends, he was intensely dispirited, feeling a deep disconnection from his African ancestry and a strong urge to know more about it.

He was about to get his wish.

It happened halfway through the ceremony. I was making my rounds checking on each client when a band of African warrior spirits appeared outside the circle. They were half-naked, holding spears and shields, and decked out in amazing animal skins. They asked to be let into the ring.

I asked my Healing Family if they were friendly, and when they checked out, I invited them in. As soon as they entered the circle, the group surrounded Emil and began performing a spirited dance, hoisting their spears and singing. The songs and the dancing were imbued with the harmonies of African culture, which, I could see, were being channeled into Emil. Usually during a ceremony I avoid speaking up, but on this occasion I felt motivated to call out, "Hey, Emil, your ancestors are here to meet you!"

The tribal visitors danced for several minutes, then a few of them sat down next to Emil, placing their hands on his shoulders. One of them then whispered in his ear for several minutes, telling him what he had craved to know about his African heritage. After the ceremony, he told me that it was as if he had been injected with the strength of his clan, and that this contact did a great deal to clear up his feelings of displacement.

But the next day he was not so certain. Was it possible, he asked, that what he saw was a hallucination triggered by the medicine? Not to worry, I told him, and then I described the visions

I had witnessed of his African rendezvous, which corresponded exactly to those he had seen, convincing him that a visit from the spiritual world had truly taken place.

Revelations

Revelations divulged to clients from the spirit world often provide counsel that certain experiences from the client's past and present are causing them suffering.

A common Revelation message shows the damaging things done to the client's parents when they, the parents, were children. This Revelation, in turn, explains why the parents did the same hurtful things to the client as a child, and why the grown-up client now feels lonely and alienated. Once this previously unidentified chain of influence is revealed, clients can begin the process of forgiving their parents and themselves as well.

Apropos of past Revelations, once during a ceremony I worked with a lady from an Asian country who in a vision saw her parents selling her as a baby because they had too many children. She also saw that a short time later her parents regretted what they had done and bought her back. Never knowing anything about these transactions, the woman nonetheless felt a mysterious aura of guilt and shame permeating her household as she was growing up, making her feel anxious and insecure. After her plant ceremony she talked to relatives—her parents were dead by then—and they confirmed the visions she had seen, immediately helping relieve the woman's feelings of insecurity and uncertainty that had disoriented her since childhood.

Revelations about the present, on the other hand, provide guidance for ongoing activities such as work, friendship, health, studies, relationships with loved ones, and so forth.

A woman in one of my plant sessions was deeply concerned over the fact that her teenage son suffered from chronic bouts of depression. During the ceremony she and I shared the same visionary Revelation, seeing her son beaten up by students in his high school but being too embarrassed to ask his mother for help. After the ceremony, this woman urged her son to talk to her about his ordeal, and he was soon doing well in therapy.

Another typical present Revelation can occur when a client's loved one suffering from a physical disorder is either unaware of the condition or does not want to tell others about it for fear of burdening them. In either case, when it is revealed to the client that a loved one is unwell or unwilling to speak about their problem, a present Revelation allows the client to step in and provide their loved one with whatever support is needed.

Finally, there are also Revelations that predict future events that may cause fundamental changes, either good or bad, in a client's personal life.

Future Revelations may, for instance, show visions of a coming illness or recovery, a change in financial obligations, moving one's residence, getting married or divorced, losing someone close by separation or death, the beginning or end of a romantic relationship, even visions of a coming earthly cataclysm like a flood or earthquake. The times and dates when these Revelations are destined to occur are rarely revealed. I have, though, noted that clues are given, and that predicted life changes tend to materialize within one to two years after a ceremony.

Once in a jungle ritual a client saw a wooden chest in his visions and at the same time heard a voice telling him he might want to open it, but he should beware: What he found inside would be protective but perhaps painful as well. Screwing up his courage, the man opened the lid and inside found a photograph of his girlfriend wrapped lovingly in the arms of a stranger. His reaction to the picture was uncompromising: Such a thing can *never* happen! He and his girlfriend loved each other too much.

More than a year later, my client and his girlfriend were at a social gathering where they met a guest who was clearly the man in the photograph. Even then, my client refused to believe that his partner was cheating on him. But, of course, after a few months his girlfriend did leave him for the man, and, adding insult to injury, he later happened to see the exact same photograph he saw in his vision hanging on the wall of his ex-girlfriend's cousin's home. This Revelation, it should be said, was not sent as a punishment but as an aid to help my client prepare himself emotionally for his upcoming loss. Unfortunately, he did not listen.

Flying

Participants in a sacred ceremony are sometimes invited to fly on the back of a winged animal or spirit or even on their own. This flight is not simply to see the sights but to visit people whose expertise and hard work creates objects of otherworldly beauty, which in turn inspires clients to strive with greater dedication in their work.

If, for example, a client is an architect, he or she may be invited to fly over a temple where engineers are designing cities of unimaginable beauty and doing so with great enthusiasm, achieving a mastery beyond anything the client has seen on earth. Clients may also see the world guardian of architecture, an ancient sage, half man, half spirit, and repository of all known architectural knowledge who is just now working on a blueprint for monuments that might well line the streets of heaven.

One fact that many people realize when flying over such scenes is that the spirit beings they see below are giving every iota of effort and love to the task they are working on, be it painting, gymnastics, doctoring, manual labor, teaching, or a thousand other pursuits. Sensing this total dedication helps clients realize the potential of their own skills for reaching a higher order of creation. "Flying over a space where masons were building these regal and perfect towers," a biologist client told me, "made me want to work harder to do comparatively excellent work in my laboratory."

When Nature Comes to Meet You

When nature greets us during a ceremony, it speaks to us in a tender voice: "Look at me, know me, appreciate me, love me: I am here for you all the time."

This epiphany comes sooner or later to anyone who works with the sacred plants, as all of us, whether we know it or not, desperately need to take Mother Nature into our hearts and recognize her flourishing perfection in the same way we did as children.

In this regard, I have noted that people who are ambiguous about the validity of plant ceremonies often receive a visit from Mother Nature at the very beginning of a ceremony. This contact occurs with particular frequency to clients from an urban and/or intellectual or business environment who rarely have time to appreciate the natural world. In such cases Mother Nature takes the first steps, taking doubting visitors on a journey over her vast and incalculably magnificent wilderness.

A case that I remember with particular fondness involved a group of Australians who were deeply involved in shamanism but who had not yet taken part in an Amazonian ritual. I had worked intensely with these people in their country, and some of them were good friends. Now they were visiting my lodge in the jungle to see how things worked firsthand.

One member of the group was a sophisticated businessman who came to the compound to accompany his wife, but who was not particularly enamored of the wilderness and showed no interest in participating in a plant ceremony. For him, besides serving as a chaperone, this trip was a chance to take a short vacation from his hectic financial ventures back home. Yet strangely enough, the day before the first ceremony the man announced that he did, in fact, want to experience a ritual.

The next day, I began the ceremony, and almost immediately the man launched into one of the most violent physical purges I have ever seen, with countless rounds of vomiting and expulsion of fluids from every orifice. Disoriented and severely weakened, he was unable to reach the toilet and was forced to finish the ceremony on the floor in front of the bathroom covered with a blanket and reeking of his purge.

The following day we all praised him for the amazing psychic clean-up he had allowed himself to go through. He answered in a gruff voice, "Never again," a decision, I thought, that was certainly appropriate under the circumstances. But then a couple of days later, before the second ceremony began, the man once again volunteered to join in. Apparently, he wished to see if he could experience the same meaningful and life-changing experiences that his wife and other members of the group were talking about after the first ceremony. Once again, the man went through the same cruel expulsions with round after round of nonstop vomiting and diarrhea that were even more enervating than the first night.

The following morning, unsurprisingly, the man once more told us, "Never again!"

The third ceremony approached, and to everyone's amazement, he asked to take part, a decision no doubt helped by the fact that his wife and companions kept telling him how clear and physically fit he looked after his first two nights in the circle.

When the third ceremony began, the man once again started his expulsions. Watching him with my shaman's eye, I could see that a myriad of selfish choices, bad behaviors, and self-defeating habits had clustered together and were being exploded out of him in a kind of psychic tsunami. At the same time, he was deluged with visions of landscapes and natural beauty; nature was calling him back and at the same time helping him expel his negative energies. The outpouring seemed as if it would never stop.

Then suddenly, in the middle of the ceremony, the man's demeanor abruptly changed. He stopped vomiting, became placid and in-turned and, I could see, was being embraced by a soothing energy, protected and healed inside a warm cocoon.

This experience was exceptional, but the aftermath of the man's Amazonian purge was even more extraordinary. Not only did he have one of the deepest cleansing experiences I have ever seen, but he applied the Second Golden Rule with an almost superhuman determination, changing his entire life. The moment he returned home, he gave up alcohol and distanced himself from disreputable associates. He focused his attention on caring for relatives, friends, and especially his wife. What was most outstanding was that during the three ceremonies he participated in he had received no teachings from the spirit world. The changes that took place in him were due entirely to the power cleanses he had so bravely endured and to the visions of nature that he embraced once he was purified.

The Sun and Moon

During a ceremony the spirit of the sun and the moon often play a major role.

When the sun's spirit vision first appears during a ceremony, it comes up over the horizon of the ceremonial circle as it does at daybreak, dispelling darkness and tinting the atmosphere with celestial colors. When this rising occurs, *curanderos* encourage clients to see it as the Force of Life, bringing warmth and healing.

Once the spirit sun reaches its zenith, it beams down golden shafts of light. When clients feel confused and alienated, these rays clear up their psychic fog. When this release occurs, the turmoil caused by Suffering Consciousness is burned away and the sun's beams, in conjunction with the Soul Consciousness, encourage prudent behavior. "I never saw a man go wrong," an old saying goes, "by taking the right road." As in so many cultures and religions around the world, the sun symbolizes both Divine understanding and the higher self. When it appears in the ceremonial circle, most participants have no idea how fortunate they are to have such a glorious ally working on their behalf.

Then there is the moon, which also comes up from the ceremonial horizon. Its light is iridescent, giving off a crystal-like aura and bathing clients in milky tints and tones. When it appears, it is always full, even if the real moon that night is new or waning.

In shamanism the moon has magical qualities that are valued by both black magicians and white. Its most essential feature is its ability to make whatever magical activity a practitioner is performing fixed and permanent. For this reason, many shamans implement acts of magic under the light of a full moon, knowing its rays will make their healings and spells last for many years, if not for a lifetime.

When I was still in the training phase with my teacher Pedro, he declared that skunks can be useful animals in shamanism. If you are setting up a ceremonial space, he told me, and you use skunk urine to mark the boundaries, nobody will ever cross these lines, not even spirits. Skunks are helpful in our work in all kinds of ways.

How else? I asked.

Well, if you capture a skunk—by the way, you have to trap it yourself; you can't buy it or steal it—you can use it as part of a nighttime ceremony that brings you enormous power.

How does it work?

First, you have to eat moon powder. This energizes your trans-action with the skunk and blends the power of its spirit with your Healing Family.

What does that mean, moon powder? I wanted to know.

You stand under a full moon holding the skunk and wearing light pants and no underclothes, Pedro explained. You can't feel constricted in any way when you perform this rite. Avoid wearing a belt and allow your penis and testicles to hang freely. You look up at the moon, open your mouth as wide as possible, and act as if you're drinking in its beams. Let the moonlight shine on the back of your palate for several minutes until you get a particular chalky taste in your mouth. This makes the spell complete, and the full effects of its power are released, arming you with protec-tion against envy, bad charms, and sorcery. The skunk spirit will now be your ally for a lifetime.

Why do it under a full moon? I asked.

To solidify the spell, he replied. The glow from a full moon acts as a kind of glue. It fixes things and makes them stable. That's why all over the world so many shamanic rituals are done under the light of a full moon. If you acquire a particular magical power under moonlight, this power will never diminish. It is yours for-ever. Light from a full moon makes things permanent.

Can anyone perform this kind of ceremony? I asked.

No! he snorted. Only a trained man of medicine. If you go through all the motions of a spell step by step but don't have the knowledge to activate it properly on a psychic level, nothing will happen. It can even hurt you. It's the same for all magic spells, he added. If you don't know what you're doing and haven't been trained, they're a waste of time. Like these people who get hold of old books of curses and magical formulas. The spells never work, and then these people go out and blab to everybody that magic is a lot of nonsense. That's a good thing, though, Pedro added. The magic protects itself by using people's ignorance about it as a shield.

Architectural Constructions

It is not uncommon during a ceremony for a large, spectacularly well-built structure to suddenly materialize overhead in the sacred circle. It makes no difference where the ceremony is taking place. It can be in a *maloca*, the jungle, the desert, inside or outside, it makes no difference. Wherever they are, clients find themselves gazing in wonder at the architectural masterpiece that surrounds them. The workmanship on this spectral complex, as one client described it, "seems as if it's woven by spiders and crafted by angels."

Architecturally speaking, a structure can take the form of any classic style, from a gold-sheathed Inca temple to a Persian citadel—arches, pillars, arcades, towers, domes, high walls made with giant chiseled stones. Sometimes clients find themselves inside an Egyptian temple, a baroque church, or a large Celtic hut. They may be enclosed in an Amazonian wooden edifice with geometric designs on the walls and rooms inside of rooms.

Important for clients to understand is that these structures are not works of art built for aesthetic enjoyment. They symbolize the spiritual sanctum *inside clients themselves*, the place where self-transformation and states of higher awareness are born. Indeed, the physical temples, cathedrals, and sanctuaries of worship built around the world are all graphic simulations of visions that originate inside the builder's elevated consciousness, each one a metaphysical idea from the higher world materialized in brick and mortar. It is my personal opinion that sacred architecture is not only the physical expression of sacred principles but also a visual representation of higher imagery seen during prayer, meditation, and sacred ceremonies. Every sacred shrine is, as it were, the soul of the person who worships there.

Sitting inside one of these havens makes clients feel buoyant and overwhelmingly optimistic. Healing energy radiates from the structure's roof and floor no matter what its design or cultural provenance. Some report that the architecture seems to suck away their negative energy and replace it with peace and gratitude. Yet no matter how substantial the structure feels, it can suddenly change shape at any time according to the needs of the moment and the lessons clients need to learn.

For example, clients may be seated under a golden dome. The shaman sings a particular sacred song or plays his drum, and suddenly the dome turns into a bamboo roof. Whatever design the shrine takes, it makes clients feel that for a few golden moments they are allowed to sit in a hallowed place that spans heaven and earth. This memory alone is curative.

I should add that many ancient religious structures were decorated by images designed to make the invisible world visible, and to pass on spiritual information so deep it can only be represented by symbols.

The paintings and petroglyphs on cave walls and rock cliffs, for instance, are transcendental messages left for future generations to remind them of their sacred past. In petroglyphic drawings by Native Americans bears stand for inner strength, an eye means supernatural discernment, a broken arrow represents peace. True, not all of these designs are religious. Some were meant to warn local people of nearby predators, some to describe events in daily life or to teach children lessons. By and large, though, most of the art and architecture that have come down to us from long ago are earthly symbols of both contemplative wisdom and the Divine.

The Tree of Life

For shamans working in the spirit realm, the Tree of Life is literally a tree. Its roots burrow into Mother Earth, its broad trunk thrusts upward energized by the Force of Life, and its branches brush the heavens. When seen in a vision, it is a ladder representing the connection between the three worlds of creation: the material plane, the spirit world, and the home of the Divine.

During a ceremony, the Tree of Life can normally be seen only by the *curandero* and by clients who have worked long and hard to subdue their Suffering Consciousness. This is not a rule but a tendency. For those with eyes to see, the tree radiates many different colors, sometimes a whitish hue or more commonly an iridescent rainbow of light that contains all the colors of the natural world. When the tree appears as a vision, clients may hear a harmonic chord that sounds much like a hymn. When this happens shamans raise their arms in an act of greeting, celebrating this archetypical sound and celebrating the structured order of the universe. When the Tree of Life appears before clients with inner vision, they are invariably overwhelmed with humility and awe.

At times the Tree of Life may first be seen as two serpents, one moving earthward and the other heavenward. Their movements accelerate until they merge, transforming themselves into a tree whose trunk opens, showing a prism of colors like those on a peacock's plumage. As this display unfolds, clients hear the harmonious chord once again. Their bodies fill with spiritual energy, and certain members of the group feel they are being reborn. When this gift of grace occurs, other spirits may also appear, gazing on the tree in a state of ecstasy, witnessing the universal manifestation of the Life Force.

There is not much more I can disclose about the Tree of Life without transgressing the rules of what can and cannot be said about the spirit world. I will add simply that the tree is a mirror image not only of the three worlds but of our own spiritual anatomy with our abdomen as root, our chest as trunk, and our head as branches reaching toward the sun and sky. Though no words can really describe the Tree of Life, the best way I know to say it is that the tree maps not only the universe but our spiritual constitution as well, and thus our infinite spiritual potential.

Three Things to Know about the Spirits

The invisible realm holds an uncountable number of spirits and spirit visions, only a handful of which have been described so far. The spirits we have talked about are generally native only to Peruvian shamanism and to adjacent South American countries. Imagine, then, the multiple forms they take in shamanic rituals around the world.

When interacting with the spirits during a sacred ceremony, there are three important things to remember:

First, as has been mentioned, the appearance of a spirit, be it as an elf or demon or jaguar with the head of a man, is a costume or camouflage created by the beliefs, expectations, and spiritual creed of the culture it belongs to. In reality, most spirits have force but no form, which is why they are called *spirits*, a word derived from Latin meaning "breath of life." This is not to say that certain spirits do not have a permanent shape. Some do. But most are ethereal and ephemeral shape-shifters.

Second, when interacting with spirits, it is fine to politely ask them for help with a particular problem. But avoid trying to manipulate them or tell them what to do. Sometimes they may follow your directions, sometimes not. But even if they do, they become perturbed when a client tries to control them. When relating to the spirits, it is thus best to minimize your demands and allow these wonderful beings to do their work. The fact is, most of them already know what you need anyway. Meanwhile, though the human mind works with billions of wheels within wheels, the world of spirits is infinitely more complex, and clients are wise to avoid trying to plumb its depths. Its lessons and healings come from an uncountable range of sources; they should always be accepted but never dissected.

Third, during any part of a shamanic ceremony, especially at the session's end, remember to thank the spirits for the healing and wisdom they bring. If you do this in a sincere way, assuring them that you appreciate their remarkable kindness and would very much like to meet them again, the spirits will return the compliment in kind with the promise that they would very much like to meet you again as well.

PART III

WORKING *with the* SACRED PLANTS

CHAPTER 6

ABOUT THE

SACRED PLANTS

A Different View of Evolution

In general, it can be said that humanity believes itself to be seated on top of the pyramid of life, with the plant kingdom many levels below. Humans use tools, speak languages, create works of art, imagine a past and a future, display emotions. Plants simply grow, feed us, and look pretty. There is, it would seem, minimal grounds for comparison.

What is ironic about viewing ourselves as the monarchs of the natural world is that from shamanic eyes—that is, from a spirit-oriented point of view—humanity is on the bottom of the evolutionary scale, not the top. Plants, animals, and other forms of life are not trapped like humans between Suffering Consciousness and Soul Consciousness; between choices that harm and choices that heal. They have two purposes only. One is material: to survive. The other is spiritual: to help the world, including the struggling human race.

Can this be true? Are humans really the lowest and neediest beings in the cosmic order?

Clearly not from a Darwinian frame of reference. And in fact, most *curanderos* would never dispute biological evolution. Indeed, the men of Knowledge I know never think about evolutionary theory at all. Some have never heard of it. From the shaman's perspective the qualitative hierarchy of life is spirit-based rather than biological. The theory of natural selection considers reason and intellect to be the result of eons of evolutionary progress. When *curanderos* talk of evolution or its equivalent, which they almost never do, they do not mean bodily or mental mutation but the upward progress a being can make toward the transcendent.

Curanderos may also ask why it is so necessary to think of our species as evolving into a race of omniscient geniuses with giant brains. As if human progress is measured purely by intellectual aptitude, and the heart and soul mean nothing. In fact, the shamanic muse insists that we are complete as we are. There is no "progress" to be made. We are not going anywhere. We are already there. We already have all the raw materials necessary for higher consciousness. The problem is that our capacity for spiritual transformation is buried beneath the clay of the Suffering Consciousness and needs to be unearthed. Once this faculty is liberated, whether through sacred plants or meditative techniques, we become what we have always been in potential, a fully conscious and spiritually transformed person living entirely in the present.

The Gift of Plants

The plant realm: beautiful, mindless, silent.

But maybe not so mindless. Or silent either. Plants, as zoological research is beginning to reveal, have their own language that is both coherent and complex, but is spoken on a largely untraceable plane. Even non-psychoactive plants seem to see and understand the people who handle them and are aware of their inner feelings.

There is no space here to begin to describe the immense number of gifts we receive from the vegetable world, though as we will see in the final chapter, many people believe that plants can and will play a part in helping the human race survive in a drowning and burning world. Yet while gratitude toward the plant universe is a basic human debt, it is largely unpracticed, even though it is the basic way we can link our souls to green growing things. So, water your plants, talk to them, treat them like companions and mentors, and if you are open to enchantment, you will feel their love coming back at you.

Plants for Good or Evil

Those interested in sacred plants should avoid the assumption that psychotropics are used either for entirely satanic or entirely benevolent purposes. In truth, they can be used for both, with the exception of certain plants that are always benevolent. One of these is the Ayahuasca vine, which always heals and never harms. This is the reason why sorcerers avoid using Ayahuasca in their magical brews, knowing it is a compassionate medicine that refuses to harm others, and worse, that during a ceremony it frequently mirrors back to magicians the dark stain on their hearts. I will speak a good deal more about Ayahuasca in a section below.

The plant world loves to work with human beings, especially sacred plants. The happiness they derive runs so deep that most plants never say no to anyone who wishes to use them for magical purposes, whether this use be helpful or harmful.

An example of this ambiguous relationship can be seen throughout the Andean regions of South America vis-à-vis the coca plant, a tall, lush bush with shiny green leaves that for thousands of years has been considered a gift from the spirits.

Those who live high in the Andes chew the leaf, usually with quicklime or the powdered ash of certain roots and barks. The blend strengthens their breathing and speeds up their hearts, making its energetic effects more intense and helping users function lucidly in the thin air. As a medicine, coca juice has soothing and analgesic properties, providing relief from headache, rheumatism, altitude sickness, and a number of common complaints. It reduces the torments of childbirth and helps reduce pain. Most of all, the leaf provides users with long-term—*very* long-term—endurance. Growing wild in fields and along trails throughout Peru, hikers chew the leaves to relieve cold, hunger, and most of all fatigue.

The coca plant also plays a role in many sacred ceremonies in the Andes where only the freshest and most beautiful leaves are offered in gratitude to the spirits and the Divine. Sometimes power objects are placed near the leaves on a cloth altar to charge them with extra force. During the ceremony a shaman may throw the leaves in the air, make packages of them bundled with other rare vines and herbs, or arrange them in the center of the ceremonial circle. Its placement there is not meant as homage to the plant's stimulating effect but as a commemoration of its sacred spirit and as a gift to Divinity.

In the mid-nineteenth century, a German chemist, Albert Niemann, extracted one of the many alkaloids in the coca plant, producing what he called cocaine hydrochloride, or simply cocaine. Put to use for medical purposes such as calming gastrointestinal spasms, cocaine was touted as a wonder drug, its only side effects seeming to be euphoria and clarity of mind.

Sigmund Freud was personally fond of cocaine, declaring it a cure-all for depression and prescribing it for several clients, who soon became addicts. In 1886 John Pemberton created a cocaine-laced refreshment that he dubbed Coca-Cola, and which quickly became the country's favorite soda. After twenty years of addicting countless drinkers, the narcotic was finally removed, though half of COCAine's name remained on the bottle. The Czar of Russia, Thomas Edison, Queen Victoria, and Pope Pius X, among many other celebrities, regularly drank a cocaine-based wine known as Vin Mariani. While writing his autobiography, Ulysses S. Grant was a confirmed user at the end of his life as a means of reducing the pain of the throat cancer that was killing him.

Finally, in 1914, when the pernicious qualities of the drug became too evident to ignore, cocaine was officially outlawed. But the genie was out of the bottle. Its rise in the 1970s and 1980s as the dope of choice for the Go-Go generation led to the creation of far worse drugs, like crack and methamphetamine, substances that continue to plague the lives of millions of Americans today.

None of these abuses are, of course, the fault of the coca plant itself, which is impelled to surrender its leaves to anyone who picks them, be the picker saint or sinner. From a spiritual point of view, breaking down coca in the lab to produce an addictive drug is an enslavement of the plant that shows it great contempt; instead of exploiting the rich mixture of healing alkaloids that it offers, and which has served as an ally for human beings over the millennia, cocaine makers take only the parts of the plant they need to make their narcotic and throw the rest away. This same dissection is done to hundreds of other leaves, roots, flowers, and bark by chemical and pharmaceutical companies, a technique decidedly antithetical to the ancient and respectful way of intersecting with the vegetable world.

This process of enslaving plants by extracting substances for industrial use and discarding the remainder is felt by the vegetable spirits as a deep, sad form of disrespect.

This is not to say, though, that when sacred plants are misused, they do not strike back.

An interesting example is chiric sanango, a psychoactive flowering shrub that grows in the Peruvian jungles and is a member of the *Solanaceae* family, which includes a range of fruitage from deadly nightshade to tomatoes. Chiric sanango is sometimes taken alone, usually during a long-term Dieta, or meditative retreat. It can also be mixed in brews with other psychoactive plants including Ayahuasca. During a ceremony, clients may feel shivers or waves of cold rolling over their spine when the plant does its work. Hence the word *chiric*, which in Quechua means "cold." (Its full name can be translated as "the sanango that brings cold.") But while the roots of this shrub provide therapeutic benefits, it has strict guidelines as to the way it should be harvested, and woe to the practitioner who ignores these rules.

Here is how its protocols work. To pick sanango properly, a *curandero* is obliged to approach it early in the morning after having fasted for twenty-four hours. He is forbidden to indulge in sexual activity for several days before the picking, and may not take part in any type of angry disagreement at home or at work during this time.

Especially important is the way the sanango is harvested. First the *curandero* courteously asks permission to uproot it. The worker must then remove it from the ground in a single pull. If the first tug does not do the job, the shaman must immediately walk away without making any further harvesting attempts and without looking back.

I have known cases where a poorly trained shaman continues

to yank at the root several times, sometimes shredding it or pulling up the root in pieces. Within several hours he almost invariably begins to feel a tormenting itch, and soon large parts of his body are covered with a red, purulent rash. The more he scratches it, the faster it spreads. If the shaman then goes to a hospital for treatment, medical professionals will apply a range of topical ointments or medicines, none of which can reduce the inflammation. The only possible source of help comes from other *curanderos* who are well versed in sanango's ways, and who know how to make a curative lotion by boiling the leaves of the same plant that the untrained shaman molested. The errant shaman is also obliged to have a repentant attitude toward the abused plant, and to apologize to it for having manhandled and dishonored its root.

The Marriage between a
Shaman and His Plants

The knowledge of how to administer the right plants at the right time in a sacred ceremony rarely comes to a *curandero* from experience or trial and error. Perhaps revelation would be a more accurate description—revelations from teachers in his lineage, from the invisible realm, and on rare occasions directly from the Divine.

During a ceremony there are many plants a *curandero* calls on constantly. Others are close associates that he uses in certain situations. Still others are put to work only two or three times in his career.

A shaman's relationship with a plant can also change. He begins by using a plant from time to time, then with increasing frequency. The relationship evolves over the years, the same as any human relationship, and the better plant and shaman get to know each other, the closer they become. Until one day they are literally in love. This bond gives the *curandero* a powerful tool to add to his

Healing Family, assuring him that the venerated plant will always have his back and never let him down.

Several remarkable things happen when a sacred plant and a *curandero* become bonded. First, as often occurs in a happy marriage, plant and shaman develop a telepathic empathy, knowing what the other is feeling and thinking without need for words.

For example, during a ceremony a shaman may need Medicine from a certain plant he is friends with in order to cure a particular somatic problem. But the plant may not be available. No matter. The plant's physical presence is unnecessary because the shaman carries its essence inside himself. During a session all he needs to do is *think* about the plant and *feel* it, and its healing energies go to work for him at a distance.

Many times, when I am overseeing an urgent case far from the source of a needed plant, even one that grows many hundreds of miles away, I sense its smell or taste, bringing its Medicine when no other plant I am using can help. Occasionally clients also see the spirit of a plant and sense it working inside them. Several longtime clients have told me that they still experience the taste or smell of a certain plant years after they were cured by it.

Some powerful trees, bushes, and vines are so remote they are unfindable, and I would never have made their acquaintance but for the fact that these plants seek *me* out and ask to be part of my Healing Family. When I do touch-healing, either in private or in a ceremony, simply conjuring up the mental image of these volunteer allies inspires them to lend me their Medicine and transfer their power into my hands.

The second notable transaction that takes place vis-à-vis the plant-shaman bond is that some plants prefer to heal in concert with other plants or vines. For instance, during a ceremony when a client needs the help of a particular flora but it is not included in the night's cocktail, one or more plants in the mixture may have a friendship with the missing plant and communicate with it via the spirit realm, asking to borrow its Medicine. This remarkable cross-healing takes place due to the mysterious affinity that exists between growing things, and because of the mutable attributes of plant Medicine, which are able to lend their help outside the bounds of our three-dimensional topography. If sacred plant healing worked only with chemical and molecular components, such a healing could never occur. In a shamanic ritual, healing almost always has its origins on the subtle plane.

Finally, it should be made clear that work with plant spirits is not always a deadly serious affair.

I mean it is always serious. But in the same vein there are moments of lightness and even humor that bring delight to clients and shamans alike. Sometimes when the *curandero* chants, the plant spirits drop into the circle like sprites in a party mood. Hand in hand, they dance gleefully in the ring or around certain clients. The energy generated by these festivities can reach such excitement that both clients and shaman begin to laugh in an ecstatic way, a laughter that transcends both tears and joy, the way all true laughter should. Indeed, certain games and ritual frolics that children have indulged in for centuries are based on unconscious memories of dancing and singing modeled for them by the spirits long, long ago.

Master Plants

Among the healing herbage common to Peru, there are innumerable green growing things used to treat a variety of disorders. There is also a smaller group of medicines known as Master Plants.

Master Plants, all of which are psychoactive, instruct us as well as cure us. They provide a more profound therapy than common medicinal plants, and they operate on an especially high plane of spiritual energy, bringing us closer to Soul Consciousness during a ceremony.

In the Amazonian region of Peru, the Ayahuasca vine is the most famous and sought-after Master Plant and is usually the principal conductor of spirits in a shaman's brew. But other Master Plants play leading roles as well.

There is, for example, an important healer we have already met, the sanango, which is actually a group of plants including the blue sanango, uchu sanango, lobo sanango, chiric sanango, and others. Medically these plants have many uses, including help for chronic fatigue and joint diseases like arthritis and rheumatism. In spiritual work, they are incredible "extractors" of deep emotional wounds, literally sucking out the grief and pain of old memories. Each sanango variety works a bit differently and has its own spirit appearance. Commonly its spirit appears in visions as a bird-like body.

Two other major healing plants are both known as bubinzana, though botanically they are unalike, growing in different regions of the jungle and having entirely different appearances. The best-known form of bubinzana is a small tree with lustrous pink-red flowers. The other is a thick fern-like growth with long leaves. Both are robust healers, having a wide range of uses connected to the archetypal healing powers of fire and heat. For instance, both plants warm old people and young children who are exposed to cold temperatures. They strengthen the body by repelling winds that invade the joints and organs. They also help open the heart and inspire forgiveness and the power of will. Bubinzana leaves are frequently used by soldiers and athletes, bolstering their determination, physical strength, and endurance in harsh weather. The plant likes to work with the chacruna plant. When used together they have a warming effect on the heart.

Also high on the list of Master Plants is sapo huasca, a vine whose bark is rough like the skin of a toad (in Spanish, *sapo* means "toad," and *huasca* means "vine"). In Peru frogs and toads are traditionally a symbol of the malleability of life, as they transform themselves from long-tailed tadpoles swimming in the water into square, spotted creatures hopping on the ground. The plant is known for reducing pressure in the heart and for calming arrythmias and tachycardia. It also strengthens the immune system, though sapo huasca's most appreciated quality in traditional communities is its use for controlling women's fertility cycles. Its cooked resin stops ovulation for up to six months, according to the size of the dose given and the way it is administered. If ingested for a long period of time, it produces permanent sterility if so desired. For many centuries the plant has also been used widely by women in tribes throughout Peru to provide birth control.

Finally, sapo huasca is related to the mystery of life. When mixed in a sacred brew, it not only brings renewal but inspires people with a wondrous sense of being alive.

Another powerful staple, a variety of tobacco known as mapacho, is one of the most widely used Master Plants in sacred rituals, both for preparing the ceremonial space and for enlarging a shaman's perceptivity and powers of mind.

When, for example, a shaman needs to burrow down to the root of a client's problem, smoking mapacho tobacco focuses his mind into a deep tracking mode, piercing through internal and external distractions and helping him pinpoint the cause of the problem. When healing, mapacho strengthens a *curandero*'s will, allowing him to break through the walls surrounding a client's Suffering Consciousness or helping him slice through barriers placed by a well-crafted curse.

In ordinary life, the use of tobacco for focusing thoughts reveals itself via the habit of lighting a cigarette when sitting alone thinking about a problem, or when a group of people light up together before discussing a complex issue. When smoking was still fashionable, politicians, writers, celebrities, and artists often smoked during an interview or while being photographed. Even today inveterate smokers look at cigarettes, loaded as they are with damaging and addictive chemicals, as a tool for calming their minds and helping them zone in on thought-provoking questions.

For shamans mapacho tobacco has a protective use as well as a healing one. At the beginning of a ceremony when a *curandero* builds a psychic dome around a ceremonial circle, he blows mapacho smoke into this space to dissolve negative energies. Indeed, the use of tobacco to diffuse negativity is one of humanity's oldest magical rituals.

A good example is the Native American practice of smoking a peace pipe to finalize a treaty between warring tribes. Participants from clans or lineages once in conflict sit in a circle inhaling the tobacco smoke, passing the pipe from person to person. They use its calming and focusing properties to resolve lingering disputes, the power of the tobacco creating a new paradigm of goodwill between them.

Yet another Master healer is toè, a member of the *Datura* family of plants, several varieties of which grow in diverse geographical areas of Peru, where they are used in different forms of medicine. In general, toè requires special handling. Its preparation and dosage are more exacting than most other plants, and there is the potential for a poorly mixed potion to cause serious physical and mental harm if not carefully monitored.

During the years I worked on the north coast where the common name of *Datura* is *misha,* I heard a story about a gang of young men who carelessly and frequently used recreational drugs. One of them heard about a new way to get high using an especially strong type of *misha*, a local variety that grew as a small bush close to the ground. Smoking it without any spiritual preparation, they not only had an evening of nightmarish visions, but several users became mentally disturbed and had to be institutionalized.

Misuse for fun and frolic—a big mistake. But the red, yellow, white, and violet flowers of toè can also trigger powerful healings. If used properly, it provides self-insights, amazing visions, and even telepathic powers. On the other hand, if its use is driven by the needs of the Suffering Consciousness, as it often is, it can take users deep into a self-destructive maze, bringing out the darkest and most dangerous parts of their psyche. For this reason, the plant is frequently used by sorcerers.

As a result of its volatility, both the flower and the leaves of toè are usually reserved for advanced clients. To mix it into a beginner's drink in order to make their trip more hallucinogenic is both physically and mentally hazardous. And since toè contains the poisonous chemicals atropine and scopolamine, if a dose is too large, the substance becomes lethal. In fact, a majority of reports of Ayahuasca fatalities in the Amazon are not due to Ayahuasca at all but to toè overdoses given by inept practitioners, or to hard drugs and nightshades mixed into the medicine by inexperienced and occasionally unscrupulous shamans.

A seeker must, therefore, only use this plant under the auspices of a *curandero* who has overseen many toè sessions, and who knows how to remedy the situation if it causes a paranoid or psychotic reaction. Toè is not a bad plant or a good plant, as people on both sides of the aisle insist. Its effects depend entirely on how it is used; and when all is said and done, our limited human judgment cannot fully understand the dimension of the spirits that belong to it.

✻

Since the turn of the century, I have met and worked with a large number of medicinal and sacred plants, many of which I keep stored in my home pharmacy—leaves, flowers, roots, seeds, some fresh, some dry. Others I plant and cultivate in my compound. Still others I have mapped and identified in the deeper parts of the jungle, hoping they will remain untouched by poachers.

Besides growing, I also purchase old, thick Ayahuasca branches from vines close to my property. I make every effort to protect the roots and trunks of these plants from poachers, who sell them in the marketplace for fifty to a hundred dollars a bag.

Rarely mentioned in botanical circles is how scholarly texts written about the healing effects of sacred or medicinal plants can be contradictory and sometimes downright incorrect. Not always, of course, but more commonly than is supposed. The authors are no doubt honest and well versed in their subject, but most have little experience working in a shamanic way with the plants they write about.

For example, suppose you read the description of a plant indigenous to a certain part of Peru. Then you consult another book about the same region. After reading both, you find it difficult to reconcile the fact that the two books are talking about the same plant, so different are the medical benefits they attribute to it. In one text a plant is listed as a remedy for lung disorders. In another it is said to help diseases of the ovaries. Some specialists report that the flower of a certain tree stops hair loss. Another that its primary use is as a purgative.

Besides the fact that many botanists have little in-the-field training, there is a deeper reason why so many different and unrelated healing powers are attributed to the same plant. A client's difficulties may start with an emotional conflict, such as, say, overweening guilt. Depending on the person harboring it, this problem can then trigger a crowd of entirely different symptoms, some organic, some psychological.

For example, ingrained guilt may cause infertility, lack of appetite, depression, anemia, and loss of vision, to name a few. A well-taught shaman understands that these seemingly unrelated symptoms are all due to a primal source: the emotions of guilt and shame. He then prescribes a single medicinal plant mixture. In this way one plant elixir given in the proper way can cure clients of a problem, though its standard healing attributes seem unrelated to the ailment. This is why in most *curanderos'* eyes intuition and schooled word-of-mouth are often a good deal more efficient at profiling the cause of a sickness than modern studies.

A Scholarly Error

While on the subject of botanical misinterpretations, I would like to mention the work of certain scientists who insist that there are only three Master Plants native to Peru, each plant coming from one of the three distinctive regions of the country: the San Pedro cactus along the desert coast, coca in the Andes, and Ayahuasca in the jungle. That's it; just three. This theory was first put forth by an anthropologist at the end of the 1970s, and scholars have been repeating it ever since.

But from my experience the theory is simply not true.

In my thirty years of traveling in Peru, besides San Pedro, I have come in contact with three other species of cactus that are all powerfully medicinal. Several of them generate healing dynamics that are quite different from those of the better-known San Pedro cactus, and all of them deserve to be considered Master Plants. These little-known cactuses grow along the desert coast but also in transitional areas of the lower northern mountains and toward the east.

Meanwhile, though identified as a mountain Master Plant by certain botanists, and though it has some medicinal uses, coca does not provide the kind of superstrong healing that defines a Master Plant. Nor is it found only in the mountains, as many botanists maintain; it grows in the jungle and the flatlands as well. The Incas and their predecessors in the highlands used coca leaves as offerings and energy tonics for workers doing manual labor. They did *not* consider coca to be a visionary Master healer.

I likewise know of at least seven rare Master Plants that thrive in the Andes and in the swampy areas close to the high mountain lakes. These plants are ecologically quite vulnerable, yet they are also extremely therapeutic. Their identity is not a secret to locals, and I am always appreciative when speaking with villagers in remote areas to discover that they know a great deal about these plants and their magical purposes, a sign that sacred plant lore still thrives in some parts of the country. However, I do hope these plants remain unknown to outside visitors, as the fragility of the environment they grow in will not withstand the heavy demands that come with popularity.

In the lush abundance of the jungle, meanwhile, a number of little-known psychoactive plants can also induce spectacular healings and certainly deserve to be considered Master Plants. I have described a few of these plants, such as Ayahuasca, chacruna, and sanango, though there are many others, some of which are trees whose resin, rather than leaves or roots, is medicinal.

In short, I believe strongly, from both instruction and practice, that the "three Master Plants" theory needs revision, hopefully by scholars sympathetic to shamanism and to the experience of its practitioners.

As part of my practice, I often use two core recipes that include Master Plants plus supplemental companion plants. The first, as mentioned earlier, I call my *yunga* recipe, *yunga* being the Quechua name for the coastal region. This formula consists of ingredients I learned about in my northern Peruvian training and includes at least one Master cactus and several companion plants that grow in the arid planes and valleys of the lower Andes.

My other recipe is Amazonian and is based on the functional relationship that exists between Ayahuasca-chacruna and other companion plants, and that uses a variety of vines, barks, resins, roots, and flowers as well as leaves. Here I would like to emphasize the importance of companion plants, even the non-psychoactive kind. They are sometimes considered secondary in a mixture, but in some cases they are almost as curative as the Master Plants.

There are, for instance, companion plants that enhance memory and psychic capacities and sharpen the senses. There are species I refer to as "soaps" because they wash away turbulent behaviors like panic, stage fright, uncontrolled grief, and phobias. Finally, without the presence of companion plants, many Master Plant recipes will not work well if at all. In a certain sense, then, as far as the healing effects of a brew go, Master Plants and companion plants stand *almost* on equal footing. The knowledge of these two formulas and their protocols is one of the greatest treasures of our Craft, symbolizing for me the attention that countless generations of natural healers have invested in this beautiful Art.

Animals Know about the Medicine

Besides the innate generational wisdom in every animal, there is a compelling phenomenon that has been observed by shamans all over the world: that like human beings, animals are aware of the healing power present in medicinal and sacred plants.

For example, when an animal knows it is sick, it may attempt to cure itself by fasting, then by ferreting out certain healing herbs, leaves, or flowers and ingesting them. Ailing animals are also known to chew and drink the juices of psychoactive shrubs, an act that sends them full-bore into visionary states. While under the influence of these remedies, animals, like human beings, purge, learn, and heal. Having seen such behaviors more than once, I myself believe that animals everywhere have their own version of what I call the Ancient Alliance—that is, rapport with and knowledge of the fundamental powers of nature and creation.

Growers, Harvesters, and Traders

During different phases of my practice, I have worked with a group of individuals that I honor as a critical link in the chain of traditional shamanic knowledge. I am speaking of the plant growers and merchants who today, after thousands of years, maintain the same farming and harvesting techniques as their ancestors. These tradesmen follow ancient trading routes all over Peru, some of which were built by their ancestors, delivering healing plants and in the process making sure they are sold only to those who will use them for the public good.

Over the years these tradesmen have acquired a deep understanding of the plant world. They are remarkably well-informed about weather and seasonal changes. They know the best times to harvest according to the cycles of sun and moon, the most efficient way to preserve and transport a crop, and so forth. Many growers are among the sixth or seventh generation to practice their trade, while a few trace their lineage back to civilizations that thrived centuries before the Incas.

Besides their expertise, what's more, many harvesters and sellers provide medical assistance for poor villagers. Using the principles of natural healing gained from years of contact with shamans and healing plants, they provide medicinal help to peasants who cannot afford the price of a physician. Townspeople also go to traders for recipes and prescriptions, or to seek agricultural information.

Yet like so much else in Peru, things are changing. When I first began training during the 1990s, several teachers told me how the workmen who harvest and transport rare plants from remote areas of the northern highlands were gradually disappearing. Since that time many have died, while others have retired or turned their work over to incompetent family members. As a result, valuable plant medicines are becoming increasingly difficult to obtain, and when these growers and sellers disappear entirely, their knowledge will disappear with them.

Sadly, there are also providers of herbs who have renounced their legacy and willingly sell fake sacred plants or backyard-grown Ayahuasca to unwary buyers. Hoards of money pouring in from tourism have caused many growers to abandon the work of their family line, opting instead to sell trinket jewelry, "spell casting" wands, plastic skulls, and foreign goods from China in the marketplace. Instead of procuring medicine from the elements, they now peddle gewgaws and worthless plant mixtures. Like so many essential aspects of the shamanic Craft, the means by which sacred plants are supplied, as well as their use in a ceremony, is being compromised more and more each year by those who would be better advised to preserve what remains of their own medicine heritage.

Vine of the Soul

When working with clients, I tell those eager to know more about sacred plants that these medicines, especially Ayahuasca, are not simply off-the-shelf hallucinogens but sentient botanicals that think and reason, have likes and dislikes, and carry a deep love in their hearts for humankind. Since Ayahuasca is the Amazonian Master Plant best known throughout the world, I would like to discuss some of its salient features in some detail.

Ayahuasca is a woody vine that twines around trees throughout the jungles of the Amazon basin and up into parts of Central America. It is especially common in Peru, Brazil, Bolivia, Colombia, and Ecuador. Over the centuries it has been used primarily for one reason: to heal human afflictions. The stuff of psychotropic Ayahuasca reaches deep into the boiler room of the mind, finding and dealing with the fundamental causes of physical and mental ailments alike, and helping cure maladies of the soul that Western medicine finds difficult if not impossible to treat; diseases such as post-traumatic stress disorder, addiction (hard drugs of all kinds, cigarettes, sex, alcohol), eating disorders, intractable depression, sociopathic behavior, criminal tendencies, and more. But besides psychological remedies, sacred plant medicine has an extraordinary reach, working also with physical ailments and with the spiritual realm. It is medicine for everyone.

While those who have only a newspaper or magazine knowledge of Ayahuasca may think of it as just another psychedelic, nothing could be further from the truth. Intoxication is a by-product of Ayahuasca, not a goal, and traditional Peruvians who hear it mentioned in the same breath as cocaine or LSD are offended. In fact, Ayahuasca is never referred to among traditional Amazonian people as a "drug." It is, as we have seen, always spoken of as "the medicine."

When native Peruvians talk of a sacred plant ritual, they may describe it as an "Ayahuasca experience." Embedded in this common term, however, is an unspoken understanding that sacred plant medicine is greater than a single root or vine, and that during a ceremony, trance states are induced by Ayahuasca *plus* a mixture of other plants, sometimes many other plants, all creating a kind of cosmic motherboard triggering visionary encounters. Ayahuasca is more than a vine; it is a collective event.

Though Ayahuasca is illegal in many countries outside of South America, Peruvians look on sacred plant legality in an entirely different way, believing the medicine to be a fundamental part of their nation's spiritual heritage. Several years ago, the president of Peru spoke of Ayahuasca as "one of the basic pillars of the identity of the Amazon peoples." In 2008 the National Institute of Culture of Peru told the United Nations, in what has to be one of the more unique statements ever heard by members of the UN, that Ayahuasca "constitutes the gateway to the spiritual world and its secrets, which is why traditional Amazon medicine has been structured around the Ayahuasca ritual."

In Brazil an even more remarkable event took place. In the late 1980s, under pressure from the US "war on drugs," Ayahuasca was banned. The public's reaction was so outraged that the Brazilian government appointed their federal drug agency to look more deeply into the pros and cons of Ayahuasca use. As part of their investigation, government agents did the unimaginable, taking part in an Ayahuasca ceremony overseen by a traditional shaman. After a night of life-changing visions and realizations, the agents unanimously agreed that Ayahuasca was indeed a safe and nonaddictive agent of human growth, describing it as "a wise or teaching plant, which shows to initiates the very foundations of the world and its components." In 1992 the Brazilian government made Ayahuasca legal again, and it remains so today.

AYAHUASCA'S NAME

The first part of its name, *aya*, means "soul" in the Quechua language, as well as "ghost," "spirits," or "the dead." The second part, *huasca* (also *wasqa*), means both "vine" and "rope." Other Spanish words used for vines include *bejuco*, *liana*, and *soga*, which also means "rope." In some northern areas of the Peruvian jungle, Ayahuasca is known to villagers as *Jayahuasca*. *Jaya* (pronounced "haya") means "bitter" or a "strong taste," a probable connection to the shamanic saying that "Bitter medicine is the best medicine." Some people think that Jayahuasca was the vine's original name and that it later morphed into Ayahuasca by non-Quechua-speaking people. Indeed, only a small number of Amazonian ethnic groups speak Quechua. Most of the jungle nations speak languages from totally different linguistic groups.

DO PLANT SPIRITS HAVE A GENDER?

Some time ago when I first began lecturing in other countries, I was introduced to a community of dedicated people who were performing plant rituals using Ayahuasca. They frequently referred to the vine as "Mother" or "Mother Ayahuasca." Though this term was new to me at the time, nowadays it is found in many communities around the globe.

Which brings up the intriguing question of whether sacred plants have a gender.

Speaking with townspeople in the outback, I have found a great deal of ambiguity over this question. Some insist that rounded mountains are female and peaked mountains are male. If a forest is populated with straight trees, the forest is masculine. When twisting, curving plants dominate, it is feminine.

This approach is no doubt borne by our tendency to think of things in a binary way—something must be either *this* or *that*. But is this true? Dualistic thinking, I believe, can at times prevent people from experiencing the great mystery of being: the sacred marriage of opposites merging into One, producing something greater than the sum of its parts. In terms of gender, stories I have heard from my teachers maintain that spirits from the invisible world can not only choose their sex, but can change it at will and at a moment's notice. Or they can choose to be both sexes at the same time. Many older references to Ayahuasca maintain that its spirit takes the form of an old man who counsels and heals. Still today you can see a mural painted long ago in the old Quistococha zoo in Iquitos depicting Ayahuasca as a seasoned elder. Yet in many jungle towns in the Amazon Ayahuasca is also talked about as the "lady of our visions."

Similarly, some people who regularly take the San Pedro cactus refer to it as grandfather. Others report the cactus guides them with a goddess-like presence. There seem to be no absolutes, and in fact when I was working with the cactus myself in the north under the direction of my teacher Pedro and elder patients in the hospital, we never thought of assigning a male or female label to the spirits. They were far more knowing than we were, and we dared not interpret their personal ways of manifesting. All things considered, then, it is wise to avoid fitting plant archetypes into categories. In their immense wisdom, the spirits manifest in whatever gender or combination of genders they know will best help their client get well.

PREPARATION BEFORE AYAHUASCA IS HARVESTED

A few days before harvesting Ayahuasca, a healer must follow strict dietary restrictions, avoiding coffee, black tea, spices, red meat, alcohol, chiles, and other stimulating food and drink. Sexual activity of any kind is also prohibited for a few days before the harvest begins. It is likewise urged that before harvesting, shamans spend three or four hours a day in meditative seclusion, and that during this time they not interact with people, even friends and family. They should also avoid harvesting plant medicine around the time of the new moon.

AGE AND GROWTH

An Ayahuasca vine ordinarily grows by wrapping itself around a tree like a twisted rope or intertwining web that can be so complex and beautiful it resembles a work of art. The vine's tendril-like foliage branches out a good deal over the years, reaching trees and stumps as far as thirty feet away.

When young, the Ayahuasca vine is an inch or so in width. The trunks of older specimens—forty or fifty years—measure six to seven inches thick and look almost like a tree. As a matter of protocol, an Ayahuasca vine should be at least fifteen years old before its branches are harvested. Younger vines are a bit anemic in their psychoactive effects and tend to provide fewer connections to the invisible world. In addition, cutting vines when they are too young brings sadness to the spirit of the plant itself.

VARIETIES OF THE AYAHUASCA VINE

Once I met a man from Europe who was traveling through different regions of the jungles of Peru, Ecuador, and Brazil attempting to experience every variety of Ayahuasca he could find, and to catalog the precise mental effects each one produced. To me this seemed a difficult and perhaps absurd task, as the man's experience taking each of these varieties would depend as much on the expertise of the shaman he worked with as on the vine itself.

In terms of plant varieties, shamans identify an Ayahuasca vine by the color it shows when scraped—red Ayahuasca, black Ayahuasca, white Ayahuasca, and pink. Some varieties are used for clients with weak physical constitutions and others are for the strong. Certain vines are also defined by the degree of intoxication they produce, though it should be said that specific types of Ayahuasca, such as heaven (*cielo*) Ayahuasca, thought to be gentle and mild, under certain circumstances produces a night of tough love, while thunder (*trueno*) Ayahuasca, famous for its raw power, sometimes treats a client with kid gloves. With sacred plants there are no absolutes.

When journeying to different regions of the northern Amazon jungle, I have come upon a number of psychoactive vines besides Ayahuasca that are unidentified by botanists. These powerful creepers are known by the local people, who think of them as part of the Ayahuasca group, but which actually belong to a different species entirely. All things considered, then, shamans define types of Ayahuasca not by biological categories but by their appearance or by the particular psychoactive effects they produce.

HARVESTING AYAHUASCA

As a rule, a shaman has three or four local Ayahuasca vines he is friendly with and which he has worked with many times in the past. When in the jungle he approaches a favored vine quietly, like tiptoeing into a sleeping child's bedroom. He sits next to it for a few moments, touching it, talking or singing to it, and connecting with it emotionally. Usually he brings gifts for the vine, such as flower petals, fruit, or dry tobacco leaves, which he buries near its roots, and which act as both a vitamin and a food.

After several minutes of bonding, the shaman asks the vine permission to take a piece of it for healing purposes. He awaits the vine's answer, which can take many forms. Sometimes it comes as an inner perception, sometimes as the call of an animal or the sudden flight of a bird passing overhead. A nearby plant pod may fall to the ground for no apparent reason. Sometimes a piece of the vine falls off by itself.

Once permission is given, the shaman thanks the vine with deep sincerity. He then rhythmically pulls off a few of its branches. If the vine is tall, he may have to do some climbing, though usually the limbs are within reach. When the shaman feels a branch loosening and drooping, this means it is offering itself to him, and he takes it with gratitude. Each time he picks the vine, he takes only what is needed. Never more. Most importantly, he *never* touches the vine's roots. In this way the *curandero*'s needs are fully met, and the plant is unharmed and joyous to be contributing parts of itself for a sacred gathering.

After taking as many limbs as he needs, most of them about a foot long, the *curandero* places them on a slab of hard wood, where he cleans them while in a kind of trance, then beats them with a stick from the quinilla tree, which has a light, thick wood. He pounds the vines until their bark breaks open, revealing fibers entwined around themselves like rope. The *curandero* weaves these strands into snake-like spiral cords, places them in a container, and brings them back to his hut for cooking.

PREPARING AND COOKING THE BREW

To cook an Ayahuasca blend, a shaman uses a large ceramic or metallic pot that he has likely owned for years, and in which he has cooked hundreds and perhaps thousands of brews.

He first arranges the Ayahuasca fibers along the inner walls of the pot, leaving an empty space in the center. In it he places a mixture of psychotropic roots, bark, vines, and leaves. As explained, though the chacruna leaves are a common companion for Ayahuasca, the shaman ordinarily uses many other plant parts as well, especially for his most common remedies. When cooked, each ingredient in the recipe works in harmony with the others like musicians all playing their parts in a concerto.

The cooking pot is filled with water and put to boil. Delicate ingredients like flowers or filmy leaves are added after the mixture has brewed for several hours to prevent them from being overcooked. According to tradition, when cooking the brew, a shaman should never close the lid of the pot. The liquid must boil in the open. I have heard stories of practitioners who cook a mixture with the lid closed, only to find that when they serve the brew it has little or no effect on their clients.

The shaman simmers his preparation for varying lengths of time—many hours at least, but more often an entire day, depending on which flowers, roots, or leaves are in the mix. During the cooking he sits close to the pot, frequently chanting or meditating. His presence is important for the activation of the Medicine, and focusing his attention in this way is considered an active ingredient in the preparation. The same way one cooks a dish with loving hospitality for family and friends, the medicine person maintains a mood that is joyful and bright while cooking his elixir.

Usually when preparing a blend, the *curandero* makes several reductions, observing the liquid's color and texture and occasionally taking a taste. Weaker reductions are set aside for casual or community use, or to provide milder servings for clients who are sensitive to plant preparations. At the end of the day's cooking, the shaman has a thick brownish mixture that he carefully strains before pouring it into bottles or storage pots. When served up to clients, the drink is a thick, dark syrup with a pungent taste. The time required to locate the plants, harvest them, and cook the preparation usually takes at least two days and sometimes longer.

Once the relationship between a *curandero* and his clients is established before a ceremony begins, the healer can best decide which roots or leaves to use for a particular group or even for a single person in the group. When there are no specific needs, he uses his standard brew, which he knows is sufficiently effective.

In some cases, a shaman may also purchase plants from harvesters and traders described in a section above. These workers, as we have seen, are part of a spiritual community, not just machete hackers. They harvest plants from remote and rarely traveled areas, knowing the pathways in Peru's jungles, deserts, and mountains better perhaps than anyone in the country. They also have intimate knowledge of unknown trails and ruins, and where to locate plant specimens that no one else can find.

A point that should be stressed is that preparing the medicine is not only about cooking it but activating it with prayers and the *curandero*'s personal Medicine to wake up the plants' spirit. This technique is the very *essence* of shamanic Craft. I am always vexed when outsiders and even those who have participated in ceremonies claim that the plants do all the healing. The plants are obviously critical, but so is the psychic participation of the shaman. At times he may not even use plants, healing his clients with telepathy or with hands-on energy alone.

STORING THE AYAHUASCA BREW

Once in my travels through the mountain jungle I met a medicine man who lived with his family in a hut away from the village. After a bit of conversation, he offered to perform a ceremony with me the following evening. As we talked, I saw his brew sitting in a covered container, and I could immediately tell it had been cooked some time ago. Though well protected and in the shade, the preparation had fermented from the steaming jungle heat, and to my dismay, when opening it the shaman removed a mass of fungi floating on top of the brew. Even though the taste of plant medicine is normally unpleasant, his brew was beyond foul. Nonetheless, I participated in the ceremony, and in the process saw the wonderful work this man was capable of performing. His brew was aged and awful tasting, it was true, but the spiritual effects it produced were marvelous.

In modern times when the cooking of a brew is complete, the liquid is poured into containers and kept in a cool, dry place. For long-term storage the best method of preservation is refrigeration, which keeps the brew fresh for many months, but which is not always available deep in the jungle. In such situations shamans must transport their brew to the nearest settlement that has access to electricity.

To ensure that a brew stored for a long period of time is still potent, I use a trick my teachers taught me. I fill a plastic bottle with the liquid, squeeze it, forcing out all the air, and then cap it. If I see that the fluid bubbles or fizzes in the bottle or that the bottle has expanded, I know the liquid has become fermented. While at times I can reboil the drink to allow the fermented gases to escape, this method usually produces a half-hearted brew. It is always best during a ceremony to use a well-preserved mixture that you know for certain is fresh.

HOW OFTEN SHOULD A PERSON TAKE AYAHUASCA?

I know of commercial healing centers in Peru that encourage clients to come to them at least once a week for a plant session. To me this seems like a lot of sessions. People who are told they need dozens of Ayahuasca ceremonies in a short period of time are, I believe, making themselves dependent on a shaman who profits from their visits. This kind of exploitation is polluting our Art.

I also know clients who have done, say, close to a hundred Ayahuasca sessions in a year, and who complain that their problems are still unresolved. The reason for this frustration is usually that a *curandero* performs all the prerequisite outer maneuvers, administering plants, playing the drums, singing *icaros*, and so forth, but does not know how to apply the invisible Medicine force and stimulate the powers of the Soul Consciousness needed for a true recovery.

The only cases in which a large number of plant ceremonies in a row is needed is when a physical ailment is extremely serious and requires intense work and follow-up. Also, in certain instances curses that have been well engineered will grow back in a client like weeds unless the shaman performs a number of ceremonies one after the other to track the curse to its very roots.

In what I consider the best-case scenario, beginners should participate in a few sessions during a one- or two-week period of time and then go home. These initial ceremonies can be enormously awakening, providing first-timers with self-knowledge, both positive and negative, that their Suffering Consciousness has blocked from their awareness all their lives.

These realizations will remain emblazoned in clients' minds

for years to come. So the next time they take the brew, they start where they left off, using their insights from the previous ceremonies as a tool to dig even deeper into their hearts and minds. For clients participating in a second series of Ayahuasca sessions, it is like reading a book twice. The second time readers absorb information they missed in the first reading. The same is then true for a possible third reading, and a fourth.

As to the question of number of trips over time, I suggest that clients take one round of sacred plant mixtures once a year or every two years. Each round consists of two to four ceremonies with several days in between each session for rest and recreation. To say it again, beware of participating in too many ceremonies in too short a time. In certain cases, as mentioned, a serious diagnosis may require a number of ceremonies back-to-back. Otherwise, at least in my experience, three or four ceremonies per visit get the job done.

Finally, it should be said that some clients are content with what they learn in their first round of ceremonies and feel no need to ever take the brew again. Others want to make that trip to the jungle as often as possible. But as said, please do be careful of any shaman who has you taking two or three ceremonies a week for months on end. This way lies dependence and eventually disillusionment.

WHAT SHOULD THE RELATIONSHIP BETWEEN PLANTS AND HUMANS BE?

When we work with sacred plants, we are obliged to relate to them with humility and trust. In shamanic terms sacred plants are considered to be above our level of being, and we must treat them that way, the way we might treat an illustrious teacher or the ruler of a kingdom, which in a sense they are.

When you pay the plants homage in this way, they are happy to return the respect by bathing you in their Medicine, though in an experiential rather than analytical way. By this I mean that if a plant is releasing you from years of anxiety or calming the chaos of your Suffering Consciousness, it will not explain the logistics of how it gets the job done. You will just feel better. The plant lets you know what it is doing by doing it. It is the same when you meet a musician and ask what kind of music she plays. Instead of offering an explanation, she picks up her instrument and plays it for you.

The relationship between plants and people should, therefore, be one of gratitude on the part of the client and the joy of healing from the plant. This mutual kinship is one reason why it is healthy to have plants, trees, and bushes growing close to where you live—in your garden, around your house. You should cultivate these plants not only because of their beauty but because you are living in the force field of their Medicine. In certain areas of traditional Peru, when people need answers to life questions, they sleep near a certain tree or bush known for its wisdom, believing that the answer to their questions will be sent to them in a dream. We will talk a good deal more on this subject in the final chapter.

BEAUTY IS IN THE DOING, NOT THE SEEING

Once upon a time my teacher took me on a long journey in the northern mountain jungle. We searched for interesting plants, known and unknown. He taught me to read signs and secret markings in the landscape that an untrained eye might miss. We visited a number of powerful spiritual healers, both young and old.

One day we were pushing through a mass of thick brush when he stopped abruptly and pointed to a large plant, telling me it was used in a healing recipe that had been passed down to him from his lineage. I had seen this plant selling in the herbal kiosks of marketplaces, but I had never found it growing in the wilds. Appearance-wise, it had spikes and pointy, spiny leaves jutting out that made it look like a weird pineapple. I was also struck by its barbed and aggressive appearance, which seemed, I thought, like it was looking for a fight. When my teacher told me it was an important plant, I was not particularly anxious to learn more about it. I remember thinking that such a grotesque growth could never be of much use to anyone. Being a beginner, I believed that only shiny leaves and neatly woven vines made effective healers.

Several days later I participated in a ceremony in which my teacher served a medicine that included the same prickly cluster. Partway through the night he began singing an *icaro*, inviting a visit from the members of his Healing Family. Immediately plant spirits manifested from all directions, some of them dancing and singing, some approaching silently. Frequently they came close, caressing me with their foliage and fragrance. Several took the form of a quasi–human being, including the spiky plant I had dismissed several days before. In its spirit appearance it had a body but no face, and just like in the landscape, it was covered with pointy leaves and prickles.

As before, I was squeamish about its appearance and became unsettled when she approached me, pushing herself into my arms for a hug. I say "herself" because the moment the plant came near, a wave of feminine energy engulfed me, and my heart lit up the way it does when touching one's beloved. Whispering in my ear, she asked, "Will you love me the way I look, the way I'm made, the way I am? Will you accept me as I am in your Healing Family?"

Immediately a bond of deep affection crystalized between us. I told her, yes, yes, of course, for sure! We hugged more, and the longer we nestled the more I smelled a particular fragrance and tasted a flavor in my mouth that was entirely different from the taste of the night's ceremonial brew. Later I understood that the plant was fusing its humors into my senses so that I would always recognize it, knowing that sensory experience runs deeper than intellectual memory. When I needed it, I had only to recall this taste and smell and the spirit of the plant would come to my aid.

From this time on the plant became one of my major helpers and one of my closest friends. From then on whenever I met an ugly or malformed plant I thought of my spiky friend and of a shamanic saying that tells us, "Do not judge a plant by its face but by its heart."

Shortly after this episode I recalled what happened to me the night I spent near the Swamp of the Dead several years earlier (see Chapter 2). As you will recall, a hairy redheaded female spirit sought a lover's connection with me, which I refused. In response she held me in her arms and gave me love.

The episodes of meeting the spiky plant and the redheaded spirit were somehow connected, I thought, both telling of a being who offered me her affections and, even though I declined, ended up nourishing my spirit. It reminded me of yet another story a friend from the Amazon once told me. While performing a Dieta or secluded fast (much more on this in the next chapter), my friend was visited by three frightful-looking vegetable spirits with green eyes and green teeth. It turned out they were siblings, and one of them, a boy, sent his sisters to hug my friend. He tried to avoid their embrace and failed. But through the contact they forced on him he felt their healing powers enter his body and rid him of longtime psychological hang-ups. Again, the moral: Trust your heart and not your eyes.

CHAPTER 7

ABOUT THE SACRED

PLANT CEREMONY

Answering the Important Questions

Inexperienced journeyers ordinarily have many questions concerning their upcoming ceremony. They ask whether they will vomit or have diarrhea. They want to know how long the ceremony lasts, and to what extent their senses will be expanded. They are interested to know what they will see and learn in these few psychoactive hours. And much more.

In this chapter I offer a comprehensive description of the different aspects of a sacred plant ritual, answering often-asked questions both for seekers interested in taking part in a ceremony and for those who are simply curious to know how it all works.

In traditional societies where shamanism has long been part of villagers ethnology, awareness of plant magic is deeply embedded in their consciousness. This awareness is common in Asia, Africa, the Middle East, and especially in Amazonian countries where shamanism and Ayahuasca are considered national treasures. Even if indigenous people show no interest in healing ceremonies per se, most have a built-in respect for the tradition and for the shamans who practice it.

Up to the modern era, before science banished plant Medicine to the realm of fable, understanding the power of plants and shamanic ceremonies was shared by a majority of the human family. What follows will, I hope, confute the notion that plant Medicine is quackery, and will help return herbal healing to its rightful place as a major spiritual resource for our time. What follows will also provide a detailed outline of how a sacred ceremony unfolds from the moment a *curandero* builds a psychic shield around his clients to the lingering moments when the plant's intoxicating effects wear off and participants return to earth to ponder all they have seen.

How Many People Take Part in a Ceremony?

For Priest shamans hosting village gatherings, large crowds are encouraged and even necessary. Often the entire town takes part in the session with singing, dancing, laughter, and bustle, always with an emphasis on good-natured kinship. A party spirit underlies the goings-on, and villagers drink a brew that is mild enough to be given to children. Little or no one-on-one work takes place between shaman and participants, and personal problems are addressed in a surface way if they are addressed at all.

A Warrior shaman ceremony is a different kind of party, as we have seen. Ceremonies run by Warrior shamans like myself are a good deal smaller, less social, quieter, and more spirit oriented, with an emphasis on mental and emotional catharsis and on the mysteries of the redemptive process.

Establishing the Shaman-Client
Relationship before the Ceremony Begins

Several days before a Warrior ceremony begins, a shaman will, or at least should, spend time getting to know his clients. If vigilant, he wants his clients to approach a ritual slowly and mindfully, especially those he has never met before and who do not understand how intense a plant ceremony can be. Now is the time to explain to first-timers how aspects of the ceremony unfold and what to expect at different stages of the evening. Needless to say, the medicine person cannot be overly specific in these descriptions, as each person's experience will be unique. Nonetheless, certain basics prevail. Educated clients are good clients, and it is important that they be at least somewhat prepared for the whirlwind they are about to step into.

I also explain to clients that from the moment they arrive at my compound in the Amazon my Healing Family is watching them and will continue to do so over the next few days before the first ceremony begins. In order for the ritual to function at its best, it is essential that the medicine person carefully assess participants ahead of time, both through dialogue and by means of intuitive perceptions concerning clients' present state of mind, information about their health, and, most importantly, their hopes and goals. Before the ceremony begins, the healer may receive messages or sudden understandings about what remedial assistance certain clients will need when the night arrives. The exchange that takes place between shaman and clients during the few days before the ceremony can, if done properly, substantially enhance a client's ability to profit from the upcoming sessions.

Traditionally, there are five ways in which a *curandero* forges an alliance between himself and a client before the first ceremony. First there are one or more direct interviews. Second, observation.

Third, touch diagnosis. Fourth, group activities. Fifth, diet and physical preparation.

ONE-ON-ONE INTERVIEWS

Shaman and client usually have one or more personal interviews before a ceremony takes place, some of which may last several hours. The interviews are not only about clients' past traumas but about their goals and fears as well. By making eye contact, breaking it, and/or looking away from the client several times during these conversations, psychic responses are transmitted to the shaman that expand on what is being communicated through verbal dialogue. When these conversations go well, the *curandero* assimilates enormous amounts of information about a client's identity, and so is ready to meet his or her needs head-on when the ceremony begins.

OBSERVATION

Rather than having a formal dialogue, a shaman sometimes suggests that he and the client hang out together for an afternoon or even for several days, avoiding any discussion about the client's problems or about the healing process to come. The shaman may ask the client to walk with him on a jungle trail, sit next to him during meals, help out in the fields or in the kitchen. Keying on the client's body language and behavior, a *curandero* in spiritual listening mode absorbs many meaningful insights. Because clients and shaman are watched by the spirits before a ceremony begins, the medicine person may also be sent dreams about the needs of clients or how best to finesse their fixations or addictions.

TOUCH DIAGNOSIS

As I have said several times, the traditional healing technique of laying on hands is one of the most powerful ways I know to establish a deep personal connection with a fellow human being. In the hour or so that a hands-on session takes place, the shaman keeps his eyes closed and his psychic ears open. The information he absorbs from touching a client's body proves extremely useful for tailoring a healing approach in the upcoming ceremony. Touch is the information-gathering technique I like best. Using it, I can absorb important internal material that often goes unmentioned or unnoticed during interviews, or which, for whatever reasons, the client intentionally hides.

GROUP ACTIVITIES

Since most people attend ceremonies as part of a group, activities like swimming together in a stream, hunting for different species of plants in the forest, sharing a group walk, picking food and feasting on it at the dinner table, boating on the Amazon, or really, any friendly and cohesive group activity, provide important information to a shaman on clients' social and interpersonal habits.

DIET AND PREPARATION

Several days before a ceremony begins, clients are discouraged from eating spicy or irritating foods. If this regime is not followed carefully, the plant spirits will be unhappy and the ceremony may be ineffectual for offenders. Sex and masturbation are also avoided for some days before the ritual, as well as violent arguments or even intense discussions with others. Better to stay inward.

The process of psychological purging is related to water, and the consumption of cool, liquid-based foods is encouraged in the days before a ceremony. Fiery foods, meanwhile, are avoided. This means that several days before the ceremony, red meat, chiles, coffee, fried or barbecued vegetables, alcohol, and anything cooked in heavy oil or grease are forbidden. In some lineages, pork and poultry are a no-no as well.

The day of the ceremony a light meal is eaten around midday, allowing a number of hours for a client's stomach to empty before the night's adventure begins.

After lunch I encourage clients to sleep, relax, meditate, and prepare themselves for the coming hours in the way monks and priestesses prepare themselves for a night's devotions. I do the same, meditating, praying, then sleeping for several hours so I am fresh for the evening. I also ask clients to drink as little water as possible after lunch so that their empty stomachs allow the brew to work quickly and to do its job with little interference from digestive juices and enzymes.

Choosing the Monthly Date
of the Ceremony

During the day the sun's energy prevails. At night the moon and the stars set the rules. For this reason, when a sacred ritual is meant to help a client reach a particular goal, the date of the ceremony is aligned with lunar phases to make the ceremony more effective.

Imagine, for example, that a woman wants to overcome her fear of cats. If her shaman accomplishes this feat, she will obviously never want the fear to return. She has no desire to go home after the ceremony feeling free of her phobia and a week later scream when a kitten crosses her path. She wants her cure to be permanent.

This is where the moon comes in. By arranging the date of the woman's ceremony to take place under a full moon, the work a shaman does to banish her phobia lasts forever. It can never come back. (Recall the story in Chapter 5 of inhaling moon powder and how the moon acts as a glue, fixing things and making them permanent.) This is why lovers swear their oaths beneath a full moon; they want their promises to last till death do they part. They want their love to be eternal. At the same time, the Suffering Consciousness likes to push its own lunar agenda, which is why sorcerers and witches also use the full moon for their work. Full moon energy gives permanency to amulets and curses, making it especially difficult for an opposing shaman to neutralize them.

On the other end of the lunar cycle, the dim light that shines from a crescent moon has the power to accelerate and make things grow. When native people need to trim their hair but want it to grow back in a few days, they do so during a crescent moon. The same with planting a seed—the crescent moon helps the seed quickly bloom. However, just as the crescent moon speeds things up, a waning moon slows them down. This slowing tendency can be helpful for farmers, say, who grow plants that fruit early. The plants will normally spoil by the time they reach the mercado. But with the help of a waning moon, time is stretched and the plants ripen more slowly, arriving in the marketplace just in time for sale.

Finally, there is the day of the new moon (Peruvians call it the "green moon") that lasts for approximately twenty-four hours. This brief period of total lunar darkness is considered a time for renewal but not for beginning any new activity. If people in my nearby village need wood for construction, they never harvest it during a dark moon. Nor do they plant fruits and vegetables. In fact, they do not begin anything new at all at this time, knowing that whatever project is started during the twenty-four-hour period of the dark moon will be plagued by bad luck. The new moon is the time for recharging but not for creation.

The Best Time of Day for a Ceremony

All shamanic lineages and disciplines follow their own spiritual protocols, most of which are different. The ideal time for a ceremony is one of these differences.

In my own practice I prefer to begin a session three or four hours after sunset, say at 10 or 11 p.m., when no trace of light remains in the sky. Darkness is the time when the eyes are the least important of the senses, encouraging clients to turn inward, where the journey of the spirit demands full attention. The absence of light also discourages clients from talking to one another in the circle or looking around randomly during a ceremony.

A plant session normally runs from four to five hours and occasionally longer. As the night matures, at some point I feel that everyone in the group has received what they came for and I close the gathering *unless* a serious last-minute problem pops up, obliging me to work until the trouble is resolved.

For seasoned clients who feel a calling to participate in shamanism as a lifetime venture, plant ceremonies often start later at night, usually around 3 a.m. This means they are still in a psychoactive trance when the first light of day appears. If properly trained, clients can then draw in the rays of morning light to amplify their Soul Consciousness, boosting their ability to see beyond even the normal psychoactive levels of discernment. This technique usually takes years to learn.

At one point in an advanced client's career, ceremonies move from inside to outside, featuring walkabouts in nature. After imbibing the sacred brew, shamans lead their flock through a landscape with eyes open, encouraging clients to see the true shape and contours of the physical world. Being accustomed to looking at their environment in a "realistic" way, clients may be shocked and even dumbfounded by the altered shape of the physical world when seen through psychoactive eyes. They suddenly learn that the world has dimensions, sounds, colors, forms, and portals into the unknown they never dreamed possible. A walkabout can be done during the day or at night under a full moon. Some people doing a walkabout see spirits circulating around them, making them aware that though they cannot see the invisible world in their ordinary life, it is always just an inch above their heads.

The difference between a novice and one who is ready to do a walkabout is based on what I call "internal placement," which is the ability to transport oneself at will out of Suffering Consciousness and into Soul Consciousness.

This difficult feat can be accomplished only after seekers have learned to identify the workings of Suffering Consciousness in their daily behavior and have spent a number of ceremonies emptying their minds of psychological trash, making enduring efforts to live by the voice of their conscience. Reaching this point, they sometimes (not always) earn a permanent place (or "placement") in Soul Consciousness. Anchored in this way, advanced clients perceive hidden parts of the sensory world *and* of the spirit realm on a daily basis, worlds that are normally seen only by trained masters. The degree to which clients learn to perform inner placement as a path to spiritual knowledge is an excellent way of accessing the teaching skills of the shaman they work with.

Dressing for a Ceremony

I ask clients to wear clothes that hang loosely and are nonrestrictive. There is no hard-and-fast rule about color or style, though bright yellows and whites help prevent people from bumping into one another in the dark. There are some clients who claim that white clothes bring happy ceremonies and black clothes bring dark, but I have seen no evidence to support this idea.

Clients are also wise to bring a handkerchief to a ceremony for cleaning their nose and mouth, as fluids do drip. Also, a flashlight—that's important. Clients need it when making their way to the toilet or when searching in the dark for their backpack or flip-flops. At times ceremonies are done out-of-doors at night with cactuses and rocks littering the ground, which if stepped on will quickly ruin a client's evening. In such situations boots or shoes are mandatory. I also suggest that participants bring a blanket or pullover. Even on warm jungle nights they may experience a release of negative energy long kept under lock and key, causing them to shiver and feel icy cold. In such cases it is good to be covered. Many veterans of plant ceremonies bring sleeping bags as well.

In some ceremonies clients wear unconventional outfits (uniforms, tribal costume, indigenous Peruvian attire) to attract cultural energies or to invoke their ancestral identity. They may also feel the urge to clothe themselves in a dress or a suit and tie. They do this as a form of respect, like putting on their best evening wear for a marriage or celebration. I am very respectful of people who wear clothes that inspire them or bestow dignity in this way, and I normally encourage it.

Yet, though dressing in special attire can be helpful in certain situations and for certain people, for myself I feel that once again the practice of minimalism is best, bringing attention to the invisible rather than physical world. During a ceremony I wear only what is comfortable and what keeps me warm, such as workman's clothes, vest, boots or sandals. In the end, with the exceptions mentioned concerning walkabouts, what is seen during a ceremony with the eyes of the Soul Consciousness makes outer appearances irrelevant.

Creating the Healing Space

On the night of a ceremony clients take their position in the ring, sitting silently in the dark for some minutes before the brew is served. During this period of quiet, I transform the circle into a sacred space. If we are in the prairie, say, or on the skirt of a mountain, the shamanic circle is drawn on the ground. More commonly, it is outlined in a *maloca* or in a round enclosure specially built for hosting ceremonies.

Working from the center outward, singing and chanting prayers, I blow mapacho tobacco smoke in certain patterns to establish the circle's perimeters. While preparing the area, I ask for guidance from my Healing Family, from the Great Spirit, and from the location itself, which during a ceremony becomes a power center. I then construct an invisible dome over the circle and over the clients sitting inside it. It is like building an architectural monument, a magic cathedral in the air where everything that happens inside is dedicated to healing.

Like a material structure, the dome has six dimensions— north, south, east, west, plus up and down—assuring that all principal directions are included. The dome structure cannot be seen, but it can be sensed because it is alive, radiating an aura that is protective and regenerative. On many occasions, clients tell me they feel a strong vibrational difference between sitting in a circle covered with a dome or when standing several feet outside the same circle.

When constructing a ceremonial space, I always include a toilet inside the perimeter so that if clients want to urinate or are having diarrhea, they do not need to leave the sacred precincts to empty themselves. Of great importance, I tell clients, is that when they are finished using the facilities, they must immediately return to the circle. Occasionally participants linger on the commode for so long I have to fetch them. Because of the trance-inducing power of the medicine, they lose themselves in a mind trip while on the toilet and entirely forget where they are.

Like the positive and minus sides of a magnet, the ceremonial space attracts the healing entities I work with and repels the forces of evil. During a session a client's subconscious is wide open and vulnerable to psychic attack. The dome I construct assures that they are safe, and that what happens inside the circle is for medicinal purposes only. In a properly constructed power spot, even the particles in the atmosphere are charged with therapeutic and protective energy; nothing can go wrong.

The same is true for threats from wild beasts. Sometimes we work outdoors in an open area where predatory animals prowl nearby: jaguars, ocelots, snakes. One can hear these creatures moving about in the darkness outside the circle, but none of them can breach its circumference. Even deadly crawlies like spiders and scorpions instinctively stay out of the circle or remain passive if inside. In all my years as a shaman, none of my clients has ever been bitten by a poisonous insect or snake. A shamanic circle is both a hospital and a walled garden.

I remember one starry night I was working with several clients on a wild beach in northern Peru. After setting up our tents, I constructed a protective domed circle, and we drank the elixir. It was a hardworking session, and after a number of hours we went to rest in our tents.

Next morning when I woke up, I was surprised to see a ring of pawprints circling our camp left by a pack of wild dogs. The dogs had been wandering in our area and obviously smelled the biscuits and snacks we kept stored in our tents. Studying the prints, I could see they had circled the perimeter a number of times, but, hungry as they may have been, they were unwilling or perhaps unable to cross the protective circle. I took photographs of the prints, which I still have today.

Sacralizing a ceremonial circle is one of the most important functions a shaman can perform. The magic circle must be looked on as a portal opening into the sphere of the sacred. It is, *curanderos* in training are told, holy ground. If they do not master this skill from the beginning, they will most likely have difficulty mastering any other shamanic art as well.

Important Things to Know and Do When the Ceremony Begins

When the ceremony begins, I encourage clients to sit as straight as possible. As the night wears on, they can then lie on their back or side as long as they allow several feet between themselves and the people next to them.

The emphasis on maintaining a straight back during a spiritual event is found in devotional schools throughout the world. It keeps the mind clear and encourages Life Force to move freely up and down the spine and to circulate in energy channels throughout the body. Keeping the back straight is also a natural reflex when discussing an important social matter or while sitting with people of consequence. When facing moments of importance, we have a natural impulse to sit or stand up straight. As the tree of life is the bridge between earth and heaven, so the spine acts as an energy conduit from the bottom of the body to the top.

In a plant ceremony it is common (and strongly encouraged) for people to vomit, and a special container is provided for the purpose. If working in the wilderness, clients dig a hole near where they are sitting. During a ceremony a person with loose bowels may race to the toilet a number of times in one night. This is unpleasant, needless to say, but in fact both vomiting and diarrhea are plant-induced and are designed to clean out harmful psychic wastes. A good deal more about physical purging is discussed below.

Where to Sit in the Circle

Shamanic work is almost always done in a circle with clients spaced evenly around the circumference. In some lineages the *curandero* positions himself on a raised platform or in the center of the circle. In our tradition he sits in the ring along with the rest of the group. Within the sacred space clients are advised to sit approximately three or four feet apart from one another and farther if there are only a few participants. Clients have access to water during the night but are advised to be sparing of it, just gargling or taking tiny sips to clean their mouths.

During the evening disagreeable odors waft up—urine, sweat, gas, bad breath, vomit, feces. If clients huddle too close to one another, the smells can be overwhelming. Meanwhile, on an unseen level there are psychic energies spiraling around each person that belong to that person alone. If clients are packed too tightly together, as they sometimes are in commercial Ayahuasca compounds, the curative auras belonging to one client merge with those of another, causing an adulteration of healing energy for both.

When I see that clients are extraordinarily nervous or fearful, or when they have a painful physical problem, I position them near me in the ring. If I sense a client is brimming with harsh emotions, I also seat them close by me, knowing I will be "operating" on them throughout the evening. For clients who are dubious or reluctant, I tell them beforehand that if they simply accept and embrace whatever is happening, be it painful or confusing, their fears will fall away and a new world will open before them.

৵

In the days before a ceremony, I frequently notice that friends, partners, or family members have a strong bond between them. I make certain that these people are seated on opposite sides of the circle or at least a good distance away from one another. During a ceremony, clients experience all types of emotional anguish. If the friend of a person is having a hard time and is seated nearby, chances are the friend will reach out to give a hug or hold hands. But this is a mistake. Many clients, especially first-timers, do not understand that each person is obliged to undergo the healing session in their own private capsule, processing the effects of the Medicine without help from anyone but the shaman. Touching others or otherwise disturbing their concentration at a critical moment can break the spell, like waking a person from a meaningful dream. The fact is, each member of the group must make their journey alone and face their demons alone.

Also important to know is that a client who appears to be suffering may not be suffering at all. What looks like agony may actually be ecstasy. Even if clients are in genuine distress, strife is a necessary part of their therapy and must be allowed to play out without interruption. At times people feel overwhelmed, it is true, but this is just one phase of their healing process and soon passes. Best not to interfere with it. Time is short and precious in a ceremony and should be spent only on inner work. I cannot tell you how often at the end of a session clients who seemed to be losing their mind an hour earlier tell me what a fantastic plunge into the other world they have just taken, and how the opportunity to weep and thrash about was a cure in itself.

In some ceremonies it occasionally turns out that a client happens to have psychic abilities. During the night's goings-on this person may clearly see the problems troubling other clients and feel the urge to fix them. In the days before a ceremony begins, when I see that a client has extrasensory powers, I ask them to *please* not interfere with anyone's struggle, and to leave the process of healing to the plants and to me. I explain that a shamanic ceremony has dozens of moving parts, some apparent, some concealed, all of which make up a fragile but balanced psychic ecosystem. To tinker with this balance, no matter how perceptive or well-meaning the effort may be, can throw the system out of equilibrium and ruin the night for everyone.

Talking during a Ceremony

Though speaking is not forbidden during a session, I discourage it. If a client must speak, it should be to the shaman, rarely to another group member, and always in whispered tones. The truth is, no matter how quietly a person talks, others in the circle will hear it and be distracted. I tell people that due to the kindness of the plants, whatever difficulty they face during a ritual, and however provoking their inner struggle may be, they will almost always have the capacity to overcome their struggle without verbally asking for help from others. I say "verbally" because asking the shaman for help on a telepathic level is acceptable and even recommended.

The above advice, by the way, is usually unnecessary, as clients naturally turn inward during a session and have neither the need nor the desire to speak with others. What is going on inside them is conversation enough.

Activation of the Medicine

Before offering the brew to clients in a ceremony the elixir must first be activated and energized. Sacred plants can and will work alone, of course, at least to some extent. But when a shaman activates them, it makes their power to heal a great deal more effective. When performing this activation, a silent connection is formed between the *curandero* and the Force of Life. This connection animates the shaman's inner Medicine, turning it on for the night and connecting him with the spirits. The actual method for activating sacred plants is a secret method handed down by master to student and is an intimate and exclusive part of each lineage.

Drinking the Sacred Brew

At the beginning of an Ayahuasca session I drink the brew first, a tradition that has come down through the ages based, it is believed, on showing group members that the liquid is not poisoned. I have heard that in some shamanic practices, clients are encouraged to drink a cup of brew two or even three times in one evening. In my experience one cup properly prepared is all that is needed.

Moving clockwise around the circle, I kneel in front of each client, sometimes touching their head or shoulders. I ask the forces of my Healing Family to keep them safe and to teach them what they need to know. I then hand them the cup of brew that contains two or three fingers' width of liquid and stay with them until they drink it down. I have used the same wooden cup for holding the brew since I first began my training in the 1990s.

When attending to each client I sometimes rub natural perfume on their hands so that the agreeable scent distracts them from the bitterness of the medicine. In some shamanic centers, clients are encouraged to take a flower bath a few hours before the ceremony begins in order to be fragrant for the spirits.

After I have served the drink, there is a ten- or fifteen-minute silent time. Clients assume we are waiting for the medicine to kick in. Actually, during this silence I am entering the spirit world and consolidating my healing resources in preparation for the evening ahead.

A strange fact about a sacred plant mixture is that the same brew tastes different to each user. Some find it astringent or vinegary, others think it mild or sweet. The brew may also taste different for the same person on different nights. Ironically, I find that the clients who complain most about the brew being foul-tasting and undrinkable tend to be the ones who have the most uplifting experience. I do not begin to understand why this is true, but I have observed it many times. To remind you of the shamanic saying mentioned earlier: "Bitter medicine is the best medicine."

After a few minutes sitting in silence, I start singing sacred songs or playing a percussion instrument like a drum or a rattle. When they hear the music, most clients feel psychic ripples of energy starting to move inside them. These sacred sounds act as a catalyst to stimulate healing forces and to invite the spirits into the circle. Sometimes gradually, sometimes in a flash, the gate of each person's mind swings open, and the night begins in earnest.

Avoid Leaving the Sacred Circle

Once inside the circle clients are obliged to remain in place for the entire session. Seating themselves beneath the sacred dome is equivalent to signing a contract with the spirits, assuring that they will remain in the ring from the beginning of the ritual to the end. With so many spirits at work during a ceremony, it is discourteous, both to the spirits and to the shaman, to stroll out of the ring on a whim.

This rule of conduct, by the way, does not apply to Priest shamans. Participants in Priest shaman ceremonies are allowed to enter and leave the circle as they please, to wander outside the *maloca*, to dance, sing, play a guitar or drum, smoke a cigarette, talk and joke with one another as if they were standing on a street corner.

In a Warrior shaman ceremony, allowing people to straggle in and out of the circle can be hazardous. When a client leaves the ring without reason, a crack is opened between this world and the spirit world. It is like turning on a bright light and saying to the universe, "Hey, look, here's an innocent taking Ayahuasca and standing outside the circle." Such events attract attention, sometimes from psychic predators. This is one reason why we speak of the sacred dome as being protective. When clients wander in and out of it haphazardly, they do so at their own peril.

Important too is that every person who sits inside the circle must drink the brew. No "sober" outsiders are allowed in. Some people think a shamanic ceremony is a kind of show or exhibition, but with Warrior shamanism (as opposed to Priest shamanism), this is far from the case. An outsider's worldly thoughts, like static on the radio, can interfere with clients' visions, causing distraction and confusion. In my own work I never allow strangers to observe a ceremony.

At times, clients with weak health are brought by a companion who watches over them during a session. Before the ceremony begins, I tell the companion that if they enter the circle, they must take the medicine along with everyone else. It is interesting to see how often these chaperones, usually people who have little interest in mystical matters and are only doing their duty for a friend, end up having the most otherworldly experience of anyone in the group.

While seated in the circle clients often appear in my visions to be secluded in a psychic cubicle or kiosk. The interior of each cubicle is decorated with illustrations, patterns, and designs psychically drawn by, and unique to, the person inside. This often beautifully rendered art depicts memories and emotional moments, but also psychological concerns that are bothering clients at this stage of their lives. Images of a client's strong points tend to appear on the right side of the cubicle, images of their weaknesses on the left. I do not know the reason for this dichotomy, though right equaling positive and left equaling negative is a notion found throughout the world.

I have also noted through the years that when the interior or personal cubicles are decorated with colorless right-angle designs, this often indicates that a client's thinking is built on rationalism and logic. A kiosk with bright colors and curved forms shows a more intuitive personality with a feeling-based view of reality. Cubicles with different art or architectural drawings that are incongruously juxtaposed often suggest that clients have not committed to a single teaching. They may be searching for a path and have partially committed to certain traditions but are still seeking a spiritual discipline that fully suits their temperament.

The Shaman's Ceremonial Dance

In some ceremonies a *curandero* abruptly stands up, enters the center of the circle, and performs a turning, dervish-like dance with elaborate footwork, projecting Medicine and prosperity to everyone in the ring.

When this takes place, clients are asked to keep their eyes closed and to envision the scene telepathically. Those who do keep their eyes open, despite missing the full value of the dance, nonetheless see a remarkable sight: the shaman may leap enormously high in the air or turn at incredible speeds. Occasionally clients see multiple versions of the shaman, as if a group circle dance is taking place with the shaman as every dancer. While the *curandero* gyrates, he sings sacred songs to keep the Medicine active, sometimes using his rattles to maintain a steady rhythm. This dance is actually a form of sacrifice, as the shaman gives up some of his psychic energy to clients, asking the spirits to grant them mercy through his leaps and play.

At other times an intense night's ceremony produces such good results that at the end of the session the shaman seals the event by spontaneously leaping up and jigging in the center of the ring as an act of lighthearted thanksgiving. Clients may also be asked to stand up and make little jumps, their dance bringing blessings from the spirit world and helping them leave the ceremony feeling assured of a better future.

Purging during a Ceremony: Water, Air, and Fire

Three types of self-purging occur during a ceremony: purging with water, air, and fire. Let's begin with water.

The vegetable kingdom is a water kingdom, and water purges both mind and body.

As we have witnessed, during a ceremony spirit fountains sometimes appear in the center of the circle spraying jets of colorful water over clients along with a healing plasma. Clients may be invited to submerge in a spirit pond in the center of the ring, or to stand under a psychic waterfall where years of pain are washed away in a moment. Water also plays a part when noxious fluids are flushed out in saliva, vomit, mucus, tears, feces, urine, and sweat. And since no part of a sacred ceremony is without meaning, each type of water-based excretion has its own psychological purpose. For instance, when crying during a ceremony, tears relieve stored-up grief. Nasal snorting blows out anger. Intense sweating relieves psychological pressure at home, at work, in a relationship. Salivation and spitting represent ideas clients have always wanted to express but were too afraid to do so.

Of all water-based expulsions, the two most significant are vomiting and diarrhea.

Vomiting is nature's way of ridding a client of moral sicknesses built up during their lifetime by Suffering Consciousness. Regurgitation or vomiting, ordinarily thought of as repulsive, in the context of *curanderismo* is looked on as a precious cleansing, healing, and even sacred act. One shaman I know of is quoted as saying that to him the vomiting of his clients is not ugly or unpleasant at all but rather like music.

Though the urge to vomit usually begins a few minutes after ingesting the brew, I ask clients to keep it down as long as possible and to breathe deeply for ten or twenty minutes. The early need to regurgitate is often due to the unpalatable taste of a brew. If a client waits and then vomits when the ceremony has gone on for some time, the cleansing will be a good deal more thorough.

The fact that vomit spews out of the mouth means, according to shamanic thinking, that users are intended to *see* this excreted matter and to realize it symbolizes the expulsion of wrongs done in the past or difficult situations that a user has had to swallow. Dishonesty, greed, cruelty, hatreds are all regurgitated before their eyes, providing a graphic image of darknesses they have harbored for years; hostile behavior they could have altered but did not due to self-involvement or lack of concern. The fact that these wrongs pass in front of the eyes cautions users that they should make all attempts to not allow these misdeeds to occur again.

The natural reflex to physically expel dark energy is the same impulse in ordinary life that makes people experience nausea when they feel ashamed or disgusted by what they have done. The shamanic ethic sees transgressions as a kind of spoiled food that has rotted in a client's system for some time and is now being disgorged.

Purging oneself by means of diarrhea, meanwhile, is another form of water cleansing and is generally triggered by four causes. There are more, but the following are the most important.

The first is due to negative behaviors clients are unaware of and/or to psychological flaws they may never have seen in themselves due to lack of self-awareness.

I remember the case of a sweet but unmindful lady who performed several ceremonies in order to calm her anxiety. During each ceremony she experienced a massive cleansing, expelling heavily watered diarrhea. At the same time, she had few visions and no significant emotional breakthroughs, an example of a person who had received no training in self-observation, living her life on automatic pilot with little connection to her inner life. After finishing the ceremonies, she experienced a sense of peace and decompression. But though she was given what she had come for, she remained unaware of how the conditions in her life had produced the anxiety in the first place. She never knew what she was purging, or why, and in this sense her temperament but not her spirit was helped.

The second cause of diarrhea is due to experiences that happen to clients in early childhood and which they have long forgotten.

The most common of these are frights, assaults, and brushes with danger, real or imagined. When these clients undergo diarrhea, they rid themselves of unremembered but harsh sufferings from their innocent past.

The third cause of diarrhea is related to a client's generational heritage; that is, to negative personality traits that are inherited through their bloodline. Even if clients are aware of these generational flaws within them, their family chain is so long it is impossible to fully know where and when the trouble began. All that can be done is to ceremonially void it.

The fourth and final cause of diarrhea are spells and psychic attacks that victims never saw coming and know nothing about. During a ceremony diarrhea flushes them all out.

I remember the case of a client who was highly educated and knowledgeable in many areas but was morally corrupt, always ready to take advantage of other people's weaknesses and more than willing to practice fraud in the name of profit. He rationalized his behavior by styling himself as being "smart selfish."

Early in the ceremony this man was urgently called to the toilet and while defecating saw smiling little demons pouring from his rear and dancing in his stool. Realizing that the demons were personifications of his bad ways, he freaked out at the sight of them to such an extent that he was forced to accept that his behavior was disreputable, and that his life had been built on diabolic self-centeredness. In a word, the cleansing defecation woke up his conscience.

I had the happy fortune to see this man many times after the ceremony, and at each meeting he told me how the purging inspired him to seek self-knowledge and how it helped him make a 180-degree benevolent turn when dealing with the world. Messages from the spirit realm in a ceremony are sometimes harsh and crude, but they are always for a person's good.

✹

While water purging cleans out emotional and physical flaws, air purging works through the mind, ridding a client of contrary thoughts, ideas, and beliefs.

Purging by air can be subtle or it can be violent. Clients may blow out noxious traits by means of hyperventilation, yelling, snorting, crying, whistling, gasping, burping, sighing, hissing, farting, sneezing, coughing, even barking or making bird-like screeches. When bad energies are released in this way, shamans sometimes see smoke coming out of a client's nose and mouth.

I remember working with a tough, self-made man who had achieved a great deal of business success using his will and grit. The man's self-discipline had made him strong but also hard and sometimes unprincipled. He had received many emotional wounds in his personal life, but exposing these hurts to others went against his cherished need to dominate and his unwillingness to show his true feelings.

The night of his ceremony four people were in the circle, none of whom knew each other. Halfway through the evening the man began making a strange *pssst* noise and swishing his hand across his face as if trying to swat away a fly. He waved his hand in this way for so long it started to annoy other people in the circle, and several asked him to be still. What the other clients did not understand was that these movements were the man's attempt to dam up a mighty river of trauma inside him. After several minutes of hand swishing, the dam suddenly burst despite his efforts, and the man began wailing and weeping, getting down on his hands and knees like a child and literally baying up to the sky, in the process ridding himself of years of pain and guilt.

The day after the ceremony the man confided in me that he was having heart problems and that he thought, and I agreed, that his attempts to stifle his emotions had been making the condition worse. His coronary problems became minimal over the following year, I learned, and I cannot help but think the improvement was linked to his release of pain and remorse during his ceremonial episode.

Finally, in terms of air it is not uncommon during a ceremony for a shaman to yawn and sigh. These in-breaths and out-breaths have nothing to do with fatigue but are a way of sending healing energy to members of the group. Usually, the yawning lasts for only a few minutes, but it can be extremely remedial for clients, even if they have no notion of its true purpose.

ﭼ

Besides water and air purging, fire Medicine is also used for purification, but in a different way.

Water washes away. It cleans, unclogs, opens channels, and drains obstructions. Air purges like a divine wind, blowing away negativity.

Fire is different from both. It does not purge exactly but destroys what existed before so that something new can be born. Once fire has done its work, there is no undoing it, and no going back.

Here it is interesting to note that according to the dictates of my lineage, an actual physical fire should never be kindled inside the circle of a plant ceremony, and clients are advised not to look at a flame of any kind during the night, even the light from a match. There are thus no candles or torches in my ceremonies, and even outside in chilly weather plant takers avoid warming themselves by a bonfire. The only instance in which I use fire is when I light a mapacho cigar if needed.

Seeing a flame while on plant medicine also "dries out" the

element of water inside clients, weakening the plant Medicine and preventing one's water nature from fully flushing away psychic residues. I learned this injunction to keep fire out of the plant circle from my teachers. Other lineages do things differently.

How Many Ceremonies Are Enough Ceremonies?

As we have seen, some medicine persons encourage clients to participate in four or five ceremonies a week based on a more-is-better philosophy. As also mentioned, in my opinion two or three ceremonies in a ten-day period are enough to nurture clients for a year or more, the reason being that what participants undergo during a ceremony needs time to be worked out in everyday life. If a year or two later clients have another Ayahuasca session, they start from a higher psychic rung of understanding, having processed what they learned over the months and years as per the Second Golden Rule. Time in shamanism is an ally.

Sex, Procreation, Ayahuasca, and the Sacred Ceremony

From the reports of clients and *curanderos* alike, Ayahuasca mixtures can at times act as a carnal stimulant. As we know, a main purpose of an Ayahuasca ceremony is to strengthen the Life Force (and thus the glandular forces), clearing the mind, causing the organs to work better, and encouraging body fluids to circulate more freely. Result? Increased sex drive for both men and women.

As illustrated by the story of the wife cursed with infertility in

Chapter 5, I have also seen women with supposed biological impediments become pregnant and give birth after participating in a ceremony that has freed them from curses and spells.

There are, of course, other mental and physical reasons that prevent procreation, though in my experience most of them respond well to shamanic Medicine. Nothing is promised, needless to say, but I have seen enough supposedly infertile couples have a child within a year or two following a ritual to recommend plant medicine as a way to restore male virility and female fecundity. This work not only strengthens a client's biological forces, it dissolves the emotional barriers between couples that are so often the reason why they cannot conceive.

In the weeks following a ceremony, it is also common for clients to feel enhanced erotic vigor even when far from any type of sexual turn-on. This is due to the fact that the Force of Life flows with particular gusto after physical and psychological blockages have been dissolved with shamanic work. Remember that the Force of Life works directly with the glands of a client's body, so that the improvement of sexual drive is also an indicator that a client's overall health, and hence their libido, has improved as well.

My advice to these lucky ones is to be grateful for such a delectable benefit but not to take advantage of it quite yet. It is better, I tell them, to practice sexual abstinence for several weeks or more after a ceremony. The reason for this seeming killjoy advice is that the process of sexual enhancement continues for months after a ceremony, even if a client is unaware of it. It is wasteful, I tell them, to give away this precious grant of reproductive energy before it is allowed to develop to its full potency.

Finally, with the increased popularity of shamanism in North America and Europe over the past ten or twenty years, some users think of psychoactive plants not as a medicine but as a way to have better sex. For those who look on Ayahuasca and the Peruvian plant ceremony as a sacrament, such a notion is not only offensive; it is wrong. Based on the protocols I learned from my teachers and from high-ranking *curanderos*, a sacred plant ceremony *never* includes sexual interplay of any kind—period. To use it for this purpose may not only cause physical disappointment— biologically speaking, there is no erotic stimulation caused by Ayahuasca—but be a psychic risk as well, as the spirits that stand guard over ceremonial shamanism do not take well to being the tools of prurience.

The one exception to the above rule is that in certain lineages male and female shamans do in fact couple while in a sacred plant trance in order to conceive. The aim here is not to induce pleasure but to channel the couple's combined ancestral and natural energy into their upcoming child.

Menstruation, Pregnancy, and the Sacred Ceremony

More than once over the years I have been told by female clients whose cycle had stopped several years earlier that after a series of sacred ceremonies they began menstruating again. This phenomenon can be due to two possible causes. One, since a sacred plant ceremony wakes up the flow of the Force of Life, this force can revive dormant physical functions in a woman's body, including menstruation.

Second, besides the part it plays in discharging blood and tissues, menstruation is an extraordinary elimination system for many subtle, psychological elements. After a ceremony, it may return for a few months to expel lingering negative elements from a woman's Suffering Consciousness.

There are, while on the subject of menstruation, several situations in which women are advised *not* to participate in a plant ritual. One is when a woman is pregnant and her belly begins to show, which is usually around the fourth or fifth month. The second is when a woman is having a particularly difficult or abundant menstruation period. In such cases it is wise for women to put off participating in a plant session until their monthly period is finished. If a powerful elimination process takes place during the session, the purging force can dramatically increase the flow of the already active menstruation, producing a very uncomfortable and occasionally dangerous situation.

Suffering and Soul Consciousness during a Ceremony

During a sacred plant ceremony, with the help of the plants and the Medicine force of the shaman, clients experience their Soul Consciousness for an average of four or five hours. During this time, they are able to observe, understand, and edit their Suffering Consciousness in essential ways. While the ceremony is taking place their Suffering Consciousness is not turned off entirely. It remains present but passive, allowing the Soul Consciousness to take command.

This process of quieting the Suffering Consciousness produces powerful moments for clients, as the deepest part of their emotional life is awoken by Soul Consciousness and brought to the surface, allowing them to experience reality for several hours as it would be without anger, worry, petulance, desire, or envy to weigh them down.

When Group Members Act
Strange or Aggressive

While I normally ask clients to remain passive and inward-turned throughout a ceremony, sessions can sometimes open a Pandora's box inside a person, releasing a range of charged emotions from wrath to ecstasy.

When this dam breaks, past traumas may explode from a client in the form of shouts, sobbing, sighs, screams, laughter, and all manner of clamor and contortions. For example, I was once doing a hands-on healing session for a woman in an elegant nineteenth-century apartment building in Paris. The woman kept telling me she wanted to scream and let out pent-up emotions from the abuse she had received as a child but that the neighbors would hear the noise. I told her this might be the only chance she would ever have to let it all out, and that she should go ahead and scream. Which she did, so stridently and for so long (almost twenty minutes) that the neighbors did indeed pound angrily on the walls of the apartment while I sat there helplessly waiting for firemen to come knocking at the door.

While most of us cover over the emotional anguish that eats at us during our day-to-day life, during a ceremony the wraps come off and it is not unusual for disruptive behaviors to burst out from ordinarily sedate clients. These flare-ups can take place in personal sessions even without taking the plants, as in the case of my hands-on work with the woman in Paris.

If, in fact, clients do act in bizarre ways or become violent or hysterical during a ritual, they must be handled with both firmness and compassion. At the same time, the *curandero* is obliged to keep the rest of the group participants in a state of self-containment. One way to accomplish this dual task is to send calming telepathic messages directly to the troubled client's Suffering Consciousness.

Another is to lay hands on the client, allowing the contact to reestablish his or her equilibrium without bothering other people in the circle. Sometimes the sound of a drum or a rattle can produce a soothing healing energy that calms everyone at once.

When clients spin totally out of control and enter a state of violent anger and frenzy, which is extraordinarily rare, I should say, an energetic straitjacket may be necessary, which is the equivalent of binding a person hand and foot with psychic cords. After several minutes, these seizures almost always pass, and when the individual calms down, I "untie" them and the ceremony continues. Considering the possibility that things now and then can and do go wrong, before we begin a ceremony I usually ask clients to sympathize with other group members' anxieties, even their outbursts, but to stay fully focused on their inner work no matter how raucous the distractions may be.

And yet there are no hard-and-fast rules. I have heard that certain facilitators are extremely strict about never allowing distressed clients to thrash about and make noise. From my perspective, a shaman should recognize what is taking place in each client's inner world during a ceremony and know when moments of great purging and pain make thrashing about a necessary medicine. Since a ceremony triggers a different set of reactions in each person, in my practice it is okay at times for clients to become boisterous and even unruly when the success of their journey depends on it.

When Clients Feel Nothing during a Ceremony

Every so often clients take part in a sacred plant ceremony and at the end of the evening announce that they felt nothing, saw nothing, and learned nothing. Some fault themselves for this blank encounter. Others blame me or the medicine or other clients, the bottom line being that they feel they have wasted their time.

There are a number of situations that can cause this reaction.

The first is when a facilitator leading the ceremony is incapable of moving healing energies in an effective way. This group leader is either a pretender or an ill-trained amateur, giving his clients nothing real. As a result, clients get nothing from their ceremony and so feel cheated by the evening's events.

The second possibility is that the brew simply does not work for a particular client or is not strong enough to light up his or her consciousness. Sometimes the mixture may have been cooked improperly. Or the shaman has failed to properly perform the psychic activation of the plants. Or even that for causes known only to them, the spirits refuse to cooperate with this particular plant conductor.

The third reason why clients may be disappointed is because in the days before the ceremony they disregard the traditional pre-ceremonial obligations. They may drink alcohol or masturbate. They may secretly snack on forbidden foods or get into arguments. Slighting the rules in this way makes the plants unhappy, sometimes so unhappy that during the ceremony they refuse to connect with the client. Hence, zero response.

The fourth possibility occurs when clients spend their time wrestling with a spell or enchantment rather than purging negative emotions. You may again recall the story in Chapter 5 of the woman whose mother-in-law cursed her to never have a child. In such cases it is the shaman's task to root out the curse rather than promote insights and self-knowledge.

Fifth on this rather long list are clients who during a ceremony indulge in intense self-analysis of their ordinary life, their career, their family, their life situation, but do not make contact with the spirits and/or their ancestors. At the end of their session, these people feel deprived that they did not experience the stars and stripes visions they had hoped for. The plants, they tell me, are overrated. But in fact, visions are not a guaranteed part of the shamanic encounter. The plants used in a ceremonial brew may help a person think and see more clearly but do not necessarily produce visions and epiphanies.

For this reason, clients are advised to avoid second-guessing the reactions that sacred plants will spark in their consciousness. Certain plants act like a detergent. Others connect people with the spirits. Some make clients more intelligent and insightful. Still others destroy curses or quell phobias and addictions. Ayahuasca, the most important of the Master Plants, places more emphasis on mental analysis than on visionary flights. In fact, in traditional Peruvian towns, villagers sometimes boil Ayahuasca alone without other ingredients, their goal being not to communicate with the invisible world but to fix social problems—to patch up a broken friendship, perhaps, or to make the correct business decisions. When people take a sacred plant and experience mental guidance but no visions, chances are that self-analysis is what they need in this session rather than a visit to other worlds.

Still another cause of an unsatisfactory session is when clients enjoy an ecstatic plant night, but somehow have an intuitive feeling that in their next ceremony they will be confronted with a painful look into their Suffering Consciousness. When the next session begins, they are so fearful of what they may see that they freeze up and very little happens during the service.

And yet again, at times during a ceremony a client may sit still for hours, staring into space as if watching a film, an analogy that comes fairly close to fact. During their session they feel frozen in place, observing the activities of the spirits through a kind of psychic TV screen a few feet in front of their eyes. All they can do is watch, they tell me. It is impossible to enter the window and take part in the real-life drama of their own spiritual affairs. Why this happens is hard to say, though I have observed that people who find it difficult to believe in the unseen often have an unalterable resistance to admitting the supernatural reality of what they undergo during a ceremony, being capable only of watching it as if it were a movie in their brain and then later saying it was a hallucination.

Last, when a client reports minimal stimulation during a Medicine session, this reaction does not necessarily mean nothing has happened. Though consciously the experience seems like a dud, deep inside the client many cleansings and healings may have taken place. It is not unusual for a participant to feel numb during a ceremony but to experience a series of dynamic visions in the days that follow, both in ordinary consciousness and in their dreams.

I remember the case of a man who came from Montreal to participate in a jungle ceremony, but who sat through the session showing zero response. The next day he complained of feeling apathetic during the ritual, about wasting his money, about the phony hyping of Ayahuasca, and so forth. When he left the compound for the airport several days later, he was still irked.

It gave me, therefore, a certain amount of satisfaction when I received a phone call from him a few days later. He had boarded the plane, he told me, and in the middle of the flight began experiencing memory flashbacks, visions, and dialogues with spirits accompanied by deep emotions and tears. In reaction to this sudden paroxysm, and much to the consternation of the passengers, he spent a good deal of time pacing up and down the aisles of the plane and visiting the bathroom to purge. Now that he understood what it was all about, he announced, he asked when he could visit the compound again.

Dangers to a Shaman during a Ceremony

We know it is the shaman's job to protect clients from the darker end of the psychic scale. But in the process what protects the shaman?

Many things.

The first safeguard is moral. To be a healing shaman requires the person of knowledge to remember that the overarching purpose of his profession is to behave as a servant for the Force of Life, and to act as a kind of prism for light to shine through him from the higher worlds. A shaman is likewise obliged to live according to the dictates of his Soul Consciousness, choosing his words and actions carefully so they do no harm to others. He must be faithful to the directives he receives from the spirits, especially in the early morning (the time when a shaman is most likely to receive input from the invisible world), and to obey these messages with precision, either with or without taking psychoactive plants. If he does all this, the spirits will protect him.

When performing healings, a *curandero* is constantly exposed to the pollution of his clients' mental and emotional illnesses. But there are other forces that threaten him even more. Spells cast by a dark practitioner are hazardous to clients, needless to say, but in a sense they are more so to the *curandero* who must oppose and nullify them—no easy task.

Many people do not understand the mechanism of curses. Just as there are tools a shaman can use to find the creator of a spell, so the sorcerer who cast the spell has tools for tracking the medicine person who is tracking him. Once this sorcerer learns that a *curandero* intends to untie the knots of his curse, and worse, is building a protective shield around the cursed client, he comes at the shaman with an arsenal of weapons and blood in his eye. It is both dangerous and technical work; for just as the shaman has his own Healing Family of protectors, a sorcerer is guided by a gang of dark helpers that aid and protect his activities as well.

I do not wish to go too deeply into the subject of a black magician's tricks, as there are enough to fill a separate book. A few examples will make the point, showing the cunning tricks that shamans must overcome when sparring with the forces of hatred.

There is, for instance, a sorcerer's technique known as *vendar,* or blindfolding. The sorcerer uses this technique by spreading a spirit veil over a shaman's eyes while the shaman is trying to undo a curse, blinding him and turning off his mind screen and thus his abilities to fight the curse.

Another method is to distract a medicine person in the middle of a ceremony with, say, a noise, a light, a physical touch. When the *curandero* turns to look, the black magician tosses *virotes,* or invisible darts, into his body, which cause temporary paralysis or sometimes threaten his life; the same skills that are used when hunting in the jungle are used by sorcerers to pursue shamans. If, on the other hand, a shaman hunts the *brujo,* drawing close to his power source, he may find that the space around his enemy is filled with traps such as swamps that devour a person's soul or the swamp's equivalent, spiritual quicksand.

The way to identify and neutralize these booby traps is by means of spirit animals and one's Healing Family, both of which show shamans ways for parrying an ambush or finding a way around it, or through it. Sometimes a shaman's master hawk will provide an aerial view of the sorcerer's psychic space. Or a master fox or jaguar will show where a sorcerer's psychic weak spots lie and explain how best to attack them. Animal members of the Healing Family may spread protective wings over a shaman or weave a protective cocoon around him when assaulted. They sometimes drape his body with protective webbing or provide spirit armor that causes harmful energy to literally bounce off him.

The powers that shelter medicine workers from a black magician's aggression, in other words, are not just the warrior's know-how but the protective tools he is given by friendly spirits and by the sacred beings in his Healing Family.

᠕

In my own work, I would like to add, I have come to adopt a different stance toward self-preservation from those described above. What I do to defend myself against a psychic ambush, in a word, is—nothing.

When, for example, I am working with a client in an individual session, I imagine that I am there to heal for life's sake, for love's sake, for natural justice's sake. This approach—this devotion, if you will—gives me all the safeguards I need.

Not to say that I never use the protective techniques described. I sometimes do. But by and large, I have discovered that intention is all; that if I wish to help clients destroy a curse or fix what is broken in them, the most powerful action I can take is to generate a flow from the Force of Life and let it act as a defensive shield. Once this is done, I can do my work without any thought or worry; the Force of Life will take care of the rest. As a teacher once told me, "How can a good warrior fight well in battle if he is afraid or if he cares too much about himself? A good warrior trusts in his higher nature, not his weapons. He is unafraid of the enemy and unafraid to die. This trust is all he needs."

᠕

In ceremonies over the years, I have occasionally been threatened by a malevolent force that tries to hurt me but which I know nothing about.

Once I was working with a healing group in Australia and specifically with a young woman named Beth who suffered from advanced cancer. Beth had tried a number of conventional and alternative treatments, but nothing slowed the growth of her tumor. Since she was part of the group I was working with, I agreed to do hands-on sessions and see how well she responded.

Ordinarily, when I take on a difficult disease like cancer, my first session is spent simply observing and waiting for some visionary clues to pop up, at the same time sending a continual flow of healing force into the client. When I trained my attention on Beth for the first time, what appeared was a fifty- or sixty-year-old aboriginal woman with an angry, resentful look on her face that seemed directed at me as well as at Beth, as if she was literally looking at me as I was looking at her. Simply making eye contact with this woman made me feel strangely alarmed.

After the session was over, I discussed what I had seen with Beth and asked if she was friends with an older native woman. At first, she shook her head no. I had been told that generally speaking, aboriginal people rarely have close relationships with Anglo Australians, and so this answer made sense. Then suddenly she remembered. She was currently working for a government agency that distributed financial aid to the poor. An older aboriginal woman had come to see her several times seeking help, but due to administrative policy, she was not entitled to state money.

"She came several times," Beth recalled. "Each time I told her I would gladly help her if I could but that she just did not qualify.

After I turned her down on her third visit, she became outraged, blaming me for personally withholding the money, and threatening revenge."

Beth was shook up by this confrontation, but over the months she more or less stopped thinking about it. To me, however, it seemed clear from my visions that the woman had the same glare in her eyes that I have seen many times in dark sorcerers. The woman, I concluded, possessed occult knowledge and had more than likely cast a spell that caused Beth's cancer.

Several days after this conversation I told Beth I had appointments to visit clients in a nearby city. I would be coming back the following week, I told her, and would like to continue our sessions. But when I returned ten days later, she was gone. Nobody knew where, and nobody ever saw her again. I did, however, continue to work on her for several more days at a distance, both because I was touched by her case, and as a counter against the evil I had seen in that native woman's eyes.

Meanwhile, in the nights following our meeting I had a series of dreams in which I saw large, dog-like creatures with their skin painted in strong colored dots similar to representations in aboriginal art. The creatures were cooped up behind a grill snarling and trying to leap through the bars to attack me. Unquestionably these were psychic attacks connected to the work I had done on Beth and to the fact that I was interfering with the woman's curse. On the third night the woman herself appeared, vowing to punish me for trying to cure Beth's disease.

How amazing, I thought: I had never seen or talked to this woman. I had nothing to do with her personal affairs. Yet she wanted to destroy me and would have if I had not been protected by my Healing Family. How dark was the heart of this sorceress who spread harm and poison even to those she did not know simply because she could not get her way. These are the types of hateful spirits that from time to time a shaman must deal with when attempting to help others.

Surprise Visits during a Ceremony

During a sacred ritual, odd and uninvited visitors, some human but a majority from the spirit world, occasionally try to join the activities. There is the story, you will recall, of how I allowed a group of African tribesmen spirits to enter the ring and dance for an Australian man who felt unconnected to his African ancestry. Though I am normally opposed to uninvited outsiders entering the circle, in some cases saying yes brings unexpected benefits.

During a ceremony several years ago, the weather was extremely eccentric, stormy one minute, calm the next. This strange flip-flop created tension in the air, as if something dramatic was about to occur. Then, sure enough, about halfway through the ceremony a group of approximately forty spirit men, women, children, and elders appeared outside the circle. The moment they arrived the weather calmed. Though they were painted and groomed in a way I did not recognize, and though I had no inkling who they were or why they had come, they were unmistakably both Peruvian and Amazonian.

Members of this crowd stared at us wistfully for several minutes until a man wearing a feathered headdress, clearly a person of authority, came to the edge of the circle and told me his group was part of a village that had been exterminated centuries ago by a neighboring tribe.

Why then, I asked, were they here?

The man explained that he and his people had been listlessly wandering the spirit world since the day of their killing, and that their enemies had cast a spell, making it impossible for them to ever return to their homeland. Seeing light coming from our circle, and knowing that a sacred transaction was taking place, they were here with a request: Allow us to make our home in the area around your compound and we will help make your life better.

Initially I was doubtful. I knew nothing about these people. Then I began to receive positive signs from my Healing Family along with a sense of compassion for these lonely outcasts. After weighing the matter, I decided to accept their offer. It was moving to see their eyes shine with gratitude when I told them they were welcome.

Since that night the group has settled quietly into the compound area around my center, and it is still an amazing surprise during a ceremony to see its members standing nearby, guarding and protecting our circle, warding off encroachments from dark spirits, warning me when a wild animal is approaching and shooing it away, or diverting questionable strangers who attempt to approach the compound. At times during a ceremony, members of the group who specialize in medicinal crafts help me perform a difficult healing. In all, the decision to let members of this kindly tribe make their home in our quarters was a sound one, both for them and for me and my clients.

The End of the Ceremony

Though ceremonies tend to run for four or five hours, no one is clocking the time, and basically the rise, leveling out, and decline of interactions with the spirit world has its own arc, which clients can feel and accommodate themselves to.

Often the most vivid encounters take place during the first two hours of a ceremony, when colors and patterns are strongest, visions and second sight are common, and energy levels are most intense. As the evening wears on, consciousness plateaus, and it is during this interval that clients are most likely to interface with spirits, ancestors, and psychic messengers. After three or four hours one feels their trance level subtly tapering off with fewer and fainter visions, though this is not a certainty, and occasionally clients have their most compelling meetings with the invisible world at the end of a session. One thing is absolutely certain: Each client in a sacred ceremony has their own unique encounter with the otherworldly.

When the ceremony feels like it has run its course, I announce this fact to clients. Around this time I often see confetti-like drops or spores rain down onto clients as a final blessing. This shower marks the closing of the ceremony. Later on participants may experience its benefits in different aspects of their life, though much of the time they do not realize that these benefits are due to the gifts they received during their last minutes dancing with the spirits.

After announcing the end of the ceremony, I dismantle the healing dome and advise clients that though the ceremony is over, the spirits may continue to work in their minds and hearts in the days ahead. After experiencing the steady drumbeat of high-charged energy for many hours, clients are tired and sleepy. Most return to their rooms without talking to others; dialogue comes the next day and the day after. Settling in, they usually enjoy a good night's sleep, often filled with dreams that continue the interplay with the spirit world.

The following morning most clients wake up feeling remarkably joyous and refreshed. Though they were up half the night, their senses are sharper than usual and their minds are calm and clear. This is not true for everyone, naturally, but it is for many. This sense of post-ceremonial clarity can last for days and even weeks. Unlike narcotic drugs, there is no "coming down" after the session. It is more like going up. Ayahuasca is spoken of as "the medicine" for good reason.

There is, needless to say, a good deal more that could be said about experiencing a sacred plant ceremony hour to hour. I think, or at least I hope, I have covered the most important aspects of it, and that for those who intend to take the plants, this information will serve as both a blueprint and a hands-on guide.

Post-Ceremony Concerns

A client's attitude toward a shamanic encounter tends to take two forms. There is overlap between them, of course, but a dual trend does exist.

First, a sacred plant session is thought of by some clients strictly as a healing tool. They come to me for help with their hypertension, their financial embarrassments, their failing marriage, their depression or insomnia. When the ceremony is over, they go their way, and I usually don't see them again. Clients of this kind tend to look on the sacred plant ceremony as the psychic equivalent of visiting a physician or attending a group session with a therapist.

The second way to look at a ceremony is as a path to spiritual education. Many people through the years have contacted me, saying they have heard promising things about *curanderismo* and would like to give it a try. Often, they have no sense of spiritual or moral urgency but simply have a yen to experience something new that might just help.

Once these people participate in a ceremony, many of them

see how deeply the plant magic has burrowed into the nooks and crannies of their unconscious, where so many of their lifetime problems have done their dirty work. They realize that the doors of an enchanted kingdom have been opened for them, and that they will never be quite the same person again. For me it is one of the most amazing rewards of my profession to hear onetime skeptics speaking after a ceremony, telling friends or family how their heart has been opened, and how the spiritual parts of them have been awakened. At the end of the night they realize, as so many people do, that the sacred ceremony is as much a teaching as it is a healing. I often see these clients again, many of whom come to Peru every year or so to attend a ceremony.

When a ceremony has come to an end for the night, the next day I meet with each member of the group to discuss their experience, hear their feedback, and make suggestions. During our conversations, I mention that when a ritual is over there is a Golden Rule to consider, the Second Golden Rule in this instance.

Remember that the First Golden Rule maintains that clients in a ceremony are never exposed to a demand or a psychic encounter that pushes them beyond their limits or harms them in any way. Whatever challenges confront them in a ceremony can always be overcome. No one is asked to do more than they can do.

The Second Golden Rule, as you will also remember, has to do with the future and with a client's behavior in the weeks and months that follow a ceremony. This rule is not the biblical "do unto others," though there are certainly parallels. It relates more to the fact that when dark mechanisms of the Suffering Consciousness are dismantled (which in older times was known as exorcism), participants are then free of these repressive influences. But though their inner trash can has been partially emptied, this does *not* mean that all the negative patterns of a client's personality have disappeared. A certain vice may and often does return to tempt them. When it does, in the best of possible worlds clients are no longer controlled by this vice and can make life choices based on their new knowledge rather than on their former behaviors and misbehaviors.

During the weeks and months that follow a ceremony some people have dreams and visitations in which they are given a better understanding of the visions they saw in the ceremony. Others are shown patterns and medallions in their imagination and are told how to make these designs into amulets for psychic protection. There are endless possibilities for post-ceremony growth if a person knows what to look for and how to deal with the opportunities when they come along.

For example, during a session many participants find themselves letting go of major grudges. But this is only half of the forgiveness process. As per the Second Golden Rule, the other half is having the courage to face the once despised person—to pick up the phone or send a text or pay a visit in order to set things right. Even if the ex-friend does not understand what you are telling them or snubs your peace offering, it does not matter. What is important is that you make the gesture. The rest is up to the other person and to fate.

What happens if clients do not apply the Second Golden Rule? What happens if they forget the lessons they learned or are too distracted to incorporate them into their lives? The answer is that these lessons remain in a kind of psychological loop that circles around a person's inner consciousness, remaining dormant but ready until the lesson is remembered and applied. This does not mean that something bad will happen to the client. Only that the way clients can finally rid themselves of problems addressed but neglected is to face them squarely by means of spiritual self-work or by once again taking part in a round of sacred ceremonies, this time with a resolution to remember the Second Golden Rule.

⚘

I have observed that over time clients apply approximately 10 percent of what they learn in a ceremony to their day-to-day life. But 10 percent is a lot. If I see a client a year after a ceremony and they tell me that one or two of their problems have cleared up, I congratulate them. Come back again, I tell them, and get another dose.

When we practice the principles learned from the sacred plants, great rewards often follow. By letting go of old angers and resentments, I tell my clients, and by not expecting any special reward for these efforts, you help the healing continue inside you for years to come. "After a session ends," one of my clients once told me, "it really just begins."

Keep a Notebook or Diary

Clients often tell me that they did one of two things after a ceremony.

The first is that the next day or the day after they wrote down everything they could remember about the night's goings-on. Some even illustrated what they saw or they made an audio recording of the experience. From time to time, they then consult this report, finding that reading it brings back resonant memories of the night's events.

The second group of clients tell me how unhappy they are that during the days and weeks after the ceremony they forgot so many vital lessons learned that night, and how they regret not having written it down while it was still fresh in their minds. In short, I recommend that you write down what you experience as soon as your ceremony is over. Letting even a few days go by without taking notes will allow the memories to fade. Write it down!

Important to know as well is that the visions you see during an Ayahuasca session do not necessarily stop working the moment the ceremony is over. They continue on a subconscious level for no one knows how long. If you document these visions in writing and consult your record of them from time to time, you will feed this higher energy working silently inside you and keep it active.

Dieta Healing Practice

I have mentioned Dietas several times throughout this text, and for good reason: It is an important element of shamanistic practice, so important that a detailed description of it is mandatory.

A Dieta is a prolonged and structured period of meditative withdrawal complete with fasting, abstention, plant medicine, and prayers, versions of which are widely practiced throughout the Amazon basin. Among certain indigenous tribes, people undertaking a Dieta color their hands and faces with bright dyes or wear certain kinds of clothes so that others in the village know they are in isolation and keep their distance. This method is an excellent example of the natural courtesy found in so many tribal villages where the need for privacy is made visually clear without aggressively telling people to stay away.

The word *dieta* means "diet" in Spanish. Besides asking participants to eat plain foods, perform scheduled fasts, and avoid all sexual contact, a Dieta is also a diet from the attractions and exchanges of everyday life, requiring a long and demanding period of seclusion that can be practiced for a variety of reasons, both worldly and spiritual. For example, clients may wish to obtain a special skill or make an important event take place (or not take place) in their lives. Others require healing or physical protection.

Some wish to establish permanent contact with particular spirits or spiritual powers.

In rural parts of the country a particularly common reason for performing a Dieta is to enhance one's hunting skills, such as gaining the ability to approach an animal without frightening it away or to locate wildlife in the bush that no one else can see or hear. After performing a Dieta, one of my good friends developed the ability to spot the tiniest and most heavily camouflaged frog in a swamp and to see a green snake hiding in grassy foliage thirty yards away. He tells me that when he is looking for prey, he sees a kind of glow in the trees or brush, indicating the presence of wildlife and, I imagine, the radiance emanating from the animal's Force of Life.

Dietas are also performed to enhance night vision or to eliminate chronic laziness in a young person. Not surprisingly, Dietas also play a role in shamanic trainings, allowing apprentices to explore their personal Medicine or to bond with the spirit of a certain plant. Finally, a Dieta may be performed by people who wish to overcome one or more of their offensive behaviors in order to become better human beings.

It may be surprising to learn that Dietas are also used on animals, especially for taming wild beasts and making them friendly to humans. Special Dietas for dogs (which became common in the Amazon only several centuries ago) are designed to enhance their sense of smell for hunting or to make them more fierce or tame. In early chronicles describing the Spanish conquistadors' observations of Peruvian culture, one reads passages describing how the Spaniards saw cougars and jaguars sitting in a placid way next to the entrance of certain temples, not bothering anyone who entered. I cannot help but think that the methods used to tame these fierce creatures were Dietas performed by Inca medicine persons.

A traditional Dieta involves three interacting points of consciousness: the participant, a person of knowledge, and the sacred plants. Sometimes a plant spirit seeks out a client during a ceremony or in a dream, asking that the two of them perform a Dieta together. A shaman may suggest that a troubled or needy individual do the same. Occasionally during a ceremony, a client requests a Dieta from a plant spirit *and* a *curandero*.

During the course of a Dieta, clients are totally isolated, seeing only the shaman and his helpers who deliver food and check on the dieter's health and state of mind. Once the confinement begins, dieters are discouraged from speaking to or in some cases even laying eyes on outsiders, especially members of the opposite sex. In some shamanic schools a social exchange of any kind nullifies a Dieta, making it necessary to restart the practice several days later.

During the weeks of a Dieta clients regularly ingest sacred plants prescribed by the *curandero*. Some clients are given only a single plant to help a particular physical problem or to establish an association with this plant's unique Medicine. In other Dietas a mixture of mild plants is taken once or twice a day. Dieta clients may also ingest a mixture of plants that are not necessarily psychoactive but which connect them with important healing energies.

Some Dietas require that clients cover themselves with a plant lotion made by the *curandero* or to frequently moisten their skin in its boiling vapors. When practiced in this way, it is essential that clients apply the lotion to every corner of their body, including private areas like the crotch, the armpits, and so forth, in order to ensure that their entire anatomy is bathed.

During a Dieta clients are asked to avoid negative thoughts, to quietly acquiesce to the Dieta's rigors, and to constantly seek advice from the spirit of whatever plants they are taking. Indeed, the more time a person spends communing with their special plant, the more bonded they become with it, so that when the Dieta is finished, the plant and the human remain lifelong companions.

A person carrying out a Dieta eats a limited selection of foods. The menu includes fish that have certain physical characteristics. Their bones must be straight rather than curved, and they must have no teeth. In practice there are two types of local fish that qualify: the boquichico and the Amazonian sardina. Meat is also sometimes eaten, but it must be dry and consistent rather than juicy.

Regarding plants, boiled yuca and pituca, an edible root, are eaten, plus certain types of plantains and bananas. Vegetables and fruits must be as straight as possible and free from spots and bumps. Boiled rice is sometimes also on the menu.

These particular foods and a few others are all specially chosen. In the jungle they represent what several millennia of practice and tradition have recognized as providing the least amount of gastric interference with the subtle workings of the plant medicines. Note that the criteria for selecting the best foods for a Dieta— wholesome, plain, unblemished, etc.—are the same as those used for choosing the best coca leaves and other plants used as offerings for the gods.

Traditionally, the duration of a Dieta closely follows the influence of the moon.

I have already mentioned that the energy of a full moon crystalizes and fixes events over a period of time, making them permanent, which is why magical operations are so often done on a full moon night. Since a common objective of a Dieta is to make positive changes in one's life last as long as possible, the duration of a Dieta corresponds to a full lunar cycle, from one new moon to the next or from one full moon to the next. This time can be extended to include several lunar cycles if a user so wishes.

Nowadays with shamanism being so popular, I hear people talking about Dietas that last only several days. Such shortened sessions are normally designed to accommodate both the calendar and the personal needs of the participant, who is often from another country visiting Peru for a week or two. Which is fine. But these truncated Dietas should be called what they really are— special retreats. This is not to say that a period of meditative solitude for a week or two is not valuable. It can be quite valuable. But if we want to remain faithful to tradition and experience the complete healing power of this ancient practice, it is best to remain in isolation for a full moon cycle of time.

Needless to say, spending each day alone interacting with only invisible beings and occasionally a shaman and his helpers can be challenging. In the end, though, clients almost always emerge from isolation feeling healthier, extraordinarily clear-minded, and soon in possession of the goals they set for themselves at the beginning of the Dieta.

Spending time in isolation dieting, meditating, and interacting with spirits is a practice found in all the great world religions including Buddhism, Islam, Hinduism, and Christianity, where Jesus himself spent forty days alone in the desert, setting the precedent for the isolated retreats of the desert fathers to come. As a shaman once remarked, "If we all lived every day as if we were doing a Dieta, we would all live a very long time."

A Different and Ideal Ceremony

The following story is not connected to sacred plant work per se, but I want to share it anyway because it helps explain the wisdom and mindset of traditional communities, the same mindset that inspires work with sacred plants.

On one of my first visits with an Amazonian tribe in the northern jungle, after some days of getting to know the villagers, I was invited to a welcoming party. I soon learned that the gathering was a version of a shamanic ceremony, held during the afternoon and without the use of psychoactive plants. Village members jammed inside a large hut, which soon became so crowded it was difficult to move six inches in any direction, though the mood in the room was so spirited that no one, including myself, seemed to mind. While claustrophobic, the feeling of being squashed one against the other was somehow bonding and I would even say intoxicating. After several minutes the door to the hut was closed and the room became dark—not black dark but deeply shadowed.

In one corner of the room three musicians started playing drums and a flute. In another corner people were mixing large pods of *masato*, a mild fermented yuca root beverage. Everyone on the floor was swaying languidly to the rhythms of the music. Some couples danced together, though there was little eye contact and no hint of flirting. Rather than smiles the expression on people's faces seemed serene and distant.

We continued shoulder to shoulder in this way for several hours in a trance-like harmony, moving in perfect unison with the beating of the drums. People were passing around the *masato* in a bowl made of dried *huingo* fruit, everyone taking a sip as they continued to move about. After a while our body fluids and smells saturated the air, but in an elevating way, as if our whole group were a single sweating entity.

Suddenly a member of the group opened the door of the hut. Anticipating this event, everyone in the room dashed outside into the sunlight and continued to dance. Later, when the ceremony was over, I remember feeling I had never felt such communion with a room full of strangers who for those few precious hours were not strangers at all but brothers and sisters. All the different elements in this event had long ago been engineered by the group's ancestors to integrate the tribe. The fact that we were pushing about in a tightly closed space for a long period of time with our bodies vibrating to the same rhythm, that we were sharing the same drink, and that we were bathing in each other's breath and humors created a perfect sense of group unity in the darkness of the womb-like enclosure. Then the sudden rush into the light—it felt like a new entity was being born and we were all cells in its body. The entire occasion, I thought, reflected the highest ideals of shamanic joy and knowledge.

PART IV

REFLECTIONS *on*

HUMANKIND'S PAST

and FUTURE

CHAPTER 8

SHADOWS OF THE

SHAMANIC PRACTICE

For those individuals planning a trip to a South American shamanic compound, I feel obliged to shed a bit more light on the
troublesome sides of *curanderismo*. The reason for doing this is
to help seekers better protect themselves against inappropriate
behavior and bad shamanism, and hence make their time in the
magic circle a genuine renewal. This section is not meant to scare
anyone off, I should make clear, but rather to expose the vulnerable and sometimes adverse aspects of shamanic practice in order
to help people avoid them.

Though many influences helped me to decide to become a
natural healer, one of the main reasons I took this step, as detailed in the second chapter, was seeing how institutional medicine so often ignores impoverished elders, providing inadequate
healing attention to those who need it most. After witnessing
how the system failed to deliver medicinal care to these people,
I became involved in indigenous Peruvian healing. At the time,
these traditional healing methods were little known to the outside world.

Today I feel equally concerned, this time because the time-honored conventions of Peruvian medicine are becoming endangered by Ayahuasca tourism—that is, by the large numbers of people who are coming to Peru, some seeking real spiritual help from the sacred plants, some inquisitive or adventurous, some recreational drug users looking for a new high. Many seekers who have embraced the art of Peruvian healing through the years find that its effectiveness is being systematically reduced not only by the enormous number of seekers pouring into Peru but by commercial contractors and shamanic predators—those who take advantage of innocent seekers and who carry out a variety of false and sometimes illegal practices.

This situation is basically due to a clash of cultures. Many visitors who come to Peru for a ceremony want quick results. Two or three sacred ceremonies, usually paid for with thousands of dollars and attended by thirty or forty people, are expected to take away all the pains and hang-ups clients have acquired over a lifetime. The problem is that the primordial healing arts are not designed to be practiced on a large scale and definitely not at a fast pace. Nor was shamanism *ever* meant to be a source of financial profit, for either *curanderos* or their associates.

The origins of Ayahuasca tourism began in the 1950s and '60s, when recreational drug use began to infiltrate all sectors of American and European society, and when world travelers began visiting countries south of the US border in their quest for new exotic highs. Beat Generation writers like Allen Ginsberg and William Burroughs sampled Ayahuasca, magic mushrooms, and cactuses and wrote glowing letters to each other about their experiences. By the 1970s, when demand in the United States for substances like peyote and psylocibin was dramatically increasing, and Carlos Castaneda's Don Juan books were appearing regularly on the best-seller list, *shamanism* became a high-profile word in the popular lexicon.

In recent years, news of Ayahuasca's medicinal powers has spread around the world via the media and Internet, inspiring tens of thousands of people from across the planet to visit rain forest communities in Central and South America looking for cures. And, of course, wherever there is an influx into a developing country of wealthy outsiders desperate for relief from first-world problems, charlatanism and profiteering are rarely far behind.

Seeing a way out of poverty, thousands of Peruvian farmers and villagers are leaving their ancestral homesteads today and moving to busy Amazonian towns where they sell mass-produced Peruvian "crafts." At the same time, lodges and hotels specializing in shamanic rituals are springing up in Amazonian cities and jungle towns alike, offering pricey "ceremonial vacations" to wealthy outsiders.

Some of these lodges are built in a traditional way, while others are ultra-modern. A growing number offer plush facilities featuring suites of decorated rooms, massage tables, swimming pool and spa, bar and restaurant, making them look more like luxury resorts than spiritual retreats. Neither the government nor local municipalities require that speculators apply for legal permission to open and run such lodges, nor are there laws mandating that a shaman be vetted for authenticity. Luring visitors from America, Europe, and Asia with blogs and magazine articles, with websites and self-produced YouTube documentaries, some centers specialize in providing a streamline "shamanism to go" for quick and popular consumption.

Over the past twenty-five years the financial activity in the Peruvian jungle cities of Iquitos, Pucallpa, Tarapoto, and others, once small Amazonian backwaters, has increased dramatically, transforming many villagers into capitalists. Business in these towns is booming thanks to the planes and boatloads of visitors arriving every day. In many of these towns it is common to see newcomers courted by restaurant owners, taxi drivers, and sidewalk pitchmen peddling access to local wizards or selling commercially packaged Ayahuasca drinks. There are even so-called shaman shops where containers of Ayahuasca and other psychedelic plant mixtures line the shelves like bottles in a liquor store.

The *curanderos* who work at commercial Ayahuasca centers are often well-schooled in traditional spirit healing, and many are sincere in their desire to help. But a disturbingly (and increasingly) large number are inexperienced novices or even outright fakes—half-trained opportunists who decorate their lodges with skeletons and spooky art, and who dispense hallucinogenic plant mixtures designed to produce light shows in the head rather than to heal the soul.

For centuries in Peru, the education of a *curandero* has been a punishing and often life-threatening undertaking. Today things are changing. Besides the outright pretenders, many self-styled medicine people study for a year or so learning the bare fundamentals of the Craft, then hire out to Ayahuasca compounds. These semi-trained facilitators who know a few basic techniques often do more harm than those with no training at all. A little learning is a dangerous thing, in this case encouraging unpracticed facilitators to attempt complex healings and spell removals that even the most advanced *curanderos* would find challenging.

All along the mighty Amazon River, shamanic practice is being harmed in ways never before seen in the history of our Craft. This is a deeply troubling reality for many South American people. As the Native American leader Janet McCloud wrote: "First they came to take our land and water. Then they wanted our mineral resources. Now they want to take our religion as well." In the sections that follow, I hope to help potential Ayahuasca users discern good practices from bad, and what to avoid and what to embrace.

The Logistics of a Shamanic
Center Gone Wrong

From the earliest days in Peru the practice of plant Knowledge has operated on a small scale. Today the desire for plant enlightenment has gone from local to international.

Of course, if done properly there is little reason why large numbers of people cannot take part in shamanic gatherings without being harmed or neglected. At the same time, the greed that lurks in the hearts of some *curanderos* can be used to transform what begins as a philanthropic effort into a mercenary run-around that exploits the unwary. There are endless variations. A common one is as follows.

A well-meaning entrepreneur who has drunk the sacred brew many times and considers himself part of the shamanic nation decides to share this good thing with the world. He tells himself that creating a healing center based on proper shamanic protocols is a boon to people's search for authentic *curanderismo* and a righteous way to make a living. He will charge a fair tuition for a week or two of ceremonies presided over by a true person of knowledge. Everyone will benefit.

Empowered by this sincere vision, our entrepreneur finds a traditional *curandero* and opens a small lodge. Perhaps he advertises on the Internet and YouTube just to get the word out, he tells people. Otherwise, how will anyone know his center is there?

Within a year or two the lodge begins to attract seekers.

Soon the owner needs to enlarge the *maloca*, expand the dining area, and build more sleeping cabins. For this he needs money. He raises the fees, but people don't seem to mind and continue coming. So, he raises them again.

Though he starts with small groups of ten or fifteen, the number of clients in a ceremony increases exponentially. Because his costs are going up along with his fees, he soon finds himself less a patron of shamanic wisdom, more a CEO. At times he is forced to cut corners on costs or even cook the books. If his shaman becomes careless or mischievous, he overlooks it. Improper things happen in every business, he tells himself. Perhaps the shaman makes poor-quality medicine or harasses a client. But the people keep coming and the bills pour in.

At one point—and this is typical—the shaman decides to leave the center. Perhaps there is a dispute, usually over money. Or he feels a need to return to his family and village. Or he is tired of the hectic pace of the overcrowded compound. Or he feels the integrity of the lodge and its owner has been compromised.

The owner hires a replacement. If he is conscientious, he finds a practitioner with an honest reputation, though to find a person of real knowledge is becoming increasingly difficult. If irresponsible, he fails to vet the shaman thoroughly and may end up with a facilitator who is superficially taught or even an impostor. Meanwhile, the lodge continues to become increasingly popular—and expensive. The pretend shaman knows how to put on a good show and dispense powerful healing plants, and the clients leave happy. Increasing demand also tempts the owner to allow participants who are obviously mentally or physically unfit to participate in group ceremonies. Eventually the owner's good intentions are entirely forgotten, swept away by money, administrative pressures, and charlatanism.

The Influence of Western Occultism

Given that shamanism has its roots in the paranormal, many Ayahuasca takers are involved with Western occult practices. When visiting the Amazon, they bring their magic with them.

Many of these visitors spend time with local shamans and with workers associated with plant lodges. In the process they introduce them to European or New Age occult practices, which some shamans find so appealing that they incorporate them into their ceremonies. In some rituals we find persons of knowledge who along with administering sacred plants augment their work with crystal healing, Kabbalistic readings, theosophy, numerology, and other decidedly non-Peruvian and non-shamanistic practices.

There is a story I was told of an older shaman, a true representative of traditional jungle knowledge, who worked at one of the first commercial lodges to open in the Amazon. He was a skilled facilitator, and his reputation for honesty and competence soon spread, attracting many people from Lima and beyond.

After some years of running the center, the man grew frail and turned over his work to his sons, who had quite a different vision of how a compound should work. Having spent time with clients involved in Western magic, they began advertising their center with a menu of services that included astrology, palmistry, and tarot card readings, along with traditional shamanic practices. This offering was not an intentional con on the part of the brothers. They sincerely believed that the addition of nontraditional esoteric methods would enhance the power of their *curanderismo*. But it didn't. After a few years the once great reputation of their practice faded dramatically.

Overdemand for Plants

Due to Ayahuasca tourism, in the past decades the demand for sacred plants in Peru has skyrocketed. While the Ayahuasca vine and other Master Plants have grown in profusion throughout the hills and jungles of Peru for thousands of years, today their heightened popularity is contributing to an alarming depletion of the vine along with many other psychoactive growths.

In an earlier time, village *curanderos* harvested herbs and plants growing in nearby fields, many of which their fathers and grand-fathers had planted years before. They picked a handful or two of leaves or vines, digging up an entire plant only when an ur-gent medical case made it necessary. Today a caste of professional plant pickers has arisen who travel to areas of Peru rich in sacred flora and harvest—*plunder* is perhaps a better word—sack after sack of chopped Ayahuasca branches, chacruna leaves, sanango roots, and other sacred vegetation, both common and rare.

Few village officials make efforts to discourage this abuse. Im-poverished persons living in jungle communities are constantly being approached by professional plant pickers or members of commercial lodges who offer them the equivalent of fifty or sixty American dollars for each sack of Ayahuasca they gather, more money than they make in several months. All a villager needs to do is cross the meadow behind his house, approach an ancient stand of vines, and whack away. Cash payments are waiting. It is the equivalent of drug dealers hiring poor kids off the street to sell hard drugs for unimaginably large profits.

Seeing how easy it is to make money in this way, some villagers not only pillage crops near their homes but cut their way deeper and deeper into isolated parts of the jungle. At times I see canoes head-ing into the small, backwater tributaries of the Amazon. The men paddling them, some of whom I know, have given up a long family history of hunting or farming and now make their living stalking rare leaves and roots. Areas of the jungle where local people barely if ever went are currently being stripped of sacred greenery that has been growing there unbothered for thousands of years.

In defense of the villagers, many of them live off the electrical grid in isolated parts of the country and have no idea either that there is a world environmental crisis or that the plants they pick are endangered. For them cutting down a crop of local vines seems like an honest day's work. More importantly, it means that their children will have food on the table and they can patch up their collapsing roof. It is difficult if not impossible for people living on the margin of survival to resist the seduction of "free" money for simply cutting down a few backyard weeds. This scenario repeats itself across the country on a daily basis, leading to alarming shortages and eventually, perhaps, to the countrywide extinction of the psychoactive bushes, vines, and trees that make Peruvian shamanism possible.

Lack of Transplanting

Who replaces sacred plants once they are cut down? How can forest growth keep up with the increasing demands of Ayahuasca tourism? What responsibility do commercial shamanic lodges take for protecting the Amazon jungle?

Traditionally, sacred leaves and vines are gathered and sold by shaman-friendly growers, harvesters, and traders as profiled in a previous chapter. To refresh your memory, these pickers follow the same environmentally sound farming and harvesting methods used by their ancestors. Sharing a profound love and understanding of the plants, they never cut down more than they need, and transport and sell them only to *curanderos* they know are genuinely engaged. One of their most important practices calls for immediately replanting the vines and shrubs they pick, seeding new crops, and transplanting endangered vines or shrubs to safer, more protected pockets of the landscape.

But again, time-tested ways fade, replaced by a cadre of plant stealers who care nothing for replanting, and who show no restraint—or mercy—in stripping the fields and forests bare, leaving hacked stumps in their wake. This new wave of pickers usually loots the entire plant including the root in order to fill up more bags. Sometimes they cut down a whole bush even though they require only a handful of its leaves or branches. It's easier that way. Though they know how dire the situation is becoming, the Peruvian government does little to discipline these vine stealers and nothing to encourage them to reforest.

Fortunately, not all the new pickers are vandals. In the case of chacruna and other plants, the better pickers take 60 to 70 percent of the leaves and leave the rest so that the bush can recover. Still, when somebody puts cash on the table for five or six sacks of Ayahuasca, even the most well-meaning pickers are tempted. If you walk through the forests near my compound in the Amazon, you will see acre upon acre of tree stumps, burned fields, and ripped-up roots.

For these and many other reasons, I celebrate and support the initiatives now in place for planting, replanting, and cultivating threatened plants. There are many visionaries involved in this good work, including students and ecologically minded people, in Peru and other countries. While many Peruvians stand by passively without objection watching their forests being torn apart, the idealistic young are taking a stand. This is a great and much-needed effort and should be supported both in my country and throughout South America.

Bigger Is Not Better

As said several times, I try to keep my ceremonies small and to ensure that I am in personal touch with each participant. Most traditional shamans I know operate the same way.

But due to the ever-growing number of seekers coming to Peru, ceremonial gatherings have ballooned in size to, say, forty or fifty clients. Many of these groups are crammed into spaces meant to hold fifteen to twenty people with participants squeezed shoulder to shoulder for an entire night, sometimes without ventilation, adequate bathroom facilities, or drinking water. Those who complain are assured by lodge personnel that this "intimacy" is a traditional part of the ritual. Or conversely, the owners of commercial compounds build *malocas* so large they can accommodate a hundred clients or more, which shows how profitable the Ayahuasca business has become.

To compete in the market, many lodges advertise a showcase of magical nights, a smorgasbord of sacred plant sessions for variety-hungry seekers: San Pedro cactus on Tuesday morning, an Ayahuasca night on Wednesday, sacred mushroom tastings during the following two nights. If one center hosts three sessions a week, the next betters it by offering four or five. Some lodges offer sacred plants to beginners that are more psychically demanding than they can handle. For any newcomers to the world of the spirits, a standard sacred plant mixture is all that is needed to get them started on their healing journey.

Luring Away Village Shamans

Due to the increasing number of lodges, hotels, and spas being built to accommodate Ayahuasca tourists, there is a growing need for qualified persons of knowledge to provide guidance. Many of these lodges hire scouts whose sole job is to search the hinterlands for qualified *curanderos*, and to offer them what amounts to a small fortune to work at their center.

Though many shamans, especially in the deep jungle, have

little interest in money, the situation can become complicated. Their family members may need extra income to survive. Or the shaman's associates may all be leaving their villages for the city, inviting him to come along, if only, they tell him, for a couple of months—which can easily turn into years.

When shamans abandon a village, they often take their disciples with them, leaving no trainees behind, and thus ending a lineage that has existed in their village for hundreds of years. As a result, villages in Peru that for centuries have been socially and religiously guided by *curanderismo* suddenly find themselves without spiritual leadership. Concurrently, when remote villages are targeted by scouts, teenagers are told all about Wi-Fi, cell phones, and high-paying jobs, and so take off for the cities, where they believe fun and fortune await them. The village itself is now doubly wounded, losing both its spiritual leaders and its young. Social "progress" cannot be stopped, we know, but as far as indigenous people go, it can end up wounding an entire community. Clearly, "progress" is a subjective term.

Flawed Recipes

Recipes for a sacred plant brew often call for a highly complex mixture of plants and roots. True, healing can be achieved with a brew containing just two or three plants. But most well-crafted mixtures exert their power when a number of plants are cooked together, assuming that the *curandero* knows how the plants relate to one another and what synergistic effects the mixture will have on his clients.

Today with crowds of people filling up the *malocas*, and with many lodges holding sacred plant sessions every night, there is little time for shamans to prepare authentic multi-plant mixtures that traditionally take a day or two to infuse. Facilitators often do not know how to make these brews properly, or they concoct random plant mixtures that may or may not work. As with drugs in pharmaceutical medicine, there are certain plants that do not mix well with others, potentially harming a user. Newcomers to Peruvian plant ceremonies must be vigilant in checking the credentials of their shaman and the lodge where they are staying before taking part in a ceremony.

Overwhelmed by Work

I was once speaking with a *curandero* who had practiced plant medicine for many years.

He told me in confidence that the increasingly large numbers of people coming to his lodge were making him feel like a "ceremony-producing machine." He was performing as many as four or five rituals a week and sometimes two in one day. This, he said, made him bored, exhausted, and sad.

Although all this activity was monetarily rewarding, he said, there was no longer any time for him to practice other aspects of traditional Knowledge that he was interested in, such as dream analysis. During a ceremony, my colleague admitted, he found his mind constantly wandering. Though it went unspoken between us, we both knew that lack of concentration and interest in one's clients during a ceremony is a sign that a shaman is no longer really practicing shamanism.

Since my friend and I had this conversation several years ago, I have not seen or talked to him. I do occasionally find myself wondering whether he is still practicing *curanderismo* at his lodge, and if so, if he is still feeling overworked and overused, or if he has reduced his number of sessions to a manageable number. Shamanism, like other intense emotional professions, is hard work, and burnout rates can be high.

The Loss of Traditional Techniques

Seekers commonly misunderstand our Art, thinking the ingestion and therapeutic effects of sacred plants is the only goal of shamanism. There is, however, much more that our way has to offer besides the healing effects of plant medicine.

For example, the practice of making a pilgrimage, the contemplation of sacred landmarks like a waterfall or a special tree, ruminative prayer, meditative seclusion, communication with animals, and many other non-plant-based practices were once common in Peruvian *curanderismo* though they are rarely used today. In my own work, as I have mentioned several times, I find that hands-on therapy is a highly important tool—an ancient Peruvian system that requires nothing more than a trained shaman's touch but which is now largely neglected.

In this regard, many years ago I received a message from the spirits that I should avoid using sacred plants outside Peru, a request I still follow today. But even without this valuable tool, I have helped hundreds of people around the world with my hands alone. Hopefully, those who are working to revive the more traditional aspects of Peruvian shamanism will reintroduce many of the above neglected practices, in the process rearming humanity with regenerative methods that are so badly needed today.

Dangers to the Rain Forest

It is a stretch, perhaps, but not a long stretch, to compare Ayahuasca tourism with another invasion of Peru from Europe and North America, this one launched by agro-industrial corporations. Near my outpost in the Amazon, I have seen the obliteration of mile after mile of virgin jungle, carried out mainly by logging companies, strip-mining, cattle ranching, coffee and sugar farms, crude oil exploration, soy companies, and palm oil extractors. Most culpable in my part of the jungle are coca farms that burn and chop down hundreds of acres of trees and bushes each month, quickly replanting them with row after row of coca trees running, it seems, to the horizon.

Every day I gaze at the burned and clipped fields left behind by these companies that have turned parts of the Amazon jungle (which covers more than 60 percent of our country) into Kansas-like farmland. In the process they are killing and driving out millions of native animals, exterminating untold numbers of Master and medicinal plants, and depleting the forest of its most precious trees: rosewood, mahogany, cedar, lupuna, mashimango, and species that are already on the verge of extinction, like the beloved shihuahuaco tree. The massive amounts of toxic chemicals poured into the earth by agro-companies for fertilizer and pest sprays contaminate the soil and kill off the insect population that fertilizes plants and trees throughout the jungle. Animals are poisoned too, and their traditional migration paths through the brush are obliterated by the backhoe.

Remarkably, deforestation of jungle land is legal in Peru, while local laws that limit cutting are easily circumvented by judicial means or are simply ignored. The government does little to help, claiming the usual, that agro-businesses bring jobs and wages to the poor and bolster the economy. Most studies show this to be a questionable claim, and that the money ends up in the pockets of the wealthy few.

Meanwhile, logging the jungle is bringing in such vast profits that agro-industrial companies apparently intend to continue taking down more and more trees in the northern part of the South American continent until there is no rain forest left at all, a ransacking that experts predict, given the current (and increasing) rate of forest attrition, will be completed within fifty to seventy-five years.

Between August 2019 and July 2020 approximately 4,200 square miles of Amazonian tropical woods was cut down, an area the size of Delaware. This number is expected to escalate with each coming year unless something or someone puts on the brakes. Seeing that 20 percent of the oxygen and 25 percent of the plant life on planet Earth comes from the Amazon jungle, it is no exaggeration to say that this vegetable genocide could be a major contributor to the extermination of nature and humans. As one environmentalist said to me, watching the stripping of the rain forest is like seeing a man skinned alive.

When deforestation occurs in a certain part of the jungle, there are often small villages in the area. These settlements are reliant on plant life for agriculture but also for business, crafts, shelter, food, and much more. When their land is sold off and the trees and vegetation are cut down, a number of townspeople find themselves farmless, landless, and sometimes homeless.

Deforestation also causes major disruptions in the patterns of nature established eons ago. For as long as can be remembered, herds of *sajino* and *huangana* jungle hogs have passed through the area of my compound once a year on their food-finding migrations. Neighboring communities hunt them on a small scale, smoking the meat so that they have enough food for several months. Members of the community wait with great anticipation for this once-a-year migration to arrive as it has done, according to village elders, as far back as anyone can remember. For many villagers the yearly jungle hog visit makes the difference between hunger and a full belly.

Five years ago, the hogs failed to arrive at their usual time. The same thing happened the next year and the year after that. I eventually learned that the forest plants that the pigs eat have largely been cut down by agro-companies.

I have often witnessed the way in which representatives from agro-companies approach jungle villagers near my compound with loan offers. The landowners are usually poor and uneducated peasants living far from any bank or source of real estate information. They have little notion that the money being offered them is a fraction of their property's true value. Once the land is sold, the harvesting machines quickly arrive and take down all the trees on their ancestral land. The people in the town, meanwhile, many of them now displaced from their homes, have no choice but to work for the corporations, cutting down the very jungle they live in and love.

An even more sinister variation on this theme takes place when a company, let's say a coca company, sends a representative to a small community deep in the jungle. The representative meets with the heads of the village, most of whom know little about modern finance. He gives them gifts, makes friends with important townspeople, then offers a "package" in which, he explains, you and our company can earn a good deal of money by working together.

Here is the deal, he explains: We start by giving you a loan that you use to purchase coca seeds from us along with planting and harvesting tools, chemical fertilizers, and technological advice. You clear a small section of your land, and we tell you how to plant and cultivate the seeds.

Once this deal is firmed up—the company may also give landowners a little hard cash as further enticement—the landowner is told he must not only clear a small portion of his ancestral forestland but cut down sizable portions of it, planting the land with coca seeds and working it from sunrise to sunset, at the same time paying back the loan to a financial institution that works with the coca company. The profit the farmer was promised turns out to be minuscule, and he is obliged to pay the financial institution a monthly fee for the loan set at a percent a good deal higher than the norm.

You can see where all this is going. Often the landowner cannot afford to keep up the loan payments and is forced to take out another loan to pay for the first one. He is now paying for the privilege of working his own land for little or no profit, at the same time getting deeper and deeper into debt. When this occurs, the coca company convinces him to chop down more trees on his property to make room for further planting; then more trees, and more until the property is stripped bare.

In many cases, after some time the farmer simply cannot afford to pay off the monthly loan (or loans), and the coca company makes sure the bank forecloses on his land. It then allows the farmer to continue working the acreage that has been in his family for generations, but at such low wages that he and his family for all intents and purposes become serfs. It is all a form of soft slavery wherein the ex-landowner's survival becomes totally dependent on the whims of the corporation, while the corporation itself increases the acres of rain forest it can cut down without technically breaking any laws.

I have witnessed this nasty bit of business many times in the Amazon, sometimes in villages near my property. When smiling representatives of a coca firm visit a village, I warn local landowners and town elders that they are walking into a financial ambush, and I explain to them how the whole shady deal works. I also tell them how to protect themselves if a corporation threatens seizure of their land by showing them official-looking legal papers that "prove" the land belongs to them, when in fact the papers are doctored forms or outright forgeries. Without legal ownership, the corporations have no right to the land whatsoever. Their threat is a meaningless and, it could be argued, criminal deception. Sometimes the villagers listen to my warnings, sometimes not.

I myself have planted a number of medicinal bushes, vines,

and trees on my property, including seven varieties of Ayahuasca vine, some quite rare. Other concerned families near my compound have done the same, as have villagers across the Amazon basin. But these gestures cannot fend off the corporate Goliath that threatens to ruin life in the Amazon as it has been lived for thousands of years. I often wonder how best to help people understand the damage being wrought when an entire country's vegetable life is under threat and rare species are being made extinct by those who look on the rain forest as a source of income rather than nature at its most sustaining—and fragile.

Often when I am delivering a lecture and speaking on the subject of corporate greed in the Amazon, members of the audience ask what they can do to "save" the rain forest. When I hear this question, I give blunt answers. Reduce your consumption of chocolate, I tell them. Or stop eating and drinking it entirely. Cut back dramatically on coffee. Abstain from sugar. Refrain from eating palm oil–based foods. Avoid buying beef from cattle raised in northern and central South America. Make sure the lumber you build your house with is grown in sustainable forests. I also tell them the most useful action they can take is to personally and financially support people and organizations that are attempting to protect tropical forests in a sustainable way.

Recognizing Flawed Shamans and False Shamanism

In several chapters of this book I have talked about pretend or badly trained shamans, and the dangers their ignorance can present to both themselves and their clients.

Several years ago I was lecturing to a group in a country halfway around the world from Peru, where they study the sacred plants of the Amazon. At one of our meetings a young woman named Katherine approached me with a sad and shameful story. The moment we started talking it became apparent that she was distraught to the point of breakdown.

Katherine had been told of my involvement with Amazonian shamanism and sacred power plants by members of the group. Throughout her adult years, she explained, she had been tormented by traumas caused by a vicious authoritarian stepfather, now long dead. None of the usual remedies—antidepressants, psychotherapy, hypnosis—had helped relieve her pain and anger or erase the psychological damage inflicted on her by this man's cruelty.

One day a friend who knew of Katherine's struggles suggested that Katherine accompany her on a trip to the Amazon in Peru to visit a famous shaman who specialized in the use of sacred plants, in particular Ayahuasca. The friend knew several people who had gone to his healing center in the jungle. Each had returned with glowing reports of how life-changing these ceremonies had been, both physically and psychologically.

Katherine was no stranger to alternative medicines. She had read articles on shamanism and knew it was used in many South American countries to cure otherwise untreatable addictions and stress disorders. Might be worth a try, she decided, and signed up.

A few months later the two friends arrived at the airport in Iquitos, a small but thriving city on the edge of the Peruvian rain forest. Here they were picked up and chauffeured for several hours to a ceremonial lodge in the jungle. Once there, they joined a large circle of eager arrivals, some thirty-five or forty Americans and Europeans who, like Katherine, had come to be emotionally renewed.

Two hours before the ceremony began the shaman showed up with his entourage dressed in colorful robes and wearing a magnificent feathered headdress. He gave a short introductory talk in English, prepared a circle where the ceremony would take place using herbs and tobacco smoke, then gave an Ayahuasca-based drink to everyone seated in the circle, himself included.

At the start of the evening all went well. Katherine sank deep into a healing trance, and revealing insights emerged from buried parts of her past. Then halfway into the ceremony things started to go wrong, and her visions took a sinister turn. Within minutes her worst terrors were assaulting her in ways she could never have imagined. She began to scream.

At the beginning of the ceremony, Katherine told me, she was buoyant, even blissful. But several hours into the evening she began to feel uneasy. Suddenly a burst of frightening flashbacks erupted in her mind, most of them memories of the ill-treatment she had suffered at the hands of the man who had shamed and abused her as a child.

In response to these memories, she began yelling reproachfully at the shaman leading the ceremony, who in her altered state of consciousness became a symbol of the hated male authority figure. Later, Katherine told me, she could barely remember what she had said to him.

Meanwhile, the shaman, rather than realize that the woman's angry reaction was a psychological projection, part of the cathartic process that the plants often stir up and that many people experience during a session, took her outburst personally and began to argue with her. Within moments their exchange escalated into a violent shouting match.

For a shaman to quarrel with a client during a sacred plant ceremony is an unimaginable breach of a protocol that has been honored by traditional shamans for centuries. To make matters worse, the shaman insulted her in patronizing ways, belittling Katherine's intelligence and telling her she was ruining the ceremony for everyone in the circle. At the session's end, in front of the other participants, he gave her a final tongue lashing, informing her that she had polluted the plant sacrament, that she was an insolent troublemaker, and that she was banned from ever returning to his lodge. A few days later Katherine left Peru in an almost suicidal state of mind.

Imagine, now, a woman handicapped by a lifetime of psychic pain inflicted on her by a brutal family member traveling halfway around the world to attend a sacred observance in hope that the memories of her harsh childhood will finally be put to rest. Instead, she ends up paying several thousand dollars for a ceremony in which she is humiliated by an equally harsh male figure, in the process having her feelings of shamefulness and unworthiness more deeply confirmed.

Even more disturbing, when ingesting psychoactive plants of any kind, suggestibility levels are dramatically heightened. If a person like Katherine is psychologically victimized while in this sensitive condition, the harm done can be many times more devastating than in an ordinary state of consciousness.

How, I wondered, can a shaman presiding over a group of vulnerable individuals not understand that a central purpose of the sacred plant ceremony is to drive out the negative psychic residues inside each participant's heart and mind? How can a healer who is supposedly familiar with the plants not have the insight, compassion, and common sense to recognize that Katherine's outbursts were manifestations of her early-life ordeals, not a personal attack on his character? And even if the attack was personal, no shaman of merit would take these insults to heart. He would recognize them as a normal and even therapeutic response to the medicine and use the encounter as a tool for transforming a client's rage into self-understanding. I was amazed and a bit ashamed for my Craft to hear her story.

That day Katherine and I began working together to undo the hurt she had endured at the hands of this bumbling and vindictive group leader. It took a great deal of healing work before she began to feel that some degree of composure and confidence was returning.

For many days after my sessions with Katherine I thought about her upsetting experience. None of her anguish, it was clear, would have taken place if the shaman in charge that night had been properly trained, psychically attuned to the members of his group, and kind.

Here it was again, I thought, the abuse of an indigenous rite designed long ago by our Peruvian ancestors to strengthen and heal. Noxious ceremonies like this, I thought, overseen by an errant shaman like the one who humiliated Katherine, are becoming increasingly common all over Peru, where they are subverting our native heritage.

Protecting Novices against False Shamanism

While to some extent what follows may overlap with stories like Katherine's and with what has already been said about counterfeit *curanderismo*, I would like to provide further aid for those who are seeking authentic medicine persons, as well as for seekers about to participate in a ceremony for the first time. In the following section I will speak a bit more about sorcerers and black magicians but more about flawed and poorly trained shamans. Unlike a black sorcerer, a flawed shaman is not necessarily a bad person. He is, however, a bad shaman. Or he may simply be inexperienced or poorly trained. Most have no fraudulent intentions of any kind. However, forewarned is forearmed, even if the chances of falling victim to serious deceptions or something darker are relatively small.

There are two typical forms of flawed shamanism. The first is exemplified by a person who has had a good deal of experience using the sacred plants. Because of the powerful experiences this person has undergone during ceremonies, he or she decides to start their own version of a shamanic discipline. Studying with a traditional healer for a certain time or even just basing their teachings on their own plant experiences and what they have read and heard, they sometimes create a New Age or a quasi-religious version of the Craft that differs from traditional shamanism in a number of basic ways.

For example, the protocols followed in ceremonies overseen by people who invent their own practice are usually a good deal less formal and structured than traditional procedures. Or sometimes it is the opposite: Such people create overstructured ceremonies by borrowing a number of rigid protocols from other traditions, not all of them shamanic.

Made-up ceremonies often include large numbers of participants. Sometime during the session the facilitator may give a talk to his flock that is disconcertingly similar to a sermon delivered by a priest or pastor in a church gathering. The brew this person mixes is often a watered-down potion of Ayahuasca, chacruna, and perhaps several other plants. The ceremonies themselves may include religious prayers, bowing to the four directions, the use of tarot cards or astrology, social networking, and popular street music, activities that are far from the practices of doctrinal *curanderismo*. And while it is true that New Age shamanism can at times heal participants, it lacks the tools needed to dive deeply into the hearts of clients' Suffering Consciousness, to empower their Soul Consciousness, and to provide protection from dark forces.

On the other end of the spectrum, unlike the self-made shamans described above who, though misguided and off the mark, sincerely believe in what they are doing, there are medicine persons who quite intentionally deceive and exploit their clients.

For example, a carpenter once came to my house to do some repairs. He worked with me for several weeks, and during this time we hung out together and exchanged personal stories. In one of our conversations, he told me in an excited voice that an amazingly powerful man of Knowledge lived in his neighborhood. He had paid for this man's services several times, he declared, and was convinced that he had enormous powers, mainly because in one of his ceremonies he, the carpenter, saw evil curses literally being destroyed before his eyes.

The carpenter then described how the shaman had told him to bring a pair of his underwear to a ceremony, as a curse had been cast on him by a jealous lover that was meant to destroy his sexual potency. At the beginning of the ceremony, which incidentally cost the carpenter the equivalent of $800, the shaman placed the briefs, along with clothes and objects belonging to other members of the night's group, in a metal cauldron. After performing invocations that called on Divine beings, gods, and angels, the shaman set the contents of the cauldron on fire, saying that his powers and those of his spiritual allies would burn away everyone's evil curses.

"When the clothes and underpants were burning," the carpenter told me, "I could see long dark snakes slithering out of the pot and crawling away until they melted into the floor. The shaman told us the snakes were curses. He was so powerful, this *brujo*, the real deal!"

At the end of the night, the carpenter went on, clients were given perfume along with auspicious words of goodbye, all of them returning home feeling they had just been rescued from the terrible sufferings the curses would have caused them.

Hearing his story, I told my friend I had something to show

him. I walked him over to my computer, opened a scientific site on the Internet that I often consult, and clicked on a video of an experiment in which baking soda and powdered sugar were burned together in a pot, producing long brown snake-like forms that oozed over the sides. Seeing this, the carpenter shouted, "But those are the same snakes I saw in the ceremony!"

I explained to him that this was an old trick that has been used by false shamans around the world for more than a century. What the so-called magician showed him was not magic at all but a common chemical reaction that is often performed in high school chemistry classes. He had, I told him, been the victim of a shamanic con.

Arriving Too Late and Leaving Too Early

A primary example on the somewhat long list of unfavorable shamanistic behaviors includes practitioners who make no attempt to meet or get to know their clients, a major departure from the practice of pre- and post-ceremony bonding described in previous chapters.

Though it is normally within their power to arrive at the *maloca* a day ahead of time or at least a number of hours before the ceremony begins, these shamans may show up a few minutes before the session starts, often accompanied by a coterie of acolytes who seem to be protecting the practitioner from contact with group members rather than facilitating it. When the ceremony is finished, the shamans leave soon after, making no attempt to dialogue with clients about their plant encounter. The sacred Ayahuasca ceremony is thus truncated at its beginning and end—no talking with the *curandero* before the ceremony, no analyzing the experience once it is over.

In traditional work, as we have seen, a shaman is obliged to speak with participants ahead of time to learn about their hopes and expectations. He may ask them a number of questions, some quite personal, as well as encourage them to be as honest as possible concerning their psychological needs and hang-ups. A true shaman will also want to make sure his clients are healthy. He may ask about their medical history, about medicines they are taking or surgical operations they have recently undergone. Occasionally during the interview, the shaman determines that a client is not mentally stable enough to ingest the medicine. Or a client may be disqualified due to a chronic ailment such as a frail heart. In both cases a hands-on healing is more appropriate. Whatever the case may be, it is important that a one-on-one dialogue takes place. Those shamans who ignore this important tool are neglecting their duties.

The Hurry-Up Factor

In the past, many seekers hiked or rode horseback across large areas of Peru to visit a renowned *curandero*. If the *curandero* was not in residence when they arrived or was not performing ceremonies, seekers would wait many weeks or even months until a ceremony was scheduled—which they did without complaint, so masterly did they consider the shaman and his work.

Today the situation is reversed. Because most visitors' plane tickets limit the duration of their stay in Peru to, say, a week or ten days, and because some centers push the idea that ceremonies should be attended as frequently and quickly as possible, clients feel they are on a roller-coaster ride rather than in a boat moving gently ahead in calm waters.

When this rush-rush attitude prevails, coming to Peru takes on a frantic feeling that many people resent. When they return home and are asked about their time in the magic circle, clients report that their shaman looked on them simply as a number to be quickly processed on the psychedelic assembly line. One client told me that during her session it seemed as if her group leader was looking at his wristwatch every ten minutes. Why, it could be asked, would a shaman wear a watch during a ceremony in the first place? By definition, a sacred plant ceremony takes place outside of time and space. Beware a *curandero* who seems to be in a hurry. Slow and easy should always set the pace.

Mixed Motives

Once years ago, I visited a famous *curandero* in his hut near the city of Trujillo. He was a sane and savvy older gentleman, with a reputation among other shamans for being a first-class healer. During the visit he showed me photo albums with pictures of him standing next to celebrities from the media, entertainment world, and politics. All of them had visited him over the years for help with their problems. Apparently he saw me as a young searcher trying to learn the shamanic Craft and treated me in an extremely kindly way. He even took me into a private room to show me the esoteric symbols, swords, strange huge insects, and occult images he had mounted on the wall.

One of this *curandero*'s specialties was his seemingly omniscient knowledge of sacred plants of the region. He was intimately familiar with every variety of medicinal and psychotropic growth: the best ways of finding them, harvesting them, cooking them, storing them, all subjects I was eager to learn. In the several hours I spent with him he taught me many techniques about the sacred plants that I had no idea existed. He was a man of impressive knowledge.

Three months later I was in the medicinal plant corner of a mercado buying herbs for my clients. Standing at the counter in front of me I saw the old *curandero* making a purchase. To my surprise, he was buying a certain species of fava bean from a woman herb seller whom he obviously knew quite well. She handed him the beans with a sly smile, telling him his "special order" was ready. At first the man did not see me, but when he turned our eyes met and I greeted him. His face became pale. He looked down, covertly pocketed the beans, and quickly walked away acknowledging me with only a quick nod. He realized I had seen him purchase the beans, and also that I knew the reason *why* he had purchased them.

This particular variety of fava bean, it turns out, is an extremely powerful laxative that is ordinarily given to cattle to purge intestinal worms and parasites. The beans are definitely not recommended for human consumption, though some dishonest shamans use them anyway. I knew at that moment what the elderly shaman was up to and why he was evading me. Having diarrhea during a ceremony, as you will recall, is considered a great benefit, emptying clients of curses and the sins of their ancestors. It is easy to trigger a robust evacuation by simply mixing laxatives into a client's brew. The more explosive the bowel movement, the greater the illusion of a spiritual purge.

What I witnessed in the market that day was a paradoxical feature not only of shamanism but of human behavior in general: Though individuals may be brilliant and successful, at times they are still capable of taking the low road. In the case of the elderly practitioner, I knew, mixing juice from the fava beans into the brew was done to ingratiate himself with an important client who would no doubt believe the shaman had rid him of curses, when in fact the beans had simply given him a hefty case of the shits. It seemed quite strange to me that this skilled and highly regarded *curandero* would practice such dirty tricks. But there it was. This is not to say, of course, that every person of knowledge cheats a bit here and there. But a few do, and this is yet one more reason to vet your shaman beforehand, and to tune in to word of mouth about him before placing yourself in his keep.

Misusing the Medicines

The psychoactive materials in a plant will always light up a person's mind. But that's all. The shaman's wisdom and skill are needed to turn this light into a medicine. With a facilitator who has not made a true alliance with the plant spirits, clients will get a trip but not necessarily a healing.

In questionable ceremonies, the Ayahuasca doled out to visitors is frequently cooked using inferior or immature vines. Far worse, some practitioners drop dangerous barks and flowers into the brew or add recreational drugs to increase the drink's psychoactive effects. There are reports throughout Peru of practitioners who blend LSD or mescaline into their potions, using them to induce meteoric visions in clients hungry for mystical explosions.

Recently I took some friends to the traditional mercado in Iquitos, where we visited the booths of several natural medicine vendors. One of my friends asked a seller if she sold Ayahuasca. The lady said yes and showed us two sacks lying near a wall. Though I never buy sacred plants at this particular market, I was curious to take a closer look. When I peered into the bag, I could see that approximately half the contents included very young Ayahuasca pieces of the so-called cielo variety. The other half contained a collection of trailing plants, one of which was barbasco, a poisonous vine that contains rotenone, a venom used to kill fish and which sometimes kills the person eating the poisoned fish as well. When purchasing herbs and vines at a Peruvian mercado, it is always buyer beware.

Invented Protocols

Shamanic lineages each have their own ways of performing sacred plant rituals. But besides traditional differences there are practitioners who add their own ceremonial twists and turns to make clients feel that they are getting their money's worth.

I call these practitioners histrionic or theatrical facilitators. During a night's session such a facilitator may be singing or playing the rattle in a conventional way, then suddenly leaps up, makes warrior-like gestures, and shouts that everyone in the circle is under attack from demons. He runs to a corner of the *maloca*, where he boxes the air, as if fending off invisible invaders. He spits and sprays saliva, swears, kicks the ground, or even throws himself over his clients as if protecting them from attack.

While some participants witnessing these concocted protocols may be skeptical or amused, others panic, thinking they are in a real battle zone being hunted by diabolic phantoms. As a result, they spend the rest of the evening in terror, a condition totally opposed to the introspective state of mind required in a ceremony for peace and healing.

A Mix of Black and White Magic

I was once told of a young man in northern Peru who became deeply depressed after his girlfriend dropped him. One day a friend of his suggested that he see a shaman for an internal rewiring to get his life back in order. The young man said it sounded like a good idea, as long as his friend accompanied him. The friend had heard from several sources that the local shaman they were visiting was a capable worker, but that was the extent of his knowledge.

The two friends traveled cross-country to a small adobe house deep in the wilderness. It had just turned dark when they arrived, and a group of seven or eight people were preparing to take part in the night's ceremony. The *curandero* welcomed them and invited them to sit in the circle, which, contrary to common practice, had a fire burning in its center. The *curandero* also made a strange request. He gave every client a sheet or a blanket and asked that they cover their heads with it when requested.

During the evening the practitioner circled the ring interacting with each member of the group including the young man, who, much to his surprise, learned that the shaman somehow knew he had been dumped by his lady friend. Your girlfriend hurt you for no reason, the shaman told him, and the pain is still inside you. I will flush it out.

The young man expressed his gratitude, but the shaman continued, saying, "That bitch who caused you all this suffering should be punished for what she did. I'll roast her legs."

Roast her legs? Punish her? When he heard this, the young man was taken aback.

"No, master," he protested, "I didn't come for any form of revenge. I'm just here for my depression. Please, don't bring her into the conversation. She did nothing wrong."

The shaman said nothing but continued with the ceremony.

About five minutes later he asked the group to place the blanket or sheet over their heads. Everyone obeyed except the friend of the young man, whose curiosity got the best of him. Surreptitiously peeping out from under his covering, he was jolted by what he saw. The shaman was sitting in the center of the ring holding both his feet directly in the fire, apparently feeling no pain. His face seemed to have morphed from his normal expression into a hateful mask. Out of fear of this obviously dangerous man, the friend kept what he saw to himself.

A couple of weeks later the young man asked his friend to come with him to visit his ex-girlfriend. He had a bad feeling about her well-being, he explained, and wanted to make sure she was all right.

When the two arrived at her house the mother of the ex-girlfriend greeted them at the door and asked them to wait. A minute later she returned pushing her daughter in a wheelchair. The ex-girlfriend explained that a few nights previously the veins in her legs had suddenly burst for no apparent medical reason, becoming hot and inflamed. She was currently undergoing treatment at the hospital in the hope that the swelling would go down, and that she would be able to walk again.

Clearly the shaman, thinking he knew best and perhaps reacting to his own misogynistic impulses, had worked harmful magic on this innocent woman, doing what he said he would do by magically burning his legs and thus hers. In the end both the young man and his friend realized they had made a critical mistake by not learning more about the shaman before they hired him. As they were later told, this man was actually a dual *curandero*, half black and half white, meaning he was an adept at kindly healing *and* sadistic spells.

Eclectic Practices

We have already met the shaman who invents his own protocols along with the facilitator who spices plant mixtures with LSD and the theatrical shaman who turns the evening ceremony into a psychodrama. There are innumerable other ways to fake a ritual or to warp certain aspects of it.

A few more examples include planting a shill in a group of clients who, in the middle of a ceremony, leaps up and pretends

he is speaking words channeled through him by the gods. Or
sometimes a shaman has his clients perform "sacred" dances or
physical exercises that have nothing to do with real *curanderismo*.
Untraditional musical instruments like electric guitars or saxo-
phones are sometimes played by shamans, making a ceremony
seem more like a jazz concert than a spiritual event.

At times, moreover, a ceremony is not designed to fool clients
but rather is composed of strangely juxtaposed spiritual beliefs.
In Peru, an especially common syncretism is the blend of shamanic techniques with elements of Christianity.

Christianity is, of course, deeply ingrained in Peruvian society
and has been for centuries. When believers speak about shamanic
practice, they often use language and symbology learned from
the church. At the same time, rural Peruvians have a deep respect and trust in the natural medicine of their ancestors. This
parallelism can lead to odd forms of practice, such as chanting a
Christian prayer while drinking the sacred brew, reciting quotes
from the Bible in the middle of a ceremony, or wearing a crucifix
and fingering a rosary while having visions.

Personally, I have conflicted feelings about mixing Christianity
with *curanderismo*. As a shamanic traditionalist, I work for the recovery of the ancient mindset that places nature and the spirits at
the center of sacred practice. On the other hand, I can vouch for
the psychic healing powers present in certain aspects of religion-
influenced shamanism. The peculiar combination of Christianity
and *curanderismo* can work well together at certain times by evok-
ing oral prayers, visions, genuflections, and a fair level of purging
during the same night's ceremony. Including religious elements in
a shamanic session can also help Christian believers feel assured
they are not straying into heresy. At the same time, however, if
not integrated properly, the combination of Christian belief and
shamanism can create a ludicrous mix-up of spiritual points of

view that nullifies the power of both. I myself prefer to keep my ceremonies as close as possible to Pre-Columbian norms and not combine them with other spiritual methods.

⚜

People would be surprised to learn how many of the songs and *icaros* sung by shamans in Peru today and featured in shamanic music albums and on the Internet are actually based on harmonies brought from Europe. Since religious chants and hymns were originally designed to induce meditative states and connect listeners with their higher emotions, these hybrid *icaros* can at times create an extraordinary state of spiritual uplift in listeners.

In a more dubious scenario, some *curanderos* introduce foreign objects into their ceremonies, such as voodoo figurines, African masks, or statues of the Buddha, in essence creating an amalgam that has no relationship to our Craft. A point that my teachers often emphasized is that a sacred plant ceremony should not be added to or subtracted from. It has a more or less standard format organized according to accepted rules and practices and performed (with local variations) in a way that has been done for hundreds of years. When a ceremony is crossbred with art and sacred totems from other countries and other cultures, clients are exposed to irrelevant symbols that can cause confusion for both client and *curandero*.

Then there are also practitioners who mar shamanic tradition by offering lessons in how to perform a ceremony at home, either alone or with friends. The same practitioners may tell you how to start your own shamanic school or how to change the one you are involved in. Some facilitators allow clients to run parts of the ritual themselves. Still others include implied or even overt sexual activities as part of the night's goings-on, more on which below.

Still another questionable but surprisingly common practice is the hiring of local natives to sit in a shamanic circle and sing songs the entire night in their own tribal language while the shaman does his work. These natives often have no training in the Craft, and many of their songs are not healing songs at all but lullabies or children's tunes. The facilitator knows that the American and European audience cannot tell the difference between the two, and since the songs are tuneful, the audience thinks they are hearing the true sound of spiritual Peru.

All in all, seekers who participate in healing ceremonies deserve better than invented, improvised, or fanciful rituals. Besides being false or unethical, distorted practices leave seekers stranded in the labyrinth of their Suffering Consciousness without any maps for escape.

Sexual Molestation

A most disturbing criticism leveled against shamanism is based on complaints, launched mainly but not exclusively by women, of being sexually harassed or abused by a seemingly trustworthy *curandero*.

Over the years and especially recently there have been reports of touching, fondling, and even rape by a facilitator before, during, or after a ceremony. These abuses run a wide gamut. An intimate relationship can, for instance, develop when a shaman persuades a client he can provide her with a deeper form of healing or give her supernatural powers if the two of them have sexual relations. The alchemy of joined male and female sexual energy, he explains, will triple the power of her encounter with the spirit world.

There are many variations on this theme. Most occur when a shaman has an authoritarian character and the client a submissive devotion both to him and to shamanism in general. If he says it, it must be true. He is, after all, a spirit master. This "shaman as holy man" syndrome is a belief that opens the door to any type of exploitive behavior on the part of a disreputable facilitator. And, of course, working with a sexually coercive practitioner can never deliver any form of higher wisdom or self-knowledge.

I once worked with a woman in France who had a long-term romance with a shaman in Iquitos, but who over time began to realize she was being used by the shaman simply to gratify his lust. She abruptly broke off the relationship and returned home. For months afterward she was stalked in her dreams by the ex-lover, who was attempting to pull her back using threatening visions and violent spells.

When I met her, she asked for my help, and I subsequently spent time tracking and neutralizing her haunting. In the end, the woman was able to recover her peace but was still deeply distressed to realize how much of a victim she had allowed herself to be. In such ways is our precious Art given a bad name by a bad shaman.

Along these same lines, there are testimonies that so-called shamans grope a client's breasts, force kissing, or sometimes take a woman into a side room on some pretext and have intercourse with her—i.e., rape—then send her back to the circle while the ceremony is still in progress. There have even been reports of molestations that occur in plain sight of others during a group healing.

When reading about these abuses one is sometimes told that psychoactive plants send clients into a somnambulant trance or are hypnotized by a shaman, causing them to lose control over their will and hence their bodies. This claim is nonsense. Plant medicine will *never* make clients forget who they are, where they are, why they are there, and what is appropriate for them to do or not do in any questionable situation. Indeed, since Soul Consciousness oversees behavior during a ceremony, sacred plant mixtures help clients see things more clearly than in their ordinary state of mind. If a ceremony is conducted in a proper way, no client will ever experience any form of hypnosis or suspension of free will.

Shamans Who Cause Harm Intentionally

Finally, there are trained and accomplished *brujos* who use their powers to intentionally hurt others, usually because they are paid to do the job. In the worst-case possibility, dark sorcerers are turned on by the sheer thrill of making other people suffer.

Evil practitioners have always existed, and even traditional or ancient shamanism was not always on the side of the Force of Life. In traditional cultures, one of the most common forms of magical abuse was for a *brujo* to intentionally make a member of the community fall ill. One common method for doing this works in the following way: The *brujo* goes deep into the forest looking for a certain type of tree. There are at least three species in the jungle that I know of—there may be more—that provide good fortune and protection, but which if activated in a certain way can also make a person sick. When the *brujo* finds one of these trees, he takes an article of clothing or a strand of hair belonging to his intended victim and, making the appropriate passes and intentions over it, places it inside the tree. Within a day or so the victim becomes ill.

The family of the ailing party, when they realize they can do nothing to make their kinsperson better, knock on the sorcerer's door seeking his help. After receiving a hefty payment, he dismantles the spell and heals the very illness he has caused, telling the family that the cured relative must come back to see him on a regular paying basis or the disease will return. Both the family and the victim, not knowing the true origin of the ailment, are wildly grateful, and the shaman's reputation for curing incurable disorders spreads from town to town.

Another shady practice takes place when a shaman tries to steal a rival's expertise by finding out when he is giving a ceremony and tuning in to it. During this time the practitioner is especially sensitive, and sucking the Medicine force out him is relatively easy. Or the shaman may attack his competitor with invisible darts or send poisonous snakes to bite him while he sleeps.

If he is well-attuned to the spirit world, the attacked shaman quickly discovers he is being targeted. Or if not, he may be warned by his Healing Family or by one of his power animals, which are always on patrol during a ceremony. He in turn fights back on the psychic level, going through a number of defensive contortions that are often so frenzied that clients in the circle watching him wonder if he is mad. But he is not. He is simply being self-protective.

There is nothing new under the sun, or in the realm of the spirits. Traditional shamanism, pure in itself, is not exempt from those who would use it as a tool for their own gain and glory.

What Can Be Done?

Whenever a spiritual practice gains acclaim, it becomes vulnerable to exploitation. Shamanism's newfound popularity is no different, putting the plant world at risk along with the powerful yet fragile practice of *curanderismo* and those who seek healing from it. A delicate balance is called for to ensure that these age-old healing routines are protected, and that's what this chapter has tried to address.

When I am discussing these matters with friends and clients, the question often comes up, what can be done? Should we prevent or control the number of Ayahuasca tourists from coming to Peru with the hope that by limiting the quota of seekers, we limit the amount of fakery as well? Is this even a realistic consideration? Should we try to return to our old ways before the advent of massive Ayahuasca harvests and commercial shamanic compounds?

Realistically, this is not possible. The bottom line is that there are innumerable deserving people visiting the Amazon every day in need of relief from their suffering, and that Ayahuasca itself has reached such popularity that going back to the old ways is inconceivable. People are coming in droves; people are being cured; people are making money.

The good news is that seekers and, in fact, the human race itself are not alone in any of this. The sacred plants of the world are coming back to help. They are trying to gain our ear, saying to us: Let us in, let us in, listen to what we have to say. We can help.

And they can. We will talk about how in the next and final chapter.

CHAPTER 9

CAN PLANTS

SAVE THE WORLD?

The shamanic Art is designed to help individual clients, it is true. But it is also true that shamanism and its partnership with sacred flora has a parallel aim: to protect the body and soul of planet Earth.

Related to this aim, a magic moment occasionally occurs in the morning just as I am waking up. Still floating in the netherworld of dreams, I see a tunnel that extends through a haze to the horizon, and it is gently sucking me in. Once inside I am immediately transported to a circle of people dressed in clothes of soft colors who are far wiser than myself. I can see from the expressions on their faces that they are all Type three spirits with an extraordinarily advanced understanding.

Sitting down with this august group and with what seem to be other invitees like myself, we work together to heal a certain geographical territory on the planet, just as if we were healing the organs of a client. After stimulating my Medicine energy, I am told to focus it on a certain region of the earth that needs guidance, though I never know why; is a war going on in this part of the world, a natural catastrophe? Or is there just a good deal of suffering and grief in the hearts of its population? I never know.

After I finish sending my healing force to the trouble zone, I feel a soft mystical joy and am then immediately transported back to my morning bed. Lying there, I feel utterly content. The periodic repetition of this morning symposium through the years has reinforced my understanding that being a *curandero* has a universal as well as a personal purpose.

During the year 2011, while I was visiting several foreign countries delivering lectures, audiences seemed to always ask me the same question: What about the Mayan prophesies? Is the world really going to end on December 21, 2012?

I replied that I had never received any instruction about this prophecy, either from a teacher or from my Healing Family. These prophecies, I explained, are an oracle belonging to the Mexican people rather than to Peruvians and are not part of our tradition. Yet what the Mayans in the extraordinary depth of their wisdom foretold, I said, is similar to what other medicine people throughout the world have also seen in their visions.

Still, I was puzzled by these predictions and finally asked my Healing Family what they were really saying. The answer I received—you can see what I said on several YouTube lectures I made at this time—is that the prophecy was not to be taken literally but was a warning about a never-before-seen polarization between the different peoples and countries of the world and hence about humanity's future—that future being *right now*. During this current era, I was told, humanity is replacing compassion and tolerance with hostility and intolerance, a condition that will lead to unimaginably terrible wars—wars at home, wars between brothers and sisters, wars inside a person's mind and heart, wars that never end, wars that make peace and gladness of any kind impossible and eventually cause millions of innocents to die. This distortion of human behavior and judgment, the prophecy maintains, will blur our connection with the sentiments of the heart and turn worldwide hatred into the norm. Over the past decade this polarization has to a large extent already taken place and is, in fact, the most urgent problem we must deal with as a global community if further world degradation is to be prevented.

Yet though Mayan prophesies tell us this polarization is an inevitable phase in the chronology of human history, my Healing Family also said that concern for righteousness, truth, gratitude, and love in all its forms, if shared and promoted, will help us survive the coming dark storm, lessening the damage done by enmity and industrial greed, and revivifying our relationship with Mother Earth. Compassion, clemency, and help from the spirits of the plants: These are the tools needed to accomplish safe steering through the turbulent waters of our times.

Renewal of the Ancient Alliance

There is another powerful message that has come through the visions of many persons of knowledge. It is simply this: Many of the forgotten or lost sacred plants from around the world are already coming to help us as they once helped people in the past. The rediscovery and use of sacred plants that were seeded by the Great Spirit in all parts of the world, and that provided help for early human communities, are once again allowing us to use their power as an antidote to environmental destruction. Though these plants and fungi have always existed, they are now weaving themselves into our lives and consciousness as never before, eager to help us reestablish what I previously described as the Ancient Alliance—a deep affinity and covenant with the natural world that once made our ancestors (and even some of us today) thrive. But though the vegetal world is knocking at our door, nothing should be taken for granted. It is up to us to accept this help. It will by no means be forced on us by nature.

The renewal of the Ancient Alliance, happily, is already at work. Wherever I go I meet committed people sensitive to the power and wisdom of vegetable life—environmentalists, nature lovers, ecologists, preservationists, organic farmers, activists concerned with climate control—people who intuitively cultivate traditional knowledge and botanical wisdom to help reconnect with the medicines of the soil. At the same time, currently there is also a wide-scale rebirth of scientific interest in the healing powers of psychoactive medicines. As it turns out, researchers and psychiatrists from the 1950s and 1960s who reported on the remarkable improvements these substances triggered in their patients were onto a world-changing discovery before corruption and misuse caused governments to make their use illegal.

This Alliance with nature, as we shall see, is not confined to the Amazon jungle or for that matter to rain forests anywhere in the world. It can reveal itself where you live right now; in the place that you love and care for. It can start in your garden or in your backyard or in your flowerpots. Do a bit of research and you will be amazed to learn how many of the herbs, trees, grasses, and wild plants growing in your area can remedy a number of physical disorders, both acute and chronic, physical and psychological.

Remember that countless generations long ago made their home on the land where you now live, and that the people who lived there used the local plants as medicine. Many of these same shrubs, trees, and greenery are still growing nearby and are often the plants that heal you best. The spirits of these plants are still there and will always be there, watching you, helping you, and expecting your acknowledgment and respect in return.

An Ancient Story

I once heard the following story from an aged *curandero*.

When the Great Spirit made this world, he told me, it did so out of mystical joy. Its creation took the form of a garden with human beings appointed as its keepers.

In the beginning, the *curandero* explained, humanity did its best to fulfill its duty. But humans were often at the edge of survival due to predators, inclement weather, and lack of food. Seeing they were about to go extinct, the Great Spirit sent the vegetable world to their rescue—sacred plants that would help them live a full life; bushes and trees to be used for food, shelter, agriculture, clothing, textiles, art, and medicine for both body and soul. People did not discover these plants on their own. The plants reached out to them, helping them survive and eventually prosper.

This cooperation with the Ancient Alliance is probably one of the most important events to ever take place in human history, and remains a cornerstone of human life today and of shamanism as well. According to the aged *curandero*, modern learning tells us that our skills working with agriculture and plant life evolved over centuries of experience. Plant shamans believe that yes, this knowledge was to some extent based on hands-on learning. But much of it was also passed on to us via direct revelation from the spirits.

The Plant World Is Knocking at
Our Door. Will We Answer It?

This is a key question that has constantly been asked between the lines of this book.

No matter what optimistic technocrats tell us, an objective observer can plainly see that the powers of nature that sustain us are everywhere imperiled. Human survival is tottering on a precipice like never in all recorded history. The belief that happiness consists of harmony with the Force of Life and respect for nature's cycles has been hijacked, replaced by the notion that human beings are the center of the world, and that anything we do to maintain our pleasures and self-serving lifestyle, no matter how dissolute or destructive, is justified.

For years many informed and well-meaning people have tried to figure out ways to prevent the wanton destruction of nature. But our attempts are too small, too late, and nothing seems to discourage the impulses that drive human beings to desecrate the planet Earth. This is true, I believe, because none of these attempts address the true causes of the problem, which are neither social nor political but purely psychological—selfishness, ignorance, and insatiable greed: in other words, the Suffering Consciousness.

And yet cultures do not *have* to be ruled by such destructive impulses.

Indigenous peoples like those from the Amazon, while far from living conflict-free lives, tend to be more peace-loving, communal, and spiritually attuned than those in first-world societies who are goaded on by the "I want, I want, give me, give me!" mantra that materialism and the Suffering Consciousness encourage. In the eyes of a traditional shaman the most concordant societies are those that regulate their lives according to night and day, sun and moon, the cycles of growth and the seasons, neighborliness and kindness, and most of all by respect and care for the trees, grasses, shrubs, and vines that green our planet.

Keep in mind that shamanism was created both for and by the plant world. This is true not only because *curanderos* use plants for connecting with the spirits but because they are tutored by nature itself. They journey alone in the wilderness as part of their training. They are taught to develop rapport with mountains and wild animals. They learn healing techniques that connect them with the natural powers of field and stream. They cultivate their Art in the deserts, by waterfalls, in the valleys and forests. They learn the use of psychoactive plants. The fact is that shamanism *is* nature in its dynamic phase; or if you prefer, it is nature in a human incarnation.

It is, therefore, not by chance that the creation stories in many major world religions (including Christianity, Islam, and Judaism) begin with humans living in a garden of flowering trees and streams enraptured by an elysian sense of peace and joy. The symbolism here is clear—the plant kingdom is our original home. It is the place where we have all come from and the place to which we will all return. We are physiologically constructed to live, think, and work in a natural terrain, each night feeling the calm that comes from performing a day's labor in the fields, lulled to sleep by the sounds of the wilderness with its teeming insect and animal songs. True, the technology that does the work we should be doing brings us leisure and pleasure, health and protection. But it cancels out the unifying force of working with nature, robbing us of the physical skills, inventiveness, and creativity that make us human.

What Can We Do to Bring the Plant World Closer to Our Lives?

Besides the efforts we make to restrain consumerism, overdevelopment of land, rampant industrialization, climate destruction, and pollution, we need to set another goal as well. If we can reach the hearts and souls of the polluters themselves and help them understand that if they keep doing what they are doing their great grandchildren will never be born, perhaps we can save our planet even at this late date. We need to help individuals in denial to realize that if they place nature and human survival above profit, the earth can still be rescued. Naive? Perhaps. But surely some of the people in power still have a sense of moral duty.

Once we move closer to our Soul Consciousness and stop sabotaging our environment, technology will, I believe, take its rightful place as servant and helper to humankind rather than its ruler. When this transformation occurs, a return to our true center in nature and ourselves will take place automatically. Our mission is to make the effort. There *are* things we can do.

What follows is not meant to be a list of dos and don'ts. Obviously, the issue of alienation from nature and the steps that can be taken to remedy it are too complex to solve in a brief analysis. Still, I offer suggestions, some soft, some hard, that have come to me partly from shaman's experience, partly from the spirit world, partly from my clients. These are suggestions that we can put into practice right now to reinstate our relationship with Mother Nature and help her to help us.

And remember, when added up over time, every effort, even the smallest, matters. Do what you can when you can. All of the suggestions that follow, I hope it is clear, are based on the teachings of shamanism as explained throughout this book, and on shamanism's link to the vegetable domain below and the spirit world above.

Moderation Is Best

Seekers can dive deeply into a spiritual encounter by simply experiencing one powerful sacred brew rather than by sampling an endlessly wide variety of shamanic offerings. No need to go looking for that fabled medicinal leaf in the Himalayas if what you have access to at home can do the trick. Experimentation is not a bad thing; spiritual greed is.

I should say here parenthetically that I have dealt with people who think that to advance in their inner growth they need to experience a wide range of sacred disciplines. They believe that one spiritual way is never enough, that they should take the best part of each religious or esoteric way and combine them into their own self-crafted enlightenment machine; though, in fact, if real, one way is *always* enough. Indeed, by definition a true spiritual discipline contains all the sacred elements necessary for bringing a person to higher understanding. Nothing further is needed; and if it is, the way is not a true way. I am not trying to tell people what to do in their personal seeking. Spiritual experimentation is a rightful phase. But it is important to acknowledge that it should be a phase, not a landing place; and that the overabundance of occult and Eastern and Western religious offerings available today can cause a spiritual quest to morph into an endless search and sampling that ultimately goes nowhere.

While the psychological reactions aroused by power plants from various parts of the world are considerably different, their remedying effects are largely the same: they tame the Suffering Consciousness and open the flow of the Force of Life and Soul Consciousness. Thanks to its inexhaustible bounty, nature has seen to it that every region of the planet is blessed with its own set of Master Plants. The help offered by these plants is available to people in every part of the world, now as in the past.

For example, the ancient Egyptians used blue lotus and magic mushrooms, images of which are depicted on the walls of their tombs. The Greeks and other Mediterranean cultures were partial to lotus, poppies, and unknown psychedelic potions, some of which were said to be taken during the Eleusinian Mysteries and by the priestess at Delphi to heighten her trance.

Through the centuries Hindus and Buddhists have used a number of awareness stimulants including hashish and psychoactive herbs, while for millennia in Asia and the Middle East opium from poppy plants has both cured serious stomach ailments and lulled users into an addictive dreamworld. In the southwest of the United States and in north-central Mexico indigenous people ingest mescaline-based peyote as part of their religion along with a variety of mind-expanding cactuses and mushrooms. In Europe mandrake root, black henbane, deadly nightshade, monkshood, and many other wakeful potions induce euphoria as well as help sorcerers cast their spells. Tobacco, chocolate, coffee, snuff, black and green tea, chiles, and other kitchen cupboard substances are all classified under the rubric "drug" because they alter, if only a tad, our state of consciousness. There are many others as well, and who knows how many psychoactive plants and plant recipes have been lost over time but remain dormant, waiting to be rediscovered?

Honor the Sanctity of Nature

We delight in the loveliness of a sunset or a desert landscape flowering in the spring. But to connect with nature from the inside, shamanism believes we must understand that this beauty is not a thing in itself but a symbol of a higher intelligence. As Plato wrote, "Beauty is the splendor of the truth."

The shamanic ethic, as we know, links the natural world with the subtle world, meaning that tuning in to the song of nature is a way of tuning in to the exalted. Next time you walk outside and gaze at a nearby stream, a tree, a wooded valley, see them, as one of my teachers told me, "with your heart as well as your eyes. Hear their sounds as if they are coming from the spirits. Let the smell of flowers and mountain air remind you of the place you came from before you were born." In matters of the Force of Life and plant compassion, the door is always open to us just as long as we knock.

⁂

An easy way to draw closer to the spiritual qualities of nature is to love and appreciate water. Besides the fact that we drink and bathe in it, water is medicine, an emotional soap, a warmer, a cooler, a soother, the blood of the earth. In earlier chapters we talked a good deal about the wonders of water, but there is never praise enough for the Force of Life as manifested in the flow of streams, lakes, and oceans. When you swim in it, when it falls on you as rain, think of yourself as being immersed in the Great Spirit.

Another source of nature's wonderment is fertile land, the generous bequest from Mother Earth's body. Generation after generation has looked on land as life itself and as the most valuable asset a community can possess. This is why most ancient settlements were built alongside rich soil rather than on top of it; not just to set it aside for farming but because the fertility in the soil brings people a special infusion of vitality. One of the worst transgressions I have witnessed in my country is the covering over of fertile soil with cement and construction materials by unchecked urban development. This treasured ground, seen as the most valuable inheritance Mother Nature has given us, is now lost forever to factories, housing developments, and parking lots.

✻

Another practical way to pay homage to nature is to engage in some form of agriculture, either in your garden or in a pot on the ledge of a window in your apartment. Allow yourself the pleasure of planting a seed, watching it sprout and grow day by day, and enjoying the fruit it gifts you. I have seen people experience epiphanies of joy simply by witnessing the fully grown plants and flowers they have, as it were, given birth to.

Dig a vegetable garden. Hang ferns in your windows. Plant trees, and for every tree that is chopped down plant two in its place. Grow an ivy bed and encourage it to creep up the walls and buildings that surround you. Grow an orchard. Encourage your children to play in the soil and to become friends with stones, silt, decaying leaves, mud. Take them for walks in the woods. Show them the mossy walls of a cave and the panoramic view from the top of a hill. If you have access to land, flower beds and rows of vegetables will bring you a tiny bit closer to nature's patrimony. Growing and nourishing plants is a form of shamanic devotion. This is a message I have received from the plant spirits through the years. Though people do not always believe it, loving and caring for plants is *almost* as important as performing the sacred ceremonies that use them.

Establish a Verbal and Psychic Dialogue with the Plant World

If you talk to inveterate gardeners or people who work in small-scale agriculture, especially on organic farms, you will find that many of them speak to their plants mentally or out loud, as if having a conversation. There are, of course, people who scoff at the idea that plants understand what we say to them and that in a certain way they can speak back to us. If they understand, why don't they respond?

There are many answers to this question, one of them being that the plant world works on a temporal level that functions many times slower than our own, and that when we speak to it, time is required for a response—an hour, a day, a week, a month, who knows? Sometimes it never comes. But in some cases it does, even though we may not recognize it as feedback from our interchange. As a poet once wrote, "Throw a seed into the river, in a year it comes up in the desert."

What's more, when people who relate closely to growing things ask plants a question, an answer sometimes pops into their mind that makes sense. Societies from time immemorial have always believed—I would say have always known—that plants and human beings can communicate, and that plants can be both our friends and our teachers. It is best to approach the question of communicating with the vegetable realm as a child approaches a fantasy game. Do it in the spirit of fun and belief, and perhaps you will be surprised.

The Good Place

Here are two more basic efforts you can make to live closer to the natural world.

First, if you own or live on a piece of property, make it a sanctuary. Look on it as something inviolable and treat it that way. Those with access to land are encouraged to let the greenery that decorates their yard or garden be cropped but not molested. If you maintain a lawn, give it a year off now and then to grow to its full height. If you are constructing a house, try not to take down all the trees on the property before building it. Let everything that is green grow. A plant spirit told one of my clients, "We need every single leaf and flower bud to go unharmed if we [the plant world] are going to survive."

Once I learned of some natives from the rain forest who were shown pictures of the exquisitely groomed gardens of Versailles. Their instant impression was to feel sorry for the plants, maintaining that they had been bent into unnatural shapes and twists and were suffering because of it. It is not that you should let your land grow wild, only that it is best not to overgroom it. Look on it as a living being rather than as an ordinary expanse of grass and hedges.

The second effort you can make to live closer to the soil is to search for a nearby place in nature that you feel an affinity with— your "good place." This site should make you feel happy and comfortable, as if you've come home; it should speak to you. Once found, visit it as often as possible. No need to climb to the top of a mountain. Just look for an agreeable natural location nearby and be grateful it has invited you to be its friend.

If you live in the city, look for a place in your local park or recreational area. If you are outside the city, your good place can be a corner of the woods, by a stream, near a hill that was lived on centuries ago by people who may well have considered the spot sacred.

If possible, make periodic visits to your good place. Tell it how happy you are to see it, and praise its peace and beauty. Do, however, avoid asking it for favors or help of any kind; this would be impolite.

Be sure to approach your good place alone. There are emotional spaces inside us that we cannot reach on these outings if accompanied by another person. Also, when visiting avoid taking photographs, and try not to discuss your visits with other people. Somehow talking about your relationship with your good place discharges the energy and weakens the bond between you; it belongs to you and you alone. Finally, if you visit your good place frequently, after some time a deep rapport will hopefully develop between you. The joy of being in this special spot comes from *connection*. The relationship of humanity to nature and the plant world is always all about connection.

When visiting your favorite spot in nature, it may seem like a quiet and uneventful place. But remember, this land has a history that goes back to humankind's beginnings, and that people who lived here thousands or tens of thousands of years ago may have done remarkable things, leaving traces that you can still sense today.

When you walk down a tree-lined street in front of a library or stroll on a country path, you think it has always looked the way it does today. But remember that over the millennia untold numbers of villages, cities, or even kingdoms have risen and fallen on these grounds. Sometimes I pick up a piece of limestone or granite and study it, trying to understand that the average rock is more than a *billion* years old. Early multicellular life, dinosaurs, Neanderthal man, the Mayan and Inca empires, the French and American revolutions have all come and gone in this time, but the rock has endured. When I look at this rock as well as other geological formations around me, I realize they are all emissaries from eternity.

Respect Insects

Insects and arachnids are viewed by most of us as repellent invaders. This is a pity, as the role they play in life is a basic tool for the survival of the world as well as an essential element of shamanism.

Westerners tend to look on insects with a combination of anxiety and disgust. True, a few make the grade. Butterflies, ladybugs, crickets, cicadas, bees, ants, fireflies, and several other picturesque species are admired for their beauty or appreciated for their song or organizational ingenuity. By and large, though, bugs are thought of as creepy aliens that need to be stamped underfoot, if not eliminated en masse with poisonous sprays and pest control devices that kill every insect in the yard, the helpful kind as well as the harmful.

Traditional and indigenous communities have a different perspective on our tiny six-legged neighbors, knowing the part they play in the survival of rain forests, desert, and mountain vegetation. Without them all greenery on earth would wither, and us along with it. Indigenous people know that insects scavenge excrement and dead creatures, keeping the earth clean. They aerate the soil and recycle nutrients back into the ground, creating fresh loam. Their bodies are used to create silk, dyes, medicines, chemicals, lacquer, and much else. Bees manufacture wax and honey. Burrowing insects like ants dig underground channels that allow water to permeate fields and forests. Insects are high on the food chain, providing meals for other insects, as well as for reptiles, birds, fish, amphibians, and mammals. In some countries, including Amazonian Peru, humans dine on insects (giant ants, large insect larvae, spiders), receiving a healthy dose of protein with their meal.

Most importantly, without insects doing their job of cross-pollination, the entire fruit, crop, and human agricultural system of the planet would perish. For this reason, bees, the world's number one plant pollinators, were recently named "the most important creatures on earth" by the Earthwatch Institute in Boston.

Bees, parenthetically, are the only living creatures that carry no pathogens, and the honey they make is the only natural substance that harbors no bacteria and never decays. Archaeologists excavating 3,500-year-old Egyptian tombs have found honey in burial pots that was not only intact but still edible.

I remember a ceremony that took place in a clearing in the forest on an extremely hot evening. The usual torrent of mosquitos, flies, and gnats were buzzing relentlessly around the heads of my foreign clients, many of whom spent a good part of the evening swatting them away with their hands. The next day several indigenous people who had assisted in the ceremony asked me why so many of my clients kept hitting themselves in the face during the night. For indigenous people who live deep in a forest or jungle, swarming insects are a natural part of life. Even when bugs crawl on their hands or face they go largely unnoticed.

I often see my clients preparing themselves for a walk in the jungle by spraying their heads and hands with toxic repellents. When tramping through the forest they touch leaves, vines, and flowers as part of their discovery experience. By so doing they spread poison to the plants and to the creatures that eat them. Which is to say that if there is no pressing need to use a spray or repellent, don't. By being compassionate and by avoiding agricultural poisons, you help protect not only the insect and vegetable kingdom but human beings as well.

Finally, in the eyes of *curanderos*, the metamorphosis of certain insects is a revelation that helps explain the mysteries of life, death, and spiritual transfiguration. In the butterfly hatching cycle, they see a caterpillar enter its sleep in a cocoon, as if dead. They watch as it becomes a pupa, looking like a corpse embalmed. They see it finally emerge from the chrysalis transformed, with spreading wings and strong, radiant colors similar to those of the spirits. The symbology of this transformation from worm to god-like creature has obvious overtones of human spiritual rebirth, even to those unaccustomed to seeing nature as a book of mystical parables.

For me it is a special joy to see the huge blue morpho butterfly flying through the jungle. The sight of it reminds me of a visit from a spirit, as its intense blue is the same as the colored healing energies used at times by shamans applying Medicine Force. When a shaman does a procedure, this iridescent blue is used to psychically soak the organs or tissues of a client's body, where it acts as a healing tincture.

As we saw previously, bees are friends of humans. Also, several types of wasps, bumblebees, and cicadas can become allies, creating a lifetime partnership with a shaman. And yet, most shamans are rarely willing to explain how partnership with a creature seemingly so low on the hierarchy of creation can possibly be of spiritual value. What I can say here is that perhaps the reason for this reticence is that these creatures are not as low on the scale as people believe, and that when operating on a psychic level, ants, bees, and other higher species of insects are watching and weighing our behavior with penetrating and at times quasi-supernatural insight.

Can Plants Save the World?

Global plant support has flowed like a river through the generations, sometimes surfacing to help humanity, sometimes sinking into the unseen until it is needed once again. Today the Ayahuasca community, both in South America and around the world, is convinced that the green world is once more mentoring us, this time to prevent a worldwide level of ecological destruction that was unthinkable a century ago. Like a web of psychic vines radiating from the depths of the rain forest, the vegetable force is channeling itself into contemporary civilization in an attempt to realign us with nature's hegemony before we reach the point of no return. At this tipping point in world history, the sacred plant world is appealing to the depth of our conscience, attempting to teach us how to act as guardians of our planetary garden, and how to oppose the forces that are destroying it and us along with it.

Here, however, it could be said that the question of whether plants and especially sacred plants can save the world is bit of a misnomer and needs to be phrased in a different way. It is not really a matter of whether plants can save the world. It is more a question of whether we humans, individually and collectively, can save the natural world, and by so doing save ourselves as well. The vegetable realm is consciously offering us the full range of its support in these troubled times, yes. But this help is of value *only* if we believe it, accept it, work with, and turn its gifts into a tool for our survival.

The calamitous threats that humanity and the planet are facing today—pollution, global warming, rising sea levels, decreasing availability of drinkable water (and water in general), deadly heat waves, famine, the poisoning of our ocean and the killing of its sea life, worldwide deforestation, the extinction of animal species—all are due to the fact that nature's systems have been thrown out of equilibrium by human tampering. Yet if we look at the situation in another way, the cataclysms listed above have less to do with eco-terrorism per se and more with the plant world's distress at our behavior and its backlash via the unprecedented climactic and environmental disasters it is currently sending our way. Plant and meteorologic conditions have their own survivalist view of the world and are currently so distressed at what we are doing to them that they are forcing us to either stop exterminating them or be exterminated *by* them.

Plants can, in other words, destroy us as well as nurture us. But in its embrace of both justice and mercy, the verdant realm is by no means out to punish humankind, which it loves, but to offer it a planetary partnership. Ruin the earth, it says, and annihilate yourselves and us. Or come up with new and creative ways of controlling technology so that it helps us to survive but does not ruin the earth and the sky—and human nature—in the process. This can be accomplished by drastically cutting back on air, water, and soil pollution, deforestation, use of toxic chemicals, smokestack contamination, and all the other end-of-the-world practices that threaten us this very minute.

To say it in a sentence, plants and humans must act together and work together on a global scale or we will all die.

Summing Up

In speaking of plant intelligence and whether the vegetable kingdom can save the world, we have reached the end of our journeying in the kingdom of *curanderismo.*

I hope you feel that this book has explained in reasonably clear terms how seekers who are intending to visit a shaman should make all attempts to find a practitioner who is not only properly trained but who makes the effort to meet with them personally, to understand their needs, and to take time after the ceremony to help them absorb what they have learned.

I also hope this book has helped you recognize what shamanism is and what it is not, and about what it is like to participate in a formal shamanic ritual. I likewise hope you come away with a sense of how a ceremony dissects our Suffering

Consciousness, exposing its sinister hidden rooms one by one and at the same time revealing the vital importance of Soul Consciousness as a tool for guiding us to a more harmonious existence.

Finally, I hope this book shows how it is possible to develop the capacity I sometimes refer to as Internal Placement; that is, the possibility of moving out of the Suffering Consciousness and into the Soul Consciousness. If approached with the proper intent and respect, the sacred plants can help in this regard, showing us how to make Internal Placement a familiar daily practice.

If we learn nothing else from our contact with the invisible worlds, it is that both the bright and the shadowy sides of ourselves must be acknowledged and integrated into our self-view. Together they form who we are as human and spiritual beings. In the end, everything is about learning to use the whole of ourselves, both good and bad, to become better people. As the German poet Rilke remarked, "Don't take my devils away because my angels may flee as well."

Those clients who experience relief from their afflictions during a ceremony, it should be made clear, are not necessarily enlightened or spiritually free when the night is over. But more often than not, they feel as if a hundred-pound weight has been lifted off their back. With this burden removed, a client can tread more lightly on the earth and make greater efforts to sustain their spiritual evolution. Keep in mind that natural medicine may be caring. But it can also be unapologetically candid, showing clients disturbing qualities about themselves they may not want to know, but then helping them transform these qualities into positive self-reform.

In the end, the message that shamanism and plant life is so desperately trying to tell us is that the world is, after all, a spiritual place, a magical place, a realm of blessings, healings, and spirits. Do not doubt for a moment that the plant spirits are really there knocking on our windows and doors, waiting to meet us and take our hand. By participating in a sacred plant ceremony, we are realigning ourselves with the laws of nature, making friends with the vegetable powers, and recognizing them as allies and teachers in our quest to rescue the biosphere. As we do this, we are also guiding our attention away from our egos and moving toward a life of service to others, in the process cultivating the virtues that dwell inside us and that yearn to open the garden of our hearts. All these life-affirming practices make us better people, and protectors of our planet as well.

And that, in sum, is the purpose of *curanderismo*—to bring back the sacred, to help us help ourselves and others, and by so doing make the earth a better place to live, breathe, and love. May you go safely and carefully on your life journey, and as you do, remember the conversation a man of knowledge once had with a great spirit. "Where is this road leading?" the man of knowledge asked the spirit. "It is laid down as you travel," came the answer. Travel wisely.

ACKNOWLEDGMENTS

From Hachumak:

I want to acknowledge the help and patience of David L. Carroll, who at his advanced age had the courage to come to my place at the shores of the Amazon River. After fulfilling his personal goals, he decided to come out of retirement and offered to help me with this book. David also encouraged me to add personal stories, more examples, and a wider discussion about the principles of Natural Healing. Thanks to him the book has grown to its present size.

I want to also acknowledge the help of Sue Kagan, who introduced me to David L. Carroll and who has come several times to Peru and has witnessed what I'm trying to accomplish for the rainforest and its treasures. Through the years she has been a constant source of moral support.

Finally, I want to acknowledge Karen Rinaldi, who decided to give this book a chance after a choppy phone call to Peru where I expressed my intentions about the content. After meeting Karen in person more than a year later, I understood why. She is a true seeker with a long path already walked.

From David L. Carroll:

I would like to thank the following for their help in writing this book: Editor Karen Rinaldi for her unwavering support and deep belief in this book: Kirby Sandmeyer for her skilled editorial help; Sue Kagan, primo cheerleader; Jen Gates for her agenting skills; Karen Murgolo, for her early input for this book; Parabola Magazine, for publishing an article on the work of Jorge Araoz; Jocelyne Beaudoin, for just being there.

INDEX